Projects for HTML

Linda Ericksen

Lane Community College

▲ ADDISON-WESLEY

An imprint of Addison Wesley Longman, Inc.

Reading, Massachusetts • Menlo Park, California • New York • Harlow, England
Don Mills, Ontario • Sydney • Mexico City • Madrid • Amsterdam

Senior Editor: *Carol Crowell*
Production Supervision: *Patty Mahtani, David Noyes*
Copyeditor: *Robin Drake/Barb Terry*
Proofreader: *Holly McLean Aldis*
Technical Editor: *Emily Kim*
Indexer: *Mark Kmetzko*
Inhouse Composition: *Sally Simpson, Michael Strong, Pat Brown, Joe Vetere*
Cover Design Supervisor: *Gina Hagen*
Marketing Manager: *Michelle Hudson*
Manufacturing Manager: *Hugh Crawford*

ISBN 0-201-30421-X

Ordering from the SELECT System

For more information on ordering and pricing policies for the SELECT Lab Series and supplements, please contact your Addison Wesley Longman sales representative or call 1 800 552-2499.

Addison-Wesley Publishing Company
One Jacob Way
Reading, MA 01867
http://www.awl.com/he/is
is@aw.com

1 2 3 4 5 6 7 8 9 10-DOW-00999897

Getting Started

Welcome to the SELECT Lab Series. We invite you to explore how you can take advantage of the newest features of the most popular software applications using this up-to-date learning package.

Greater access to ideas and information is changing the way people work. With Windows 95 applications you have greater integration capabilities and access to Internet resources than ever before. The SELECT Lab Series helps you take advantage of these valuable resources with special assignments devoted to the Internet and additional connectivity resources that can be accessed through our Web site,

http://www.awl.com/he/is

The key to using software is making the software work for you. The SELECT Lab Series will help you learn to use software as a productivity tool by guiding you step-by-step through case-based projects similar to those you will encounter at school, work, or home. When you are finished with this learning package, you will be fully prepared to use the resources this software offers. Your success is our success.

A Guided Tour

To facilitate the learning process, we have developed a consistent organizational structure for each module in the SELECT Lab Series.

You begin using the software almost immediately. A brief **Overview** introduces the software package and the basic application functions. **Getting Help** covers the on-line Help feature in each package. **A Note to the Student** explains any special conventions or system configurations observed in a particular module.

Each lab manual contains five to eight **Projects,** an **Operations Reference** of all the operations covered in the module, an extensive **Glossary** of **key terms,** and an **Index.**

The following figures introduce the elements you will encounter as you use each SELECT module.

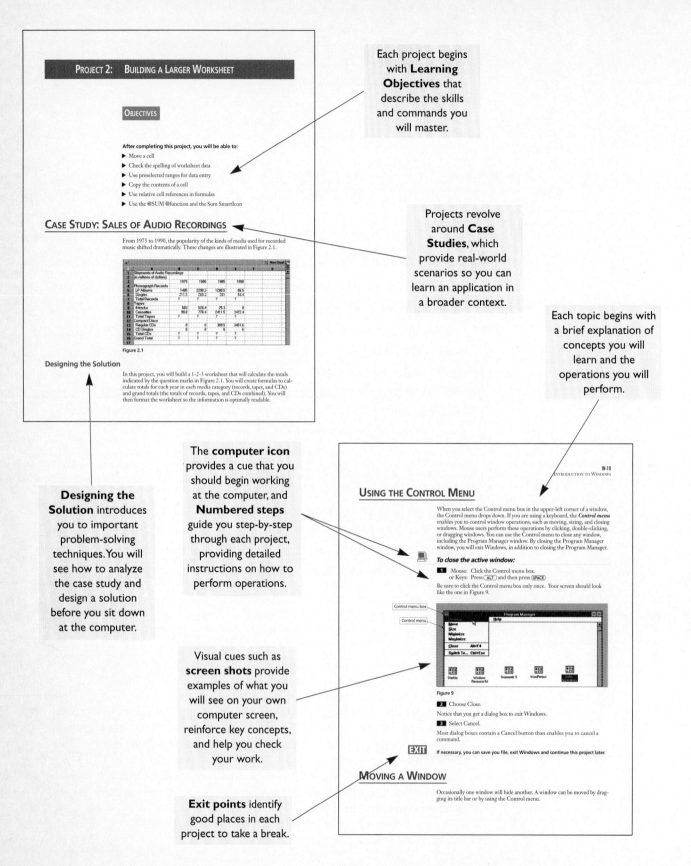

PROJECT 2: BUILDING A LARGER WORKSHEET

OBJECTIVES

After completing this project, you will be able to:
▶ Move a cell
▶ Check the spelling of worksheet data
▶ Use preselected ranges for data entry
▶ Copy the contents of a cell
▶ Use relative cell references in formulas
▶ Use the @SUM @function and the Sum SmartIcon

CASE STUDY: SALES OF AUDIO RECORDINGS

From 1975 to 1990, the popularity of the kinds of media used for recorded music shifted dramatically. These changes are illustrated in Figure 2.1.

Figure 2.1

Designing the Solution

In this project, you will build a 1-2-3 worksheet that will calculate the totals indicated by the question marks in Figure 2.1. You will create formulas to calculate totals for each year in each media category (records, tapes, and CDs) and grand totals (the totals of records, tapes, and CDs combined). You will then format the worksheet so the information is optimally readable.

Each project begins with **Learning Objectives** that describe the skills and commands you will master.

Projects revolve around **Case Studies**, which provide real-world scenarios so you can learn an application in a broader context.

Each topic begins with a brief explanation of concepts you will learn and the operations you will perform.

Designing the Solution introduces you to important problem-solving techniques. You will see how to analyze the case study and design a solution before you sit down at the computer.

The **computer icon** provides a cue that you should begin working at the computer, and **Numbered steps** guide you step-by-step through each project, providing detailed instructions on how to perform operations.

Visual cues such as **screen shots** provide examples of what you will see on your own computer screen, reinforce key concepts, and help you check your work.

Exit points identify good places in each project to take a break.

IN-10
INTRODUCTION TO WINDOWS

USING THE CONTROL MENU

When you select the Control menu box in the upper-left corner of a window, the Control menu drops down. If you are using a keyboard, the *Control menu* enables you to control window operations, such as moving, sizing, and closing windows. Mouse users perform these operations by clicking, double-clicking, or dragging windows. You can use the Control menu to close any window, including the Program Manager window. By closing the Program Manager window, you will exit Windows, in addition to closing the Program Manager.

To close the active window:

1 Mouse: Click the Control menu box.
or Keys: Press (ALT) and then press (SPACE)

Be sure to click the Control menu box only once. Your screen should look like the one in Figure 9.

Control menu box

Control menu

Figure 9

2 Choose Close.

Notice that you get a dialog box to exit Windows.

3 Select Cancel.

Most dialog boxes contain a Cancel button than enables you to cancel a command.

If necessary, you can save you file, exit Windows and continue this project later.

MOVING A WINDOW

Occasionally one window will hide another. A window can be moved by dragging its title bar or by using the Control menu.

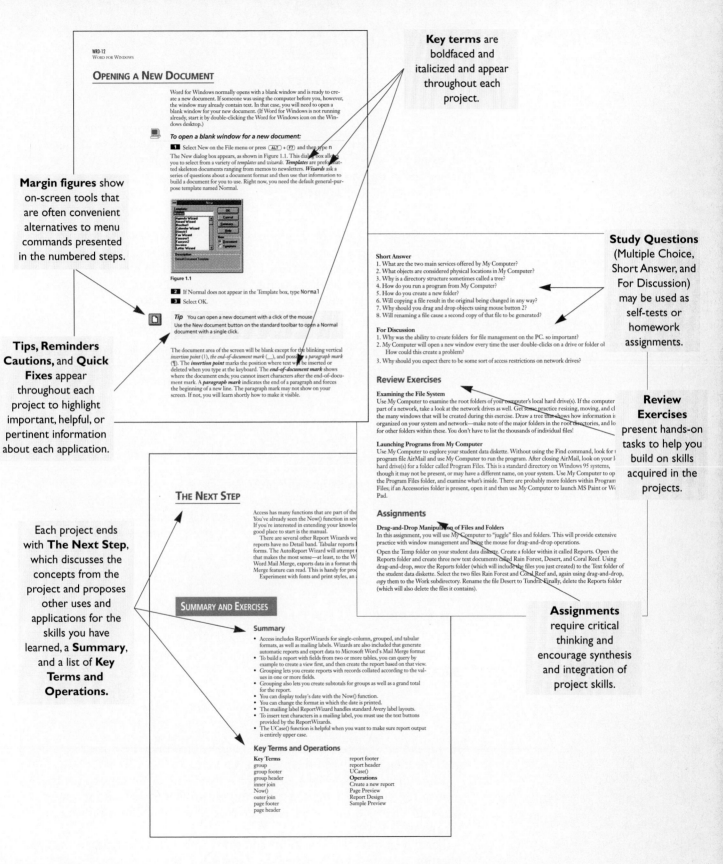

Key terms are boldfaced and italicized and appear throughout each project.

Margin figures show on-screen tools that are often convenient alternatives to menu commands presented in the numbered steps.

Tips, Reminders Cautions, and **Quick Fixes** appear throughout each project to highlight important, helpful, or pertinent information about each application.

Study Questions (Multiple Choice, Short Answer, and For Discussion) may be used as self-tests or homework assignments.

Review Exercises present hands-on tasks to help you build on skills acquired in the projects.

Assignments require critical thinking and encourage synthesis and integration of project skills.

Each project ends with **The Next Step**, which discusses the concepts from the project and proposes other uses and applications for the skills you have learned, a **Summary**, and a list of **Key Terms and Operations**.

FOLLOWING THE NUMBERED STEPS

To make the application modules easy to use in a lab setting, we have standardized the presentation of hands-on computer instructions as much as possible. The numbered step sections provide detailed, step-by-step instructions to guide you through the practical application of the conceptual material presented. Both keystroke and mouse instructions are used according to which one is more appropriate to complete a task. The instructions in the module assume that you know how to operate the keyboard, monitor, and printer.

> **Tip** When you are using a mouse, unless the text indicates otherwise, you should assume that you are clicking the left button on the mouse. Several modules provide instructions for both mouse and keyboard users. When separate mouse and keyboard steps are given, be sure to follow one method or the other, but not both.

Each topic begins with a brief explanation of concepts. A computer icon or the ▶ symbol and a description of the task you will perform appear each time you are to begin working on the computer.

For Example:

 ### To enter the address:

1 Type **123 Elm Street** and press (ENTER)
Notice that the keys you are to press and the text you are to type stand out. The text you will type appears in a special typeface to distinguish it from regular text. The key that you are to press mimics the labels of the keys on your keyboard.

When you are to press two keys or a key and a character simultaneously, the steps show the keys connected either with a plus sign or a bar.

For Example: (SHFT)+(TAB)
(CTRL)+**C**

When you are to press keys sequentially, the keys are not connected and a space separates them.

For Example: (CTRL)(PGDN)
(HOME)(HOME)(↑)

Be sure to press each key firmly, but quickly, one after the other. Keys begin repeating if you hold them down too long.

In some instances margin figures of single icons or buttons will appear next to the numbered steps. Margin figures provide visual cues to important tools that you can select as an alternative to the menu command in the numbered step.

For typographical conventions and other information unique to the application, please see **A Note to the Student** in the Overview of each module.

THE SELECT LAB SERIES—A CONNECTED LEARNING RESOURCE

The SELECT Lab Series is a complete learning resource for success in the Information Age. Our application modules are designed to help you learn fast and effectively. Based around projects that reflect your world, each module helps you master key concepts and problem-solving techniques for using the software application you are learning. Through our Web site you can access dynamic and current information resources that will help you get up to speed on the Information Highway and keep up with the ever changing world of technology.

Explore our Web site: **http://www.awl.com/he/is**

THE TechSuite

This module may be part of our new custom bundled system—the **Addison-Wesley–Benjamin/Cummings TechSuite.** Your instructor can choose any combination of concepts texts, applications modules, and software to meet the exact needs of your course. The TechSuite meets your needs by offering you one convenient package at a discount price.

SUPPLEMENTS

Each module has a corresponding Instructor's Manual with a Test Bank and Transparency Masters. For each project in the student text, the Instructor's Manual includes Expanded Student Objectives, Answers to Study Questions, and Additional Assessment Techniques. The Test Bank contains two separate tests (with answers) consisting of multiple choice, true/false, and fill-in questions that are referenced to pages in the student's text. Transparency Masters illustrate 25 to 30 key concepts and screen captures from the text.

The Instructor's Data Disk contains student data files, answers to selected Review Exercises, answers to selected Assignments, and the test files from the Instructor's Manual in ASCII format.

ACKNOWLEDGMENTS

Addison-Wesley Publishing Company would like to thank the following reviewers for their valuable contributions to the SELECT Lab Series.

Joseph Aieta
Babson College

Tom Ashby
Oklahoma CC

Bob Barber
Lane CC

Robert Caruso
Santa Rosa Junior College

Robert Chi
California State
Long Beach

Jill Davis
State University of New
York at Stony Brook

Fredia Dillard
Samford University

Peter Drexel
Plymouth State College

Ralph Duffy
North Seattle CC

David Egle
University of Texas,
Pan American

Jonathan Frank
Suffolk University

Patrick Gilbert
University of Hawaii

Maureen Greenbaum
Union County College

Sally Ann Hanson
Mercer County CC

Sunil Hazari
East Carolina University

Bruce Herniter
University of Hartford

Lisa Jackson
Henderson CC

Cynthia Kachik
Santa Fe CC

Bennett Kramer
Massasoit CC

Charles Lake
Faulkner State
Junior College

Ron Leake
Johnson County CC

Randy Marak
Hill College

Charles Mattox, Jr.
St. Mary's University

Jim McCullough
Porter and Chester
Institute

Gail Miles
Lenoir-Rhyne College

Steve Moore
University of
South Florida

Anthony Nowakowski
Buffalo State College

Gloria Oman
Portland State University

John Passafiume
Clemson University

Leonard Presby
William Paterson
College

Louis Pryor
Garland County CC

Michael Reilly
University of Denver

Dick Ricketts
Lane CC

Dennis Santomauro
Kean College of
New Jersey

Pamela Schmidt
Oakton CC

Gary Schubert
Alderson-Broaddus College

T. Michael Smith
Austin CC

Cynthia Thompson
Carl Sandburg College

Marion Tucker
Northern Oklahoma
College

JoAnn Weatherwax
Saddleback College

David Whitney
San Francisco State
University

James Wood
Tri-County
Technical College

Minnie Yen
University of Alaska,
Anchorage

Allen Zilbert
Long Island University

Contents

About the Author

Linda Ericksen teaches in the Department of Business Technologies at Lane Community College, Eugene, Oregon. She is the author of eleven computer text books and does training for government agencies and businesses. She has an MS degree in Computer Science/Education and an MA degree in English. Linda is the current President of the Oregon Chapter of the American Association of Women in Community Colleges.

Thanks to...

A project like this can only come together with a team effort. I would like to personally thank Carol Crowell for her vision and her support, Barb Terry for her dedication and good ideas, Robin Drake for her valuable input, and Emily Kim for her willingness to give this project 150% effort and her great ideas.

Overview

Objectives

After completing this overview, you should be able to:

▶ Differentiate between the Internet and the World Wide Web

▶ Describe the components required for connecting to the World Wide Web

▶ Work with addresses on the World Wide Web

▶ Use search engines to find information on the World Wide Web

▶ Design a Web document

▶ Identify HTML editors and syntax-checking programs

▶ Describe the procedure for publishing a Web document

DISTINGUISHING BETWEEN THE INTERNET AND THE WORLD WIDE WEB

The *Internet* is a network of computer networks developed in the 1960s by the U.S. Department of Defense to link military, government, and university computer networks. The result was the *Advanced Research Projects Agency Network* (*ARPANET*), which developed a method for breaking messages down into *packets* of data (standard-sized pieces of the message). These packets of data travel randomly over the network, never following the same path twice, and then are reassembled at the destination, thus providing secure communications in the case of a threat to national security. For the Internet to link various types of computers, a communications standard (*protocol*) called *Transmission Control Protocol/Internet Protocol* (*TCP/IP*) was developed and used by all the linked computers.

Over the next few years, other networks were developed for special purposes, and, in 1986, the *National Science Foundation* (*NSF*) developed a network that connected supercomputer centers across the country to the Internet. The transmission lines that link these computer networks are known as a *communications backbone*. This backbone, or *information highway*, includes telephone lines, fiber optic cables, microwave, and satellite links that now carry messages at speeds up to 45 megabits per second—and soon at speeds in the gigabytes (see Figure O.1).

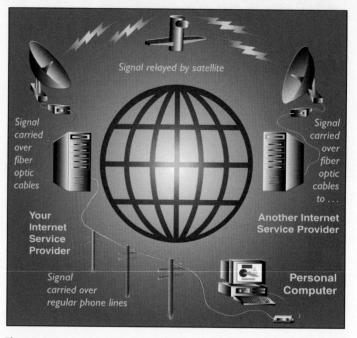

Figure O.1

For years, only the military, government, or university staff who were doing research or had computer expertise made use of the Internet. These people sent and received *e-mail* (*electronic mail*); they used *Telnet* to connect to remote host computers and used their computers as terminals; and they used *FTP* (*File Transfer Protocol*) to transfer files from remote computers.

In 1989, Tim Berners-Lee at CERN, the European Laboratory for Particle Physics in Geneva, Switzerland, developed a new set of standards (protocol) for exchanging information on the Internet. This protocol provided a way to link documents on any computer on any network by means of an easy-to-use piece of software called a *browser*. This web of documents linked together became known as the *World Wide Web*. Some people think that the World Wide Web is separate from the Internet or that the World Wide Web *is* the Internet. Actually, the Web can't exist without the Internet. The Internet is the network of computer networks that provides the framework for the World Wide Web.

For the next few years, most activity on the Web remained scientifically or academically oriented, and the browsers were *text-based*; that is, they linked text-only documents together. Until 1991, NSF set limits on the type of information that could travel over the Internet, and because the network was largely financed by the federal government, business activity wasn't allowed. The lifting of the ban on commercial activity and the development of commercial networks have helped create the current level of activity on the Web.

In 1993, the National Center for Superconducting Applications (NSCA) released *Mosaic*, developed by Marc Andreessen and others at the University of Illinois at Champaign-Urbana. Mosaic was the first graphical Web browser, allowing users to click the mouse on text, graphics, buttons, or icons to link to another location. Marc Andreessen and others went on to form a private company, Netscape Communications Corporation, that markets software to browse the Web. This software is known as *Netscape Navigator*.

Since the inception of the graphical browser, the Web has become the communications phenomenon of the late 20th century. Anyone can publish on the Web, and anyone with access to the Web has free use of the information. This is truly a revolutionary idea. No longer is publishing your ideas limited to books, magazines, or other traditional media. And on the information-retrieval end, no longer can governments or institutions control the flow of information, even though they may monitor—and, in some countries, attempt to control—the flow of information.

Information on every imaginable topic is now available on the World Wide Web. Users "surf" the Web—finding new information, looking at "cool" sites, doing serious research, or conducting business. They can contact government officials, plan a vacation, find people with like interests, or simply find out new things.

Information on the Web resides on host computers known as Web *servers*. The computer on your desk, from which you access information on the World Wide Web, is known as the ***client***.

The client computer user requests information from the Web server by clicking a ***link*** or ***hot spot***. The link contains the invisible address of the computer where the information resides, so the request immediately goes to the proper Web server. This method of linking various documents is both nonlinear and nonsequential—that is, not like a book where you read one page after another—allowing the user to design his own path through information (see Figure O.2).

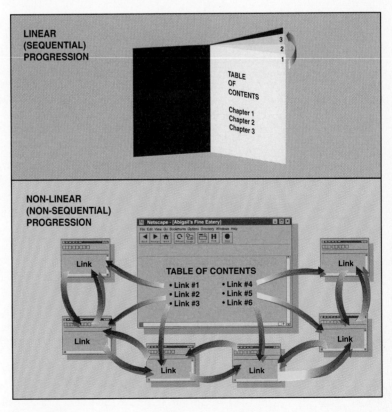

Figure O.2

The communications protocol that Web servers and clients use is *HTTP* (*Hypertext Transfer Protocol*). *Hypertext* appears in a different color from the other text, usually blue. *Hypermedia* can be images or audio or video clips. When the user clicks the hypertext or image, the computer makes a link to another location, and a document or image appears or a video or audio clip plays.

Only electronic documents have linked files. These linked files can be on computers in separate parts of the world. Space simply disappears on the Web; distance is collapsed. No longer is a person limited to the information available in his town or village or even country or continent.

CONNECTING TO THE WORLD WIDE WEB

To connect to the Internet, you need the following:

- A computer
- A modem, at least 28.8 kilobits per second is recommended, and you might want a dedicated phone line to the modem for convenience
- A connection to the Internet through an *ISP* (*Internet Service Provider*) that normally charges a subscription fee
- A Web browser
- If you want to play recorded sounds and display video, your system also needs a sound card, a video card, and plenty of random access memory (RAM)

When the client computer uses its modem to access the Internet, the call is routed over phone connections to the Internet Service Provider. The ISP has racks of modems that receive incoming calls and then connect the client to a computer on the Internet backbone by means of a fast T1 or T3 connection, a leased dedicated line. The Web server then processes the request and sends the requested document to the client through the same lines. The document that appears on the client's screen is called a *home page*, which is simply the top or first page in a Web document.

Because the cost of a personal computer with enough power and speed to use the World Wide Web effectively is quite high, the electronics industry is looking at alternatives. One such alternative is *WebTV*—a small box that attaches to your television set and connects it to a phone line. WebTV makes your TV seem more like a personal computer by providing full Internet access, a Web browser, and e-mail. By integrating a RISC computer chip and a fast modem (33.6 kilobits per second) with your television set, this new advance will mean that people can purchase the equipment for online access for about $300.

BROWSER BASICS

A browser is the software that allows you to navigate the World Wide Web easily. Unlike Telnet, which uses the PC as a dumb terminal by maintaining the connection with the host continually, the browser sends the request for information, the Web server transfers the information to the browser, and then the connection is broken. Each request by the client computer requires a new, separate connection to the Web server.

The first generation of browsers were text-based, and although they are still widely used, the newer browsers are usually graphics-based. All browsers allow you to click hypertext links, move back to the previous page, move to your opening page, open files, and print pages. If you find locations to which you want to return, you can set bookmarks or look at the history list of recently viewed pages. The three most popular browsers are Mosaic, Netscape Navigator, and Microsoft Internet Explorer.

As of the printing of this module, NCSA Mosaic 2.1.1 is the latest version of the first graphical browser (see Figure O.3, which shows the home page for Mosaic at `www.ncsa.uiuc.edu/SDG/Software/WinMosaic/HomePage.html`). Mosaic is easy to use and has some nice features, such as AutoSurf, which automatically follows links and saves them on the client's hard drive for viewing offline. However, Mosaic's popularity has fallen off in the last few years.

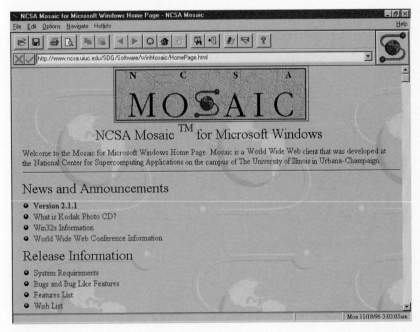

Figure O.3

Netscape Navigator 3.0 has two versions: Atlas and Atlas Gold, which includes a Web page editor for creating your own Web documents (see Figure O.4, which shows `home.netscape.com`). At print time for this module, Netscape is the most popular Web browser—claiming 85 percent of the browser market—and has been called the most popular PC application of all time. Netscape is easy to use and provides great flexibility with plug-ins—software applications that expand a browser's basic capabilities, such as allowing users to chat with each other or sign documents on the Web by using a digitizing pad. Netscape includes e-mail, newsgroup readers, and FTP (file transfer protocol).

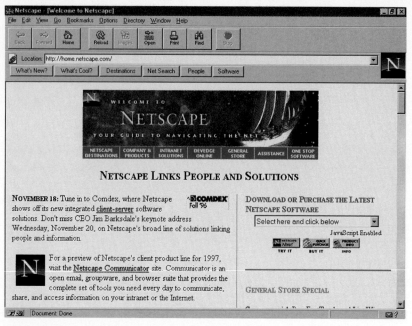

Figure O.4

Microsoft Internet Explorer for Windows 95 is becoming very popular with Windows 95 users (see Figure O.5, which shows the Internet Explorer start page). It's easy to use and includes e-mail, news programs, and FTP, and comes as part of Windows 95. In some areas such as viewing mail, Internet Explorer is even more flexible than Netscape because it allows users access to their mail without having to load any Web documents.

Figure O.5

Working with Web Addresses

Linking to any of the millions of Web documents that are on thousands of different servers in thousands of locations requires an addressing scheme. Each network has a unique address and each computer on the network has an address based on the network to which it's connected. The address, based on the *Internet Protocol* (*IP*), appears as a long string of numbers separated by periods, for example 198.168.37.186. Because the long numeric IPs are so hard for users to deal with, most networks also have *domain names*, which are converted into the numeric IP by software. The domain names are words separated by periods, for example, efn.org. In this example, org is the top-level domain name (or suffix) and efn is the second-level domain name. The suffix of the domain name specifies the type of organization to which the computer belongs. Table 0.1 lists the common suffixes.

Table 0.1

Suffix	Type of Organization
edu	Educational institution
com	Commercial organization
gov	Government
mil	Military
org	Nonprofit organization
net	Networks

Frequently, the domain name also has a suffix that identifies the country in which the server is located. For example, au tells you that the document is located on a server in Australia.

When a user requests a document by clicking a link, a *Domain Name Server* (*DNS*) matches the domain name with the IP numeric address. Once the address of the Web server is known, the IP protocol checks with a *router*—a computer on the Internet that finds routes for the packets to travel.

For this addressing scheme to work, each Web site must have a unique domain name, and somebody must keep track of all the domain names. The InterNIC Registration Service approves unique names and keeps track of domain names. Because of the explosion in the number of servers being attached to the Web, requests for registrations of domain names is now a slow process, and many domain names and IP addresses have already been used.

Although IP addresses can be used, domain names are more commonly used in the *URL* (*Uniform Resource Locator*), which is the complete address used to access documents. For example, look at the following address:

http://www.whitehouse.gov/WH/Welcome.html

In this example, http: names the protocol used and tells the browser how to deal with the document. The protocol is usually separated from the second part, the domain name, with two forward slashes (/). The domain name often begins with the three characters www to signify that the document is on the World Wide Web. The last part of the URL (preceded by a single forward slash) is the path or folder (directory) on the server where the file is located, and subdirectories may be part of this path. The file name of the desired file is the last part of the URL. If no file name is specified, the URL refers to the default file in that folder (directory).

The example just cited tells the browser to find a Web document (`http:`) on the host computer `www.whitehouse.gov` in the folder `WH` with the filename `Welcome`, and the document is a hypertext document (`.html`). Because URLs are case sensitive, you must type them carefully. Also be sure to include the punctuation exactly, and never include spaces. If you type the example address correctly into your browser, you will be connected to the White House (see Figure O.6).

Figure O.6

 To practice using the World Wide Web:

1 Start your browser software and connect to the World Wide Web.

2 Visit a museum, a library, the White House, NASA, and The Whole Internet Catalog by typing the following addresses. Be careful when you type the addresses: they're case sensitive, and spaces aren't allowed. (These addresses were accurate as of the printing of this book, but the Internet is a constantly changing entity. If you can't contact one of these sites, consult your instructor).

> **http://watt.emf.net/louvre/**
> **http://www.w3.org/pub/DataSources/bySubject/Overview.htm.**
> **http://www.whitehouse.gov/WH/Welcome.html**
> **http://www.gsfc.nasa.gov/NASA/homepage.html**
> **http://nearnet.gnn.com/wic/index.html**

3 Use some of the links at each site to jump around the Internet.

 If necessary, you can exit the browser and continue this project later.

Finding Information on the World Wide Web

Finding specific information on the Internet requires specialized electronic search tools. These tools include:

- *Archie*. This database, located on servers in various parts of the world, searches FTP sites.
- *Gopher*. This software, located on Gopher servers, steps you through a series of menus to help find the information.
- *Veronica*. This program searches Gopher sites.

With the tremendous growth of the World Wide Web, a new type of service provider has evolved. These services compile databases of information to be found on the Web, using two methods:

- Accepting new URLs submitted by users
- Using programs called spiders that follow links in documents and gather information from the documents

Most search services are free because they include advertising on nearly every page. Some of the most popular search services include *Yahoo!* (see Figure O.5), *infoseek*, *Excite*, *Lycos*, *AltaVista*, and *Magellan*. You can find these search services within Netscape Navigator or Microsoft Internet Explorer by choosing commands in the browser that help you search for information.

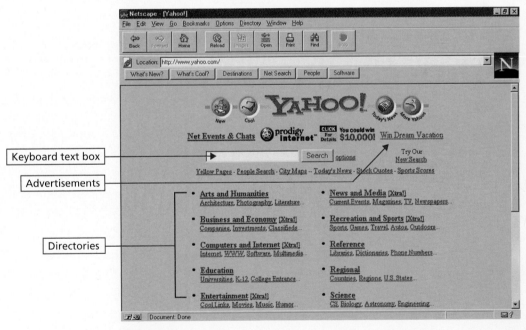

Figure O.7

You can click in the directories section and follow the path to information, or you can type a keyword or words for Yahoo! to search for. Documents that contain the keywords are then listed. You can refine your searches by using specific keywords.

Caution Keep in mind the source of the documents you encounter in your search. Anyone can place anything on the Web, whether accurate or not. Always verify your research.

To use the search engine Yahoo!:

1 Start your browser software and connect to the World Wide Web.

2 Type the address www.yahoo.com and press [Enter] to go to the Yahoo! Web site.

3 Search for information on these topics:

- HTML editors
- Web page design
- The history of the Internet
- Browsers
- Hobbies
- Areas of medical interest
- Colleges of interest
- Organizations of interest

EXIT If necessary, you can exit the browser and continue this project later.

DESIGNING A WEB DOCUMENT

Because anyone can publish on the Web, you'll see all kinds of poorly designed, hard-to-read home pages. You will be designing home pages throughout the rest of this module, so this section provides you with information and tips for designing effective home pages.

Tip You should design all elements of a Web presentation on paper before you begin creating the document. A **Web presentation** is the entire presentation, whereas the home page is just the top page of the presentation.

To begin designing your Web presentation, answer the following questions:

- What's the purpose of this Web presentation?
- What audience am I trying to reach and how does that affect my presentation?
- What information am I trying to convey?
- How will I organize the information?
- What should the home or top page have on it to attract visitors?
  After defining the goals of your Web presentation, you should define the structure. There are two basic organization styles to Web presentations: linear and hierarchical (see Figure O.8):

  - Linear organization is much like a book that's read page by page.
  - Hierarchical structure allows you to select something from the first page and move directly to that information; this scheme makes use of

hypertext links and is used extensively online. However, even a hierarchical Web presentation may contain some linear structure when you need the reader to follow a certain course.

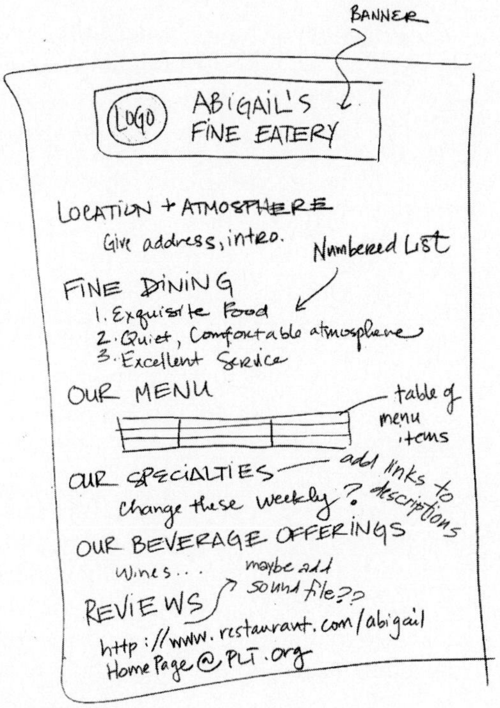

Figure O.8

> **Reminder** Keep in mind that users don't always enter from the top or home page of a presentation; they can link to any of your pages. All the pages in your presentation should be able to stand alone, and all pages should provide a link back to the top or home page of the presentation.

Once you know what you want to say and how you want to present it, you're ready to write the content of the presentation. When writing for online publication, you should follow the guidelines given in the Web Page Design Checklist.

- [ ] Be brief—use lists whenever possible; use short words in short sentences
- [ ] Be clear—avoid vague words
- [ ] Use simple language—avoid extra words
- [ ] Check your spelling and grammar—the world can visit your document
- [ ] Use the following features to tie the presentation together:
  - [ ] Use hypertext lists or menus
  - [ ] Include a link only if it's a useful way to get to relevant information
  - [ ] Use consistent terminology throughout the presentation

☐ Use consistent icons throughout the presentation

☐ Use the same banner or identifying information on each page of the presentation

☐ Use consistent layout for each page of the presentation

☐ Include a way back to the home page on each separate page and place it in the same location on each page

☐ Make sure all links are current

☐ Include a graphic only if it relates to the content

☐ Include alternative text with every graphic

☐ Make sure each page can stand alone yet remains consistent with the rest of the site

☐ Don't overdo emphasizing or formatting text

☐ Make sure the text stands out from the background

☐ Use rules to separate sections of the page

☐ Try out the presentation in more than one browser

After you've created the Web presentation and checked it out in your browser, you may want to verify that all of your HTML code is correct, by using an HTML validator or syntax checker. Many of these programs to test HTML code can be found on the World Wide Web. You can download a program and run it on your computer, or you can type the URL for your home page into a form, and the program will check your coding.

CREATING A WEB DOCUMENT

After becoming familiar with the World Wide Web, you can create your own home page. Home pages are made up of the text and graphics you want to display, along with links to other documents. You use *HTML* (*Hypertext Markup Language*), to provide information to browsers as to how to display pages and create links. HTML is the Web's universal programming language; it's not specific to any platform, computer brand, or operating system. It's a simple programming language that places codes or tags in a Web document, providing information to browsers about the structure of the document.

HTML, developed in 1989, is actually a simplified version of the programming language SGML, short for Standard Generalized Markup Language, which was developed to share documents on different types of computers. HTML contains one added feature: the use of hypertext to link documents.

The first version of HTML contained only about 30 commands (tags), which the user embedded in a document. The next version, HTML 2.0, added new tags, expanding the capability of the language to include such things as interactive forms. The third version, HTML 3.0, further expanded the programming features of the language. As a group called the WWW Consortium was discussing what should be approved as standards for this third generation of HTML, Netscape and other developers brought out versions of their own software that used many of the proposed tags and some browser-specific tags; consequently, some of these new tags or extensions of older tags aren't understood by all browsers.

HTML documents are actually ASCII (text) files with HTML tags embedded. HTML tags tell browsers how to display the document; however, each browser expresses the commands in its own way. For example, if you define a line of text on your Web page as a heading, each browser that displays the document knows to display the line of text as a heading. However, each browser might embellish the text in headings differently, so your Web document will look different when displayed in different browsers. Figures O.9 and O.10 show the Microsoft home page in Mosaic and Netscape, respectively. Notice the differences in the way the page is displayed in one browser versus another.

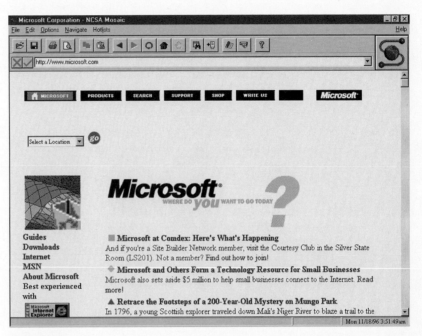

Figure O.9

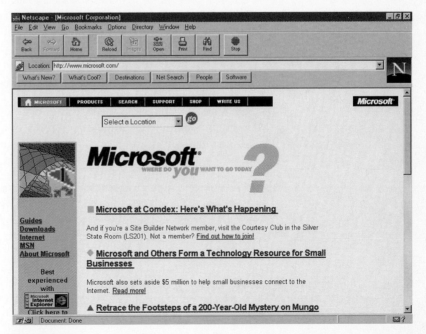

Figure O.10

Because HTML documents are just ASCII text files, you can type the HTML tags using any word processing program (such as Microsoft Word) or a simple text program (such as Windows Notepad), or you can use an editor, such as HotDog, that places many of the tags for you. Some editors can be classified as WYSIWYG (short for "what you see is what you get"), that is, you don't have to switch to your browser to view the results of your coding.

If you decide to use an editor that generates tags for you, you still need to know HTML so that you can edit your work, add elements that may not be available in an editor, or troubleshoot a problem.

Most high-end word processing programs, such as Corel's WordPerfect Internet Publisher, include HTML capabilities. Microsoft Word includes the Internet Assistant. Even some browsers such as Netscape Gold offer HTML capabilities. Other standalone HTML editors are shareware or freeware and are available for a fee or on the Web, or you can purchase standalone retail packages. Some popular HTML editors include FrontPage, HotDog, Homesite X, HTML Easy!, and HTML Assistant.

Caution When downloading software, keep in mind the prevalence of viruses on the Internet.

PUBLISHING A WEB DOCUMENT

After your Web document is error-free, you're ready to publish it. You should check with your Internet Service Provider to see whether the provider offers that kind of service, imposes any limits, and charges any fees. If you're designing a commercial site, you might explore maintaining your own Web server so that you have more control over security and management of the site.

Once you settle on a Web site for your presentation, you need to place the files on the server. Files should be organized in one directory or in a main directory with subdirectories. Naming conventions between operating systems may require you to rename your files and the link addresses. (For example, you may need to change all .htm files to .html.) Then you're ready to FTP your files to the server.

Once you have published your document and have a URL for it, you need to let people know about your home page. Be sure to include the URL on your business cards, stationery, and other business documents. Also, announce your home page online by contacting Internet search tools companies. Many are free, but some charge to list your page.

Tip After you've published your Web presentation, keep it maintained and up-to-date. Periodically check all links to make sure that they are still active, and add new or updated information to your page so that you will have repeat visitors.

THE NEXT STEP

Study the organization and layout of many home pages in preparation for creating your own. Notice elements that are unattractive and avoid these in your design, and find elements that catch your eye or simply work well.

SUMMARY AND EXERCISES

Summary

- A *client* is a computer that displays a Web document.
- A *server* is where the Web document resides.
- *Browsers* enable you to display Web documents.
- A *home page* is the top page of a Web presentation.
- A *URL* is the address of a Web document.
- *HTML* is the programming language used to create Web documents.
- *Search tools* help locate information on the World Wide Web.
- An *editor* places HTML tags in the document for you.
- A *validator* or *syntax checker* checks your HTML code for errors.

Key Terms

Alta Vista	Internet protocol (IP)
Archie	Internet Service Provider (ISP)
browser	link
client	Lycos
domain	Magellan
Domain Name Server (DNS)	Mosaic
Excite	Netscape Navigator
gopher	protocol
home page	router
hot spot	server
HTML (Hypertext Markup Language)	text-based browsers
	Uniform Resource Locator (URL)
HTTP (Hypertext Transfer Protocol)	Veronica
	Web presentation
hypermedia	Web server
hypertext	WebTV
infoseek	World Wide Web
Internet	Yahoo!

Study Questions

Multiple Choice

1. The World Wide Web is
   a. a network of computer networks.
   b. independent of the Internet.
   c. primarily for military use.
   d. a web of linked documents.
   e. all of these answers.

2. HTML is
   a. a protocol.
   b. a programming language.
   c. a Web presentation.
   d. a domain.
   e. all of these answers.

3. A URL is
   a. a protocol.
   b. a programming language.
   c. a document address.
   d. a domain.
   e. all of these answers.

4. HTTP is
   a. a protocol.
   b. a programming language.
   c. a document address.
   d. a domain.
   e. all of these answers.

5. Hypertext is
   a. a protocol.
   b. a programming language.
   c. a link.
   d. a domain.
   e. all of these answers.

6. A home page is
   a. the top page in a Web presentation.
   b. always about you.
   c. hypertext.
   d. written in HTTP.
   e. all of these answers.

7. To connect to the World Wide Web, you need
   a. a modem.
   b. an ISP.
   c. a browser.
   d. a computer
   e. all of these answers.

8. Home pages should
   a. be written in long, detailed sentences.
   b. be written in short, concise sentences.
   c. contain graphics that simply look good.
   d. never link to other locations.
   e. all of these answers.

9. You can create your own home page, using
   a. an editor.
   b. a validator.
   c. a syntax checker.
   d. graphics
   e. all these answers.

10. To advertise your Web site, you should
    a. place the URL on your business cards.
    b. notify a search tool.
    c. place the URL on your stationery.
    d. link to other documents.
    e. all these answers.

Short Answer

1. HTML codes are also called _____.

2. What software tools can you use to create a home page?

3. What's a protocol?

4. What's the protocol used on the World Wide Web?

5. What's an IP?

6. What's a domain?

7. What's a URL?

8. Define the Internet.

9. Label the parts of the following URL:

   `http://www.w3.org/pub/DataFiles/byAuthor/index.html`

10. Define HTML.

For Discussion

1. What's the difference between linear and hierarchical organization?

2. Describe the process for designing a Web presentation.

3. Describe the process for finding information on a certain topic on the World Wide Web.

4. Explain how the World Wide Web is part of the Internet.

5. Describe the use of hypertext on Web documents.

Review Exercises

Preparing to Create an HTML Document

This exercise will continue throughout this module. You'll be provided with all the information necessary to create a home page for a children's bookstore. Before you get started in Project 1, take time to look at what other bookstores have published on the World Wide Web.

Researching Information for an Animal Web Page

This exercise will continue throughout the book. At this point, you need to decide on a topic related to animals. Perhaps you know someone who raises a certain type of animal, or you're interested in a certain endangered species, or in your local Humane Society—or any other topic related to animals. You should start researching the topic, both online and offline. That is, check out similar information on the World Wide Web, and gather any materials necessary to start creating your own home page. Spend time designing the overall presentation.

Assignments

Designing a Personal Web Page

Many people use a personal Web page to find employment, and so can you. This assignment continues through the text.

If you have a business venture or just want to sell your talents, this is an opportunity. Gather your personal information, such as your résumé, and spend some time browsing the Web to see what other people have done. Spend time designing the overall presentation.

Designing an Organization or Nonprofit Web Page

Many wonderful nonprofit organizations would benefit by having a presence on the World Wide Web. This assignment continues throughout the text, and asks you to create a home page for an organization, church, team, or nonprofit organization. You'll need the permission and help of the organization, and this is a good way to help others while you learn how to create home pages.

Once the concept has been approved by the organization, ask for help in compiling information on the organization, such as the purpose statement, history, bylaws, and any other data you need. Spend time searching the Web for comparable organizations or other chapters of this one. Design the overall presentation.

> **What Is a FAQ?** *FAQ* stands for *Frequently Asked Questions*. Many online services provide a FAQ section. The questions in the FAQ are compiled from users who have had trouble getting started or problems with some aspect of the service or program. You can benefit by always checking out the FAQ section before jumping in; it may save time in the long run.

PROJECT 1: CREATING AN HTML DOCUMENT

Objectives

After completing this project, you should be able to:

▶ Create an HTML document

▶ Use headings

▶ Use the address tag

▶ Insert new paragraphs

▶ Include line breaks

CASE STUDY: CREATING A WEB PAGE

You've already learned what the Internet is and how it works. Now you're aware of its potential to change the nature of communication within modern society. Businesses, educational institutions, governments, and computer users everywhere have a myriad of opportunities available for using the Internet.

For this project, you're bringing the Internet to a local business. Imagine that the owner of Abigail's Fine Eatery has asked you to create a Web page for her restaurant.

Designing the Solution

In this first project, you create the basic structure of a Web document. You then use the structure to create a home page that you'll learn how to enhance in the remaining projects. Figure 1.1 shows the home page you'll create in this project.

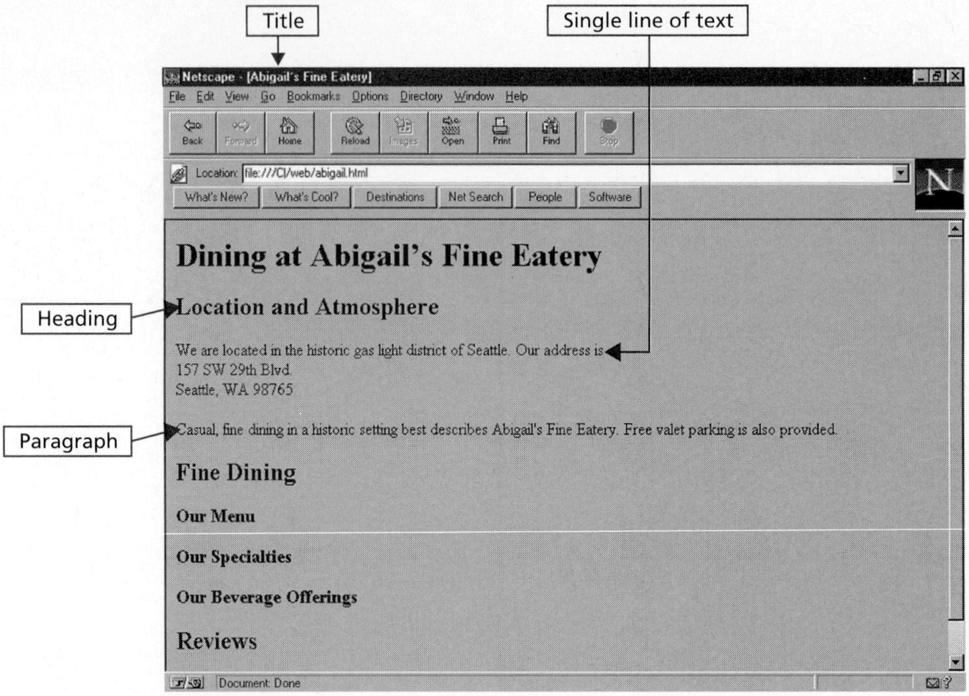
Title
Single line of text
Netscape - [Abigail's Fine Eatery]
Location: file:///C|/web/abigail.html
Dining at Abigail's Fine Eatery
Heading
Location and Atmosphere
We are located in the historic gas light district of Seattle. Our address is
157 SW 29th Blvd.
Seattle, WA 98765
Paragraph
Casual, fine dining in a historic setting best describes Abigail's Fine Eatery. Free valet parking is also provided.
Fine Dining
Our Menu
Our Specialties
Our Beverage Offerings
Reviews
Document: Done

Figure 1.1a

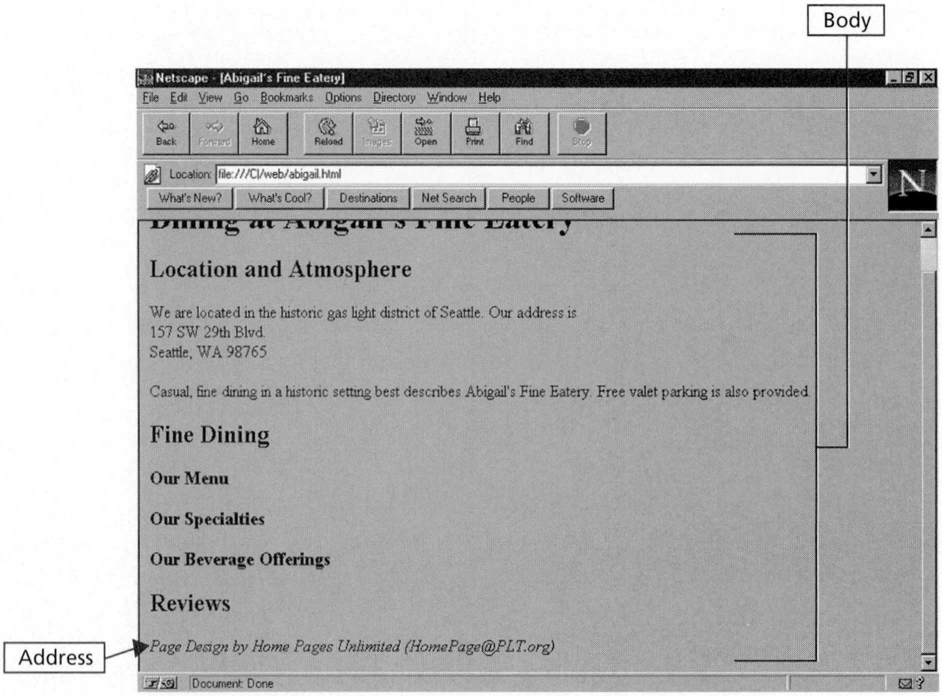
Body
Netscape - [Abigail's Fine Eatery]
Location: file:///C|/web/abigail.html
Location and Atmosphere
We are located in the historic gas light district of Seattle. Our address is
157 SW 29th Blvd.
Seattle, WA 98765
Casual, fine dining in a historic setting best describes Abigail's Fine Eatery. Free valet parking is also provided.
Fine Dining
Our Menu
Our Specialties
Our Beverage Offerings
Reviews
Address
Page Design by Home Pages Unlimited (HomePage@PLT.org)
Document: Done

Figure 1.1b

STARTING AN **HTML** DOCUMENT

HTML (HyperText Markup Language) is a set of codes that you use to create a document. These codes, called **tags**, format text or connect one file with another. These HTML tags follow a certain format, or **syntax**. Each tag begins with an opening angle bracket (<), ends with a closing angle bracket (>), and contains a command between the brackets; for example, <HTML> is the tag that designates the beginning of an HTML document.

Many of the tags are paired; that is, the first tag indicates the beginning of the command, and the second tag ends the command. The closing tag of the pair has the same syntax as the opening tag, but includes a forward slash (/) before the command. For example, the tag for the ending of an HTML document is </HMTL>. All the text between the opening and closing tags is affected by the tags. For example:

Opening tag	`<HTML>`
Affected text	`entire Web document`
Closing tag	`</HTML>`

> **Caution** If you forget to close a paired set of tags or you include a backslash or some other character rather than a forward slash, the tag won't be closed, and the command will stay in effect. For example, if you forget to put in the </H1> tag to end a level-1 heading, you may be unpleasantly surprised by seeing large bold type throughout your document.

The first section, called the **head section**, opens with the <HEAD> tag and closes with the </HEAD> tag. The head section *must* contain the title of the Web page, but it also *can* contain the **URL** (**Uniform Resource Locator**) or World Wide Web address of your document. You must include the opening <TITLE> tag, the title of the Web page, and the closing </TITLE> tag in the head section. Following is an example of a simple document head section:

Opening tag	`<HEAD>`
Words appearing on-screen	`<TITLE>Addison Wesley</TITLE>`
Closing tag	`</HEAD>`

Remember these important points about titles:

- A Web page can have only one title.
- The title should be specific and descriptive because it's used in a browser's history list, as bookmarks, and in indexes or other programs that catalog Web pages. For example, if you use `Abigail's Home Page` as the title, when the reader sees it in a browser, he might not remember that Abigail's is a restaurant; thinking that this is somebody's personal home page, he might simply delete it. `Abigail's Fine Eatery` is more descriptive, and therefore more likely to be kept in a bookmark list.
- A title should be concise because browsers place it in the title bar of the browser, not on the Web document.
- A title can't be formatted like other tags—you can't change its appearance.
- A title can't link to other pages.

> **What Is TCP/IP?** TCP/IP stands for **Transmission Control Protocol/Internet Protocol**. This protocol (standard) allows computers to communicate regardless of what brand, model, or operating system they run. The Transmission Control Protocol contains the message, and the Internet Protocol contains the address where the message packets need to go. Every message sent over the Internet is broken down into packets of data that travel to the destination independently, taking whatever route is available at the time. When all the packets arrive at the destination, they're reassembled into a coherent message. For your computer to communicate with the Internet, it must run the TCP/IP standard.

The second and final section of the Web document is the *body section*. The opening <BODY> tag must come immediately after the closing </HEAD> tag, and the closing </BODY> tag must immediately precede the closing </HTML> tag. Therefore, the entire body of the Web page is included within the <BODY></BODY> tags. Here's the structure:

```
<HTML>
        <HEAD>
                <TITLE></TITLE>
        </HEAD>
        <BODY>
        . . .
        . . .
        </BODY>
</HTML>
```

Adding Comments to Your HTML Code

Documentation is a very important step in the creation of a computer program. You may need to come back to the program months later, or someone else may need to edit or update your work. In either case, notes about the program can be helpful to you or someone else.

You can include comments in HTML to document what you've done or to provide some additional information. Comments have the following syntax:

```
<!-this is a comment->
```

You replace the text `this is a comment` with any information you want to include.

Comments show up only when the document is opened in an editor; they never appear on the final Web page.

> **Caution** Anyone who saves your Web page as HTML code will have access to your comments.

Creating a Basic HTML Document

You will now create the structure of an HTML document for Abigail's Fine Eatery. Because you should make the source code of your HTML document as readable as possible, be sure to use plenty of carriage returns and tabs for formatting. (The tabs and returns don't show up in your Web document.) Remember that the goal is clarit—so that you or someone else can come back and easily edit the document.

To create an HTML document:

1 Open your HTML editor, a word processing program, or a plain text editor (like Window's Notepad).

2 To create the structure of your HTML page, type the following code:

```
<HTML>
<HEAD>
<TITLE>Abigail's Fine Eatery</TITLE>
</HEAD>
<BODY>
<!—This section will be updated—>
</BODY>
</HTML>
```

The document should look like Figure 1.2.

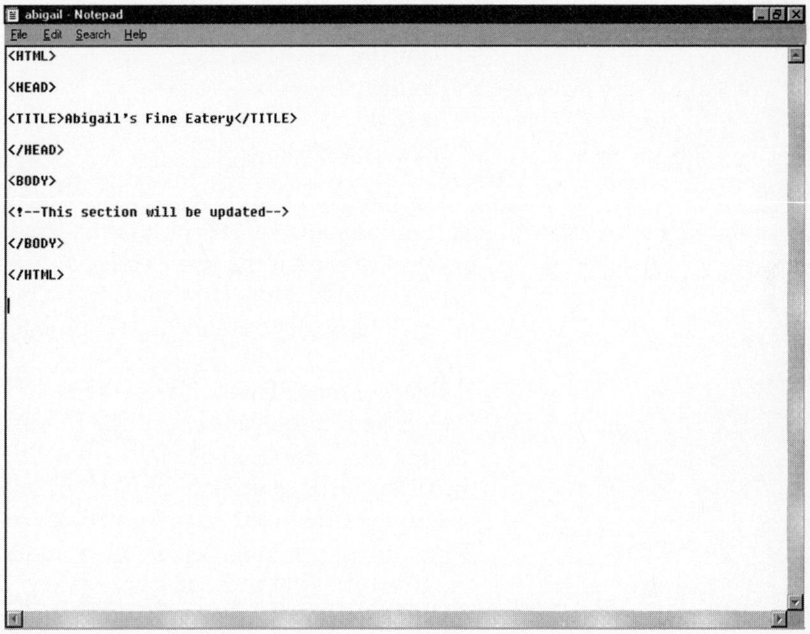

```
abigail - Notepad
File   Edit   Search   Help
<HTML>

<HEAD>

<TITLE>Abigail's Fine Eatery</TITLE>

</HEAD>

<BODY>

<!--This section will be updated-->

</BODY>

</HTML>
```

Figure 1.2

Notice that the code includes a comment that reads This section will be updated. This information will be filled in a bit later in this project.

3 Save the file as *abigail.html*.

If the operating system doesn't allow long file names, name the file *abigail.htm* instead.

4 View the document in your Web browser by opening the file from the menu in the browser.... Surprise! If you wrote your HTML code correctly, you should get a blank page. Remember, the items included so far don't show up in a final Web document and are only markers for the actual content.

> **Tip** Be sure to save your HTML code before you try to view the document with your Web browser. If you don't save the document, the browser won't read any of the changes you made since you last saved your code. Not saving could lead to a very frustrating hour of wondering why your perfect code isn't showing up on your Web page!

 If necessary, you can save the HTML file, exit the browser and editor programs, and continue this project later.

USING HEADINGS

You can use headings to organize the body of your Web documents, much like an outline can organize a conventional document. HTML has six levels of headings, designated by the following tags:

```
Heading 1 <H1></H1>
Heading 2 <H2></H2>
Heading 3 <H3></H3>
Heading 4 <H4></H4>
Heading 5 <H5></H5>
Heading 6 <H6></H6>
```

Heading 1 is the most prominent of the headings and Heading 6 the least prominent. When you use the heading tags, you're telling each browser to format the text as a heading. Each individual browser formats each level of heading its own way, so you're simply setting up a structure for each browser to follow. You'll probably use the first three levels most often.

Because the title you place in the <TITLE> tag in the head section of the Web page is displayed only in the title bar of the browser, you should include a title for the page in the body section of the document. To make the title appear as text on the Web page, use the first-level heading to restate the title of the page, or provide a more complete title. For example, if the title of the Web document is Addison Wesley, you might use the first-level heading text Addison Wesley Computer Textbooks. Then you would use the next levels of headings to organize the content of the page.

> **Tip** You aren't limited to the amount of text you can include in a heading, but you should keep all headings concise because some Web search tools use headings in their searches.

In the following steps, you will add headings to the Web page for Abigail's. You will place all headings, paragraphs, tables, and just plain text in the body section of the HTML document.

To add headings to an HTML document:

1 In the *abigail.html* document, under the words This section will be updated, type the following text:

```
<H1>Dining at Abigail's Fine Eatery</H1>
    <H2>Location and Atmosphere</H2>
    <H2>Fine Dining</H2>
        <H3>Our Menu</H3>
        <H3>Our Specialties</H3>
        <H3>Our Beverage Offerings</H3>
    <H2>Reviews</H2>
```

Compare what you typed with the HTML code in Figure 1.3. Notice that the code uses three different heading levels. The extra returns and tabs in the source code are included to make the hierarchy of headings more obvious. On a longer document, you may choose to organize the code differently, in a manner that's comfortable for you. The important thing is that your code follows some logical and clear order.

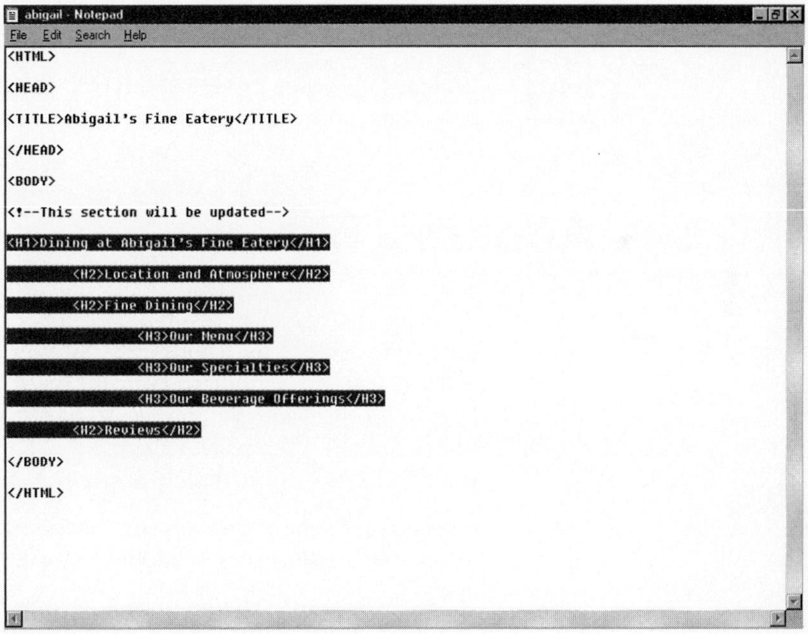

```
abigail - Notepad
File  Edit  Search  Help
<HTML>

<HEAD>

<TITLE>Abigail's Fine Eatery</TITLE>

</HEAD>

<BODY>

<!--This section will be updated-->

<H1>Dining at Abigail's Fine Eatery</H1>

            <H2>Location and Atmosphere</H2>

        <H2>Fine Dining</H2>

                <H3>Our Menu</H3>

                <H3>Our Specialties</H3>

                <H3>Our Beverage Offerings</H3>

        <H2>Reviews</H2>

</BODY>

</HTML>
```

Figure 1.3

2 Save the document. Then look at the page, using your browser. The page should look similar to Figure 1.4.

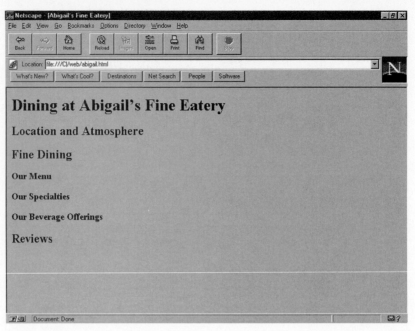

Figure 1.4

 EXIT   If necessary, you can save the HTML file, exit the browser and editor programs, and continue this project later.

USING THE ADDRESS TAG

To place the name and e-mail address of the owner or designer of the Web page, you can use the <ADDRESS> tag immediately above the closing </BODY> tag. The standard convention is to place this information at the bottom of the Web document. To have the information displayed at the bottom of the Web page, type the <ADDRESS> tag and information that you want to include immediately above the closing </BODY> tag. For example:

```
<ADDRESS>Page Design by Home Pages Unlimited
(HomePage@PLT.org)</ADDRESS></BODY>
```

In this example, the text Page Design by Home Pages Unlimited (HomePage@PLT.org) will appear at the bottom of the Web page.

 ### *To add an address to a Web page:*

1 In the *abigail.html* document, above the </BODY> tag at the bottom of the HTML source code, type the following address line (see Figure 1.5):

<ADDRESS>Page Design by Home Pages Unlimited (Home Page @ PLT.org)</ADDRESS>

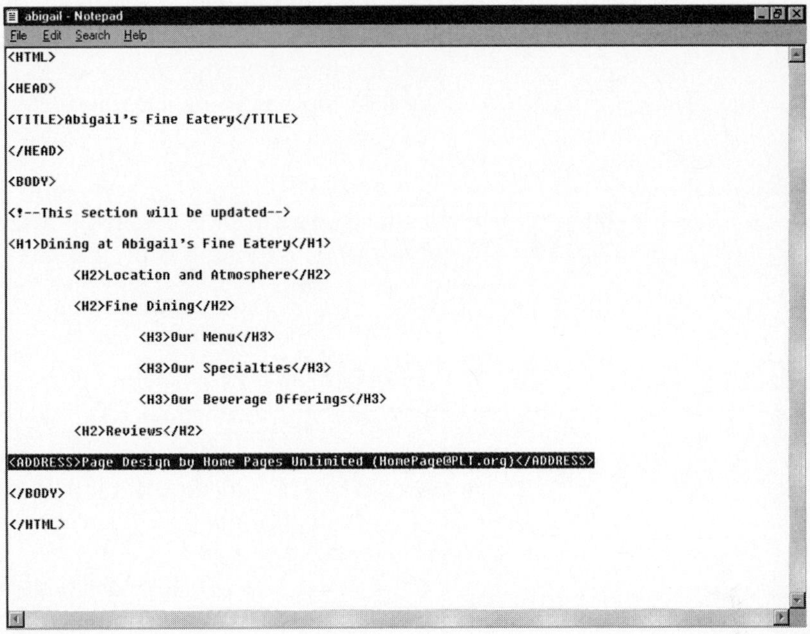

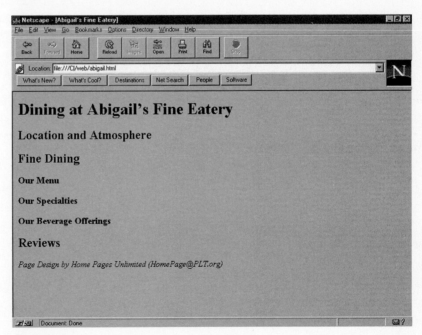

```
abigail - Notepad
File  Edit  Search  Help
<HTML>

<HEAD>

<TITLE>Abigail's Fine Eatery</TITLE>

</HEAD>

<BODY>

<!--This section will be updated-->

<H1>Dining at Abigail's Fine Eatery</H1>

        <H2>Location and Atmosphere</H2>

        <H2>Fine Dining</H2>

                <H3>Our Menu</H3>

                <H3>Our Specialties</H3>

                <H3>Our Beverage Offerings</H3>

        <H2>Reviews</H2>

<ADDRESS>Page Design by Home Pages Unlimited (HomePage@PLT.org)</ADDRESS>

</BODY>

</HTML>
```

Figure 1.5

2 Save the document. Then look at the page, using your browser. It should look similar to Figure 1.6.

Figure 1.6

> **Tip** Each browser has specific programming on how to handle the <ADDRESS> tag. With the version of Netscape shown in Figure 1.6, the <ADDRESS> tag has an italic format.

 If necessary, you can save the HTML file, exit the browser and editor programs, and continue this project later.

INSERTING NEW PARAGRAPHS

You're now ready to add text to the HTML document, just as you would in any conventional document. Note that HTML doesn't recognize when you press the (ENTER) key to end a paragraph. You need to include a <P> tag to start a new paragraph.

Each heading, <H1> through <H6>, automatically includes a paragraph break; therefore, you use the <P> tag only for new paragraphs that don't follow a heading. The end of the paragraph can include the closing paragraph tag </P>, but that's optional; however, you should get into the habit of including it for clarity and completeness.

 To insert paragraphs into an HTML document:

1 In the *abigail.html* document, insert the following two paragraphs of text under the heading Location and Atmosphere:

> **We are located in the historic gas light district of Seattle. Our address is 157 SW 29th Blvd., Seattle, WA 98765**
>
> **<P>**
> **Casual, fine dining in a historic setting best describes Abigail's Fine Eatery. Free valet parking is also provided.**
> **</P>**

Now look at Figure 1.7. The extra carriage returns and tabs format the paragraphs so that they follow exactly under the heading Location and Atmosphere. In the HTML code, notice the <P> and </P> tags around the second paragraph; they lie on the lines above and below the actual text. The reason for using such precise formatting is to make the code obvious and readable for anyone who may need to edit it; the formatting doesn't change the way the code looks in the Web document.

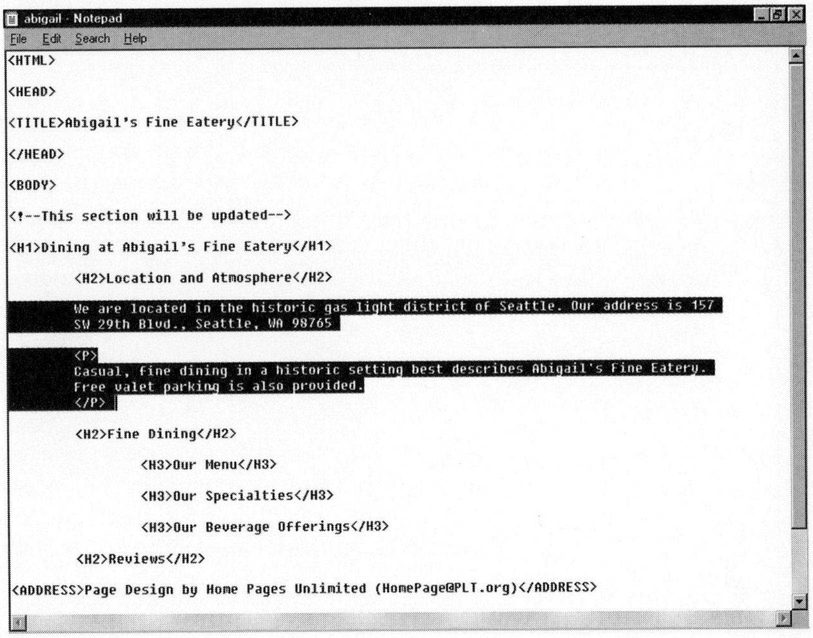

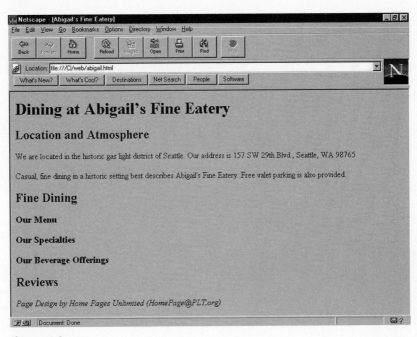

Figure 1.7

2 Save your work and look at the page from your browser (see Figure 1.8).

Figure 1.8

BREAKING LINES

When you use the paragraph tags (<P> and </P>), browsers insert white space. Sometimes you'll want to place some text on a line by itself, without including extra white space above it, thus creating a ***line break***. The line break tag <BR> provides an option for placing text on a line by itself without including white space. There's no closing tag for the line break.

In the following set of steps, you use the <BR> tag to format the address at the end of the first paragraph that you added in the preceding set of steps.

To insert line breaks in an HTML document:

1 In the *abigail.html* document, insert two <BR> tags to break the address you added in the preceding set of steps onto multiple lines. Then delete the comma following the word Blvd. (It's no longer necessary after you break up the address.) Your code should look like this:

```
We are located in the historic gas light district of
Seattle. Our address is<BR>
SW 29th Blvd.<BR>
Seattle, WA 98765
```

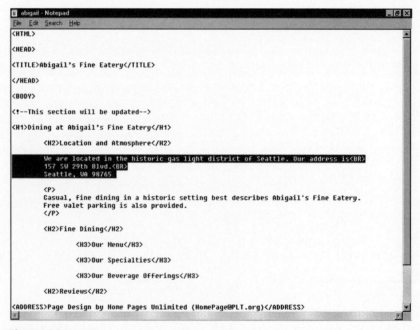

Figure 1.9

2 Save the document and then look at it with your browser (see Figure 1.10). Notice that, although the <BR> tags created carriage returns, they didn't add any extra white space, as the <P> tags do.

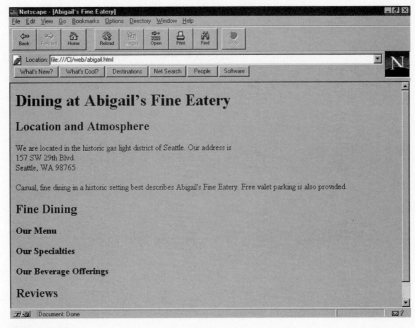

Figure 1.10

The Next Step

After creating your first Web page in this project, you might want to practice creating HTML documents, using the information provided in this project. Experiment with the heading styles to learn how to use them to organize the text you want to include on your Web page. Add paragraphs and single lines of text to the page.

Be sure to save your practice document with a different name. You will use the *abigail.html* document in the next project.

This concludes the project. You can either exit your editor and browser or go on to work the Study Questions, Review Exercises, and Assignments.

Summary and Exercises

Summary

- Each tag begins with an opening angle bracket (<), ends with a closing angle bracket (>), and contains a command between the angle brackets.
- In HTML codes that require a closing tag, the closing tag of the pair has the same syntax as the opening tag; however, it includes a slash before the command.
- The entire Web document is contained between the opening tag <HTML> and the closing tag </HTML>.
- The first section of the document is the head section, located between the opening <HEAD> tag and the closing </HEAD> tag.
- The title must appear in the head section and is contained between the opening <TITLE> tag and the closing </TITLE> tag.

- The body section of the document is contained between the opening `<BODY>` tag and the closing `</BODY>` tag.
- There are six levels of headings—`<H1>` through `<H6>`. As the number increases, the prominence of the heading decreases. All headings require appropriate closing tags—that is, `</H1>` through `</H6>`.
- The `<ADDRESS>` tag is used to place the name and e-mail address of the owner or designer on the Web page. It requires the closing tag `</ADDRESS>`.
- The `<P>` tag begins a new paragraph by placing white space above the text. Although the closing tag `</P>` is optional, it may be best to use it for consistency.
- The `<BR>` tag places text on a line by itself, without including white space above the text. It isn't a paired tag.
- The `<!-comment->` tag places a comment in the HTML document that won't appear on-screen, only in an editor.

Key Terms

address	headings
body	line break
closing tag	opening tag
comments	syntax
documentation	tag
head	title

Study Questions

Multiple Choice

1. HTML codes require a certain
   a. comment.
   b. line break.
   c. heading.
   d. syntax.
   e. mark.

2. Each tag begins with a(n)
   a. brace.
   b. angle bracket.
   c. slash.
   d. backslash.
   e. open parenthesis.

3. You use comments to
   a. keep the viewers of your browser from getting lost.
   b. prevent others from copying your Web page.
   c. make your page look better.
   d. make it easier to revise your page later.
   e. gain permission to put your page online.

4. Every Web document must begin and end with
   a. `<HTML>` and `<HTML>`.
   b. `<BODY>` and `</BODY>`.
   c. `<HTML>` and `</HTML>`.
   d. `<HEAD>` and `</HEAD>`.
   e. `<BR>` and `</BR>`.

5. Every HTML tag must
   a. have a closing tag.
   b. have a comment.
   c. follow the right syntax.
   d. have a slash.
   e. appear in the head section.

6. The `<BR>` tag
   a. is a paired tag.
   b. places no white space above the line.
   c. places white space above the line.
   d. is used to start a paragraph.
   e. begins an HTML document.

7. The `<TITLE>` tag
   a. is located in the body section.
   b. is located in the head section.
   c. should be very long and descriptive.
   d. appears in the text of the Web document.
   e. is the HTML filename.

8. Which tags should you use to make the text *University of Washington, Seattle* a title within the head section?
   a. `</TITLE>` and `<TITLE>`.
   b. `<TITLE>` and `<TITLE>`.
   c. `<TITLE>` and `</TITLE>`.
   d. `<!-TITLE>` and `<TITLE-!>`.
   e. `<!TITLE` and `</TITLE>`.

9. Which tag will make the text *Courses Offered* the second largest heading of the HTML heading styles?
   a. `<H5>`
   b. `<H4>`
   c. H2
   d. `<H2>`
   e. `<H1>`

10. Which tag do you need to make the text *The University of Washington offers courses both for credit and for non-credit* a paragraph if it comes before a heading?
    a. `<P>`
    b. `</P>`
    c. `<LB>`
    d. `<BR>`
    e. Can't be determined from the information given.

Short Answer

1. The tag to indicate the largest heading is _____.

2. What must you do to see the results of your HTML code?

3. Why should you be careful about what you write as comments?

4. Why don't you need to use the paragraph tag after a heading?

5. What must appear in the head section of a document?

6. How is a line break tag different from a paragraph tag?

7. Why should your title be concise?

8. How do you begin and end an HTML document?

9. What does URL stand for?

10. Where should you place an address?

For Discussion

1. Why would a restaurant want to have a Web page?

2. What's the difference between the paragraph tag and the line break tag?

3. Why should the title for an HTML document be carefully selected?

4. Why would including an address on an HTML document be important?

Review Exercises

Creating an HTML Document

Create a Web page for Alphabits Bookstore, using the following text (see Figure 1.11):

Title: `Alphabits Bookstore`

Heading 1: `Alphabits: The Children's Bookstore`

Heading 2: `Location and Hours`

`We are located at the corner of 12th and Broadway in downtown Eugene, Oregon. Our mailing address, e-mail address, and phone are`
`P. O. Box 206`
`   Eugene, OR 97401`
`   e-mail: Alphabits@efn.org`
`   (541)688-2354`
`   We are open from 10-6 Monday through Saturday, but we are closed on Sunday.`

Heading 2: `Special Events`

Heading 2: `Best-Selling Children's Books`

Heading 2: `Reviews of Books`

Heading 3: `Reviews from Parent's Magazine`

Heading 3: `Reviews by our customers`

`Page design by Home Pages Plus (HomePlus@net.com)`

Save the file as *alphabit.html*.

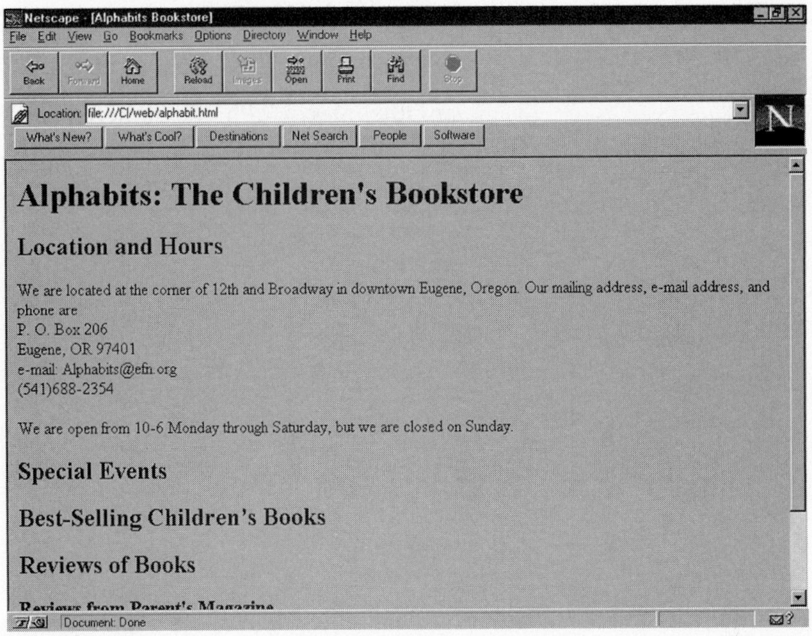

Figure 1.11a

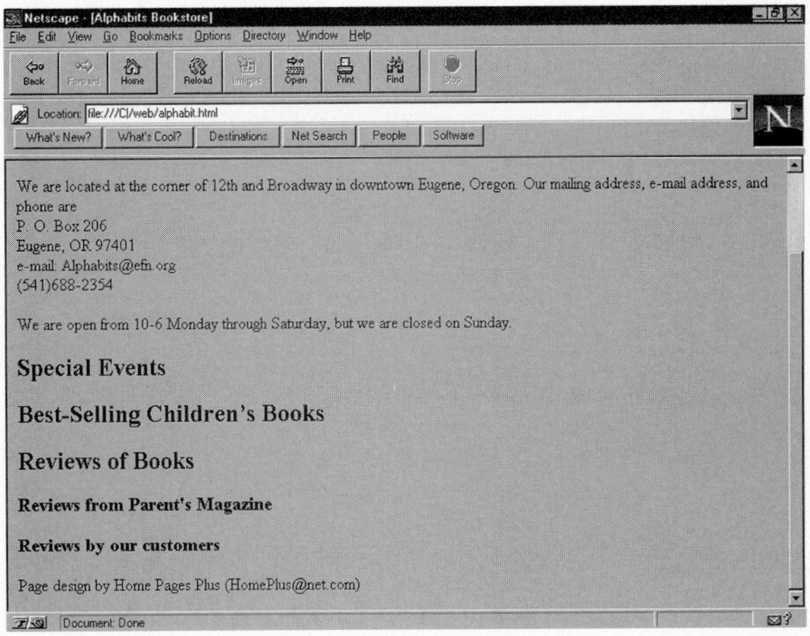

Figure 1.11b

Building the Animal Web Page

Using the information you gathered and organized in the Review Exercises at the end of the Overview, create a Web page for a small business that raises animals, or some other animal-related organization. Organize your material in an outline form, using headings to enter your material. Make use of the tags described in this project. Save the Web document; in later projects you'll add text, add links, and enhance the document.

Assignments

Creating a Personal Web Page

Using the information you gathered and organized in the Assignments section at the end of the Overview, create a Web page for yourself. Organize your material in an outline form, using headings to enter your material. Include a Work Experience heading. You'll use this heading later to link to your résumé. Make use of the tags described in this project. Save the Web document for use in later projects.

Creating an Organization or Nonprofit Web Page

Using the organization, church, team, or nonprofit organization you identified in the Assignments section at the end of the Overview, create the Web document. Organize the information using headings such as Purpose, Bylaws, Membership, and so on. Use the tags described in this project. Save the Web document; you'll enhance it in later projects.

PROJECT 2: FORMATTING TEXT

In this project, you will use logical and physical formatting tags to format individual words and characters that appear in the Web document.

Objectives

After completing this project, you should be able to:

▶ Use logical formatting to emphasize text

▶ Use physical formatting to format text

▶ Create nested tags

▶ Use attributes with tags

▶ Change font sizes

▶ Use block quotes and preformatted text

▶ Align text

▶ Insert special characters

▶ Use monospaced text

CASE STUDY: FORMATTING THE TEXT OF A WEB PAGE

In Project 1, you used HTML tags to create a home page. The page had very little formatting. However, most of the pages that you've seen as you surf the Web probably aren't as plain as the one you created.

Emphasizing text by formatting characters is common to all word processing software—you usually select the text and choose the formatting command, such as bold or italic. For the same reasons that you format characters in a word processing document, sometimes you'll want to change the format of text in an HTML document. The paired tags <B> and </B>, for example, make the text between them bold. This type of formatting is known as *physical formatting* in Web documents.

The appearance of Web documents is controlled by the browser software that the reader uses, which may or may not be able to handle some of the very specific physical tags you could use in your HTML document. Another type of HTML formatting, called *logical formatting*, is often used to get around this problem of browsers not recognizing physical tags, and thus not formatting the text at all. Logical formatting simply tells the browser how the text is to be used. Logical formatting is much like the tags you used in Project 1 for the title and headings in a Web document. These tags tell the browser to handle the text as a title or heading; the actual formatting of the title or heading text varies from browser to browser. When you use logical formatting tags to format text, you're simply telling the browser to emphasize the text, for example, rather than boldfacing it physically. That way, each browser will give the text some formatting that emphasizes that text.

Designing the Solution

In this project, you'll format the text of a Web document, insert material, and use preformatted text. Figure 2.1 shows the home page after you have formatted it in this project.

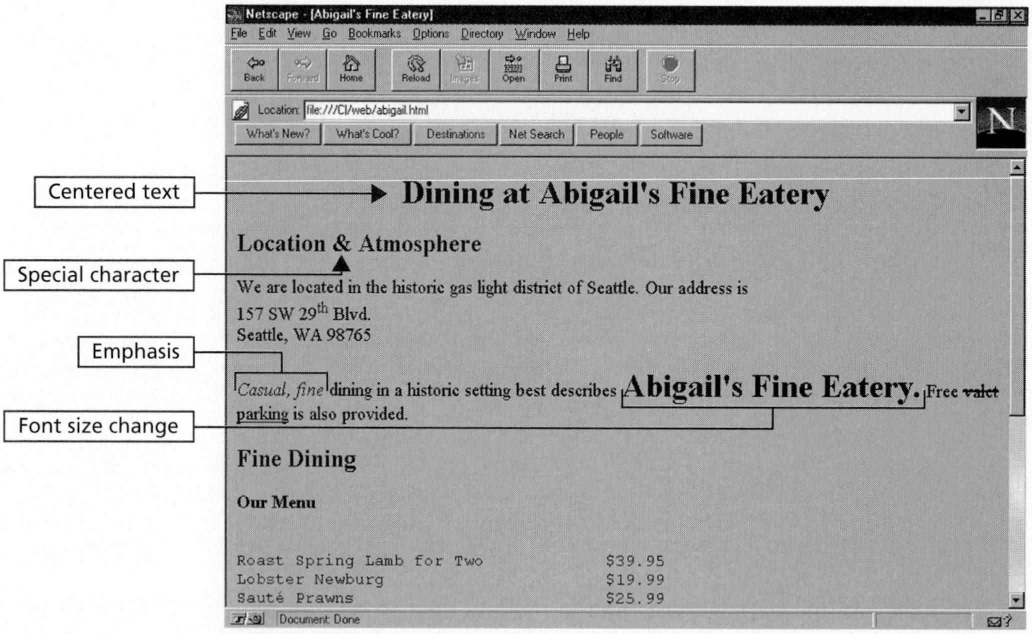
Netscape - [Abigail's Fine Eatery]
Location: file:///C|/web/abigail.html
Centered text
Dining at Abigail's Fine Eatery
Location & Atmosphere
Special character
We are located in the historic gas light district of Seattle. Our address is
157 SW 29th Blvd.
Seattle, WA 98765
Emphasis
Casual, fine dining in a historic setting best describes Abigail's Fine Eatery. Free valet parking is also provided.
Font size change
Fine Dining
Our Menu
Roast Spring Lamb for Two $39.95
Lobster Newburg $19.99
Sauté Prawns $25.99
Document: Done

Figure 2.1a

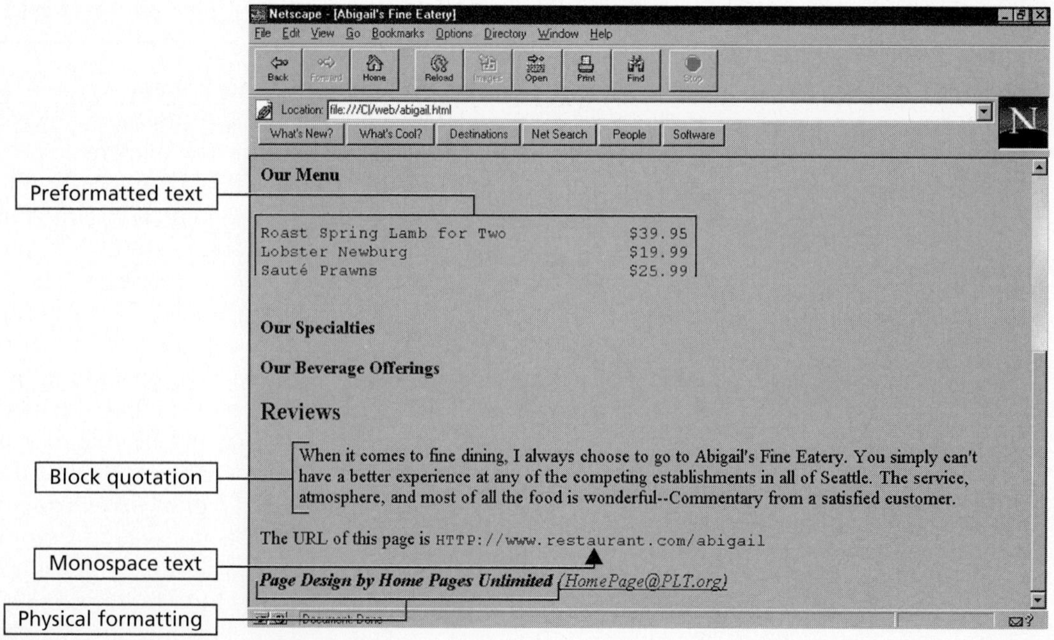
Netscape - [Abigail's Fine Eatery]
Location: file:///C|/web/abigail.html
Our Menu
Preformatted text
Roast Spring Lamb for Two $39.95
Lobster Newburg $19.99
Sauté Prawns $25.99
Our Specialties
Our Beverage Offerings
Reviews
Block quotation
When it comes to fine dining, I always choose to go to Abigail's Fine Eatery. You simply can't have a better experience at any of the competing establishments in all of Seattle. The service, atmosphere, and most of all the food is wonderful--Commentary from a satisfied customer.
The URL of this page is HTTP://www.restaurant.com/abigail
Monospace text
Page Design by Home Pages Unlimited (HomePage@PLT.org)
Physical formatting

Figure 2.1b

USING LOGICAL FORMATTING

HTML has two logical tags that add emphasis to text. One of the tags is the <EM> tag, which stands for emphasis. Many browsers place text within the <EM> tags in italics. The syntax is as follows:

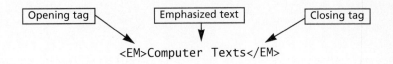

<EM>Computer Texts</EM>

Another logical HTML tag is the <STRONG> tag. This tag provides stronger emphasis than the <EM> tag. Many browsers boldface the text within the <STRONG> tags. The syntax is as follows:

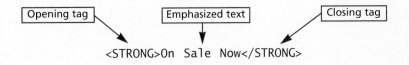

<STRONG>On Sale Now</STRONG>

As Figure 2.2 shows, the <EM> tags in the preceding example italicized the words Computer Texts and the <STRONG> tags in this example bold-faced the text On Sale Now.

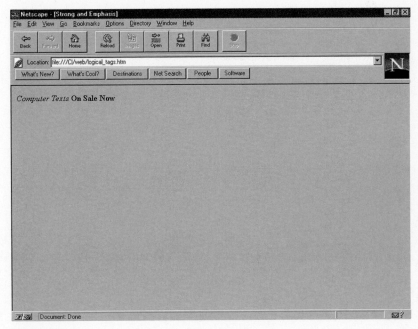

Figure 2.2

In the following steps, you will make some changes to the *abigail.html* document created in Project 1. Specifically, you will change the second paragraph that follows the heading Location and Atmosphere. Use Figure 2.3 as a guide as you type your HTML code.

```
abigail - Notepad
File  Edit  Search  Help
<HTML>

<HEAD>

<TITLE>Abigail's Fine Eatery</TITLE>

</HEAD>

<BODY>

<!--This section will be updated-->

<H1>Dining at Abigail's Fine Eatery</H1>

        <H2>Location and Atmosphere</H2>

        We are located in the historic gas light district of Seattle. Our address is<BR>
        157 SW 29th Blvd.<BR>
        Seattle, WA 98765

        <P>
        <EM>Casual, fine</EM> dining in a historic setting best describes
        <STRONG>Abigail's Fine Eatery.</STRONG> Free valet parking is also provided.
        </P>

        <H2>Fine Dining</H2>

            <H3>Our Menu</H3>

            <H3>Our Specialties</H3>

            <H3>Our Beverage Offerings</H3>

        <H2>Reviews</H2>

<ADDRESS>Page Design by Home Pages Unlimited (HomePage@PLT.org)</ADDRESS>
```

Figure 2.3

To add emphasis to text in an HTML document:

1 Open *abigail.html*.

2 Find the paragraph that reads as follows:

```
<P>
Casual, fine dining in a historic setting best describes
Abigail's Fine Eatery. Free valet parking is also
provided.
</P>
```

3 Add emphasis to the words Casual, fine by placing the <EM></EM> tags around them like this:

```
<P>
<EM>Casual, fine</EM> dining in a historic setting best
describes Abigail's Fine Eatery. Free valet parking is
also provided.
</P>
```

You may have to rearrange the tabs and carriage returns to make the code look neat.

4 Next, add <STRONG></STRONG> tags around the words Abigail's Fine Eatery in the second sentence:

```
<P>
<EM>Casual, fine</EM> dining in a historic setting best
describes <STRONG>Abigail's Fine Eatery.</STRONG> Free
valet parking is also provided.
</P>
```

5 Save the changes and then view the document in your browser to see how the browser interprets the logical tags. Figure 2.4 shows the Web page in Netscape Navigator 3.0. The <EM> tag has been interpreted as italics and the <STRONG> tag as bold.

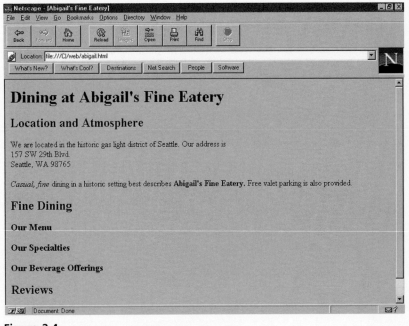

Figure 2.4

EXIT If necessary, you can exit the editor and browser and continue this project later.

USING PHYSICAL FORMATTING

You can use physical tags to format text. However, if the browser doesn't understand the physical tag, the text will appear on the page with no formatting. Table 2.1 lists a few of the tags that apply physical formatting.

Table 2.1

HTML Tag	Closing Tag	Description
`<B>`	`</B>`	Bolds text—physical formatting
`<I>`	`</I>`	Italicizes text—physical formatting
`<CENTER>`	`</CENTER>`	Centers text
`<U>`	`</U>`	Underlines text
`<STRIKE>`	`</STRIKE>`	Strikes through text—for example, ~~DON'T~~
`<BLINK>`	`</BLINK>`	Creates blinking text
`<SUP>`	`</SUP>`	Superscripts text—raises the marked text above the rest of the line, as the 3 is raised here: 2^3
`<SUB>`	`</SUB>`	Subscripts text—lowers the marked text below the rest of the line, as the 2 is lowered here: H_2O

Caution If you format text to stand out by making it blink, the text continues to blink while the page is viewed and could be disconcerting to the reader; therefore, use the `<BLINK>` tag sparingly.

In the following steps, you modify the section of the Web document under the heading Location and Atmosphere, using the physical tags `<BLINK>`, `<STRIKE>`, `<U>`, and `<SUP>`. Figure 2.5 shows the modified HTML source code.

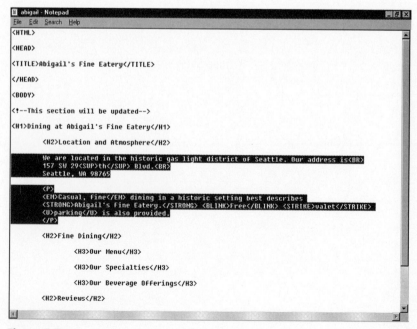

Figure 2.5

To apply physical formatting to an HTML document:

1 Add the <SUP> tag to superscript the letters th in the street address for Abigail's:

```
157 SW 29 <SUP>th</SUP> Blvd.
```

2 Modify the second paragraph, using the <BLINK> tag to make the word Free blink:

```
<EM>Casual, fine</EM> dining in a historic setting best
describes <STRONG>Abigail's Fine Eatery.</STRONG>
<BLINK>Free</BLINK>valet parking is also provided.
```

3 Format the word valet in the same paragraph as strikethrough, using the <STRIKE> tag:

```
<EM>Casual, fine</EM> dining in a historic setting best
describes <STRONG>Abigail's Fine Eatery.</STRONG>
<BLINK>Free</BLINK> <STRIKE>valet</STRIKE> parking is
also provided.
```

4 Underline the word parking by using the <U> tag:

```
<EM>Casual, fine</EM> dining in a historic setting best
describes <STRONG>Abigail's Fine Eatery.</STRONG>
<BLINK>Free</BLINK> <STRIKE>valet</STRIKE>
<U>parking</U> is also provided.
```

5 Save the file and view it in your browser. Figure 2.6 shows the document with its new formatting in Netscape Navigator 3.0. (Obviously, you can't see the word Free blinking in the figure.)

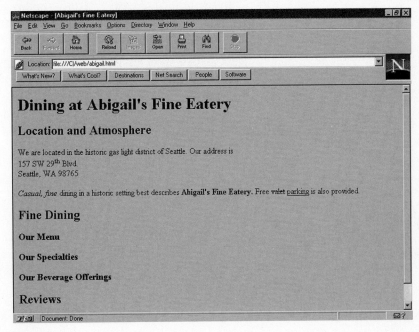

Figure 2.6

If necessary, you can exit the editor and browser and continue this project later.

CREATING NESTED TAGS

Sometimes you may want text to have more than one formatting tag, such as emphasizing and blinking the same text; tags combined in this way are called *nested tags*. If you want text in a heading to be italic, for example, you would include the italic tag with the heading tag.

In the following example, the text Computer Textbooks will appear in Heading 1 format and will be italicized:

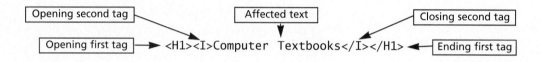

When you nest tags, pay careful attention to the order in which they are closed. The last tag opened must be closed first. The preceding example is correct; the following one is not:

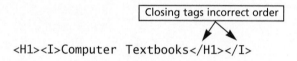

In the following steps, you will modify the <ADDRESS> section of *abigail.html* to learn the correct way to nest tags (see Figure 2.7).

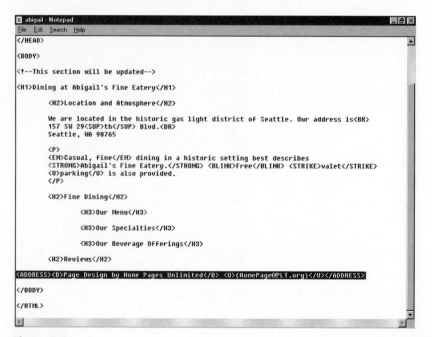

Figure 2.7

To create a nested tag in an HTML document:

1 Find the <ADDRESS> section, near the bottom of the HTML source code in *abigail.html*:

```
<ADDRESS>Page Design by Home Pages Unlimited
(HomePage@PLT.org)
</ADDRESS>
```

2 Make the words `Page Design by Home Pages Unlimited` bold by using the <B> physical tag:

```
<ADDRESS><B>Page Design by Home Pages Unlimited</B>
(HomePage@PLT.org)</ADDRESS>
```

3 Underline the e-mail address by using the <U> tag:

```
<ADDRESS><B>Page Design by Home Pages Unlimited</B>
<U>(HomePage@PLT.org)</U></ADDRESS>
```

4 Save the file and view it in your browser (see Figure 2.8).

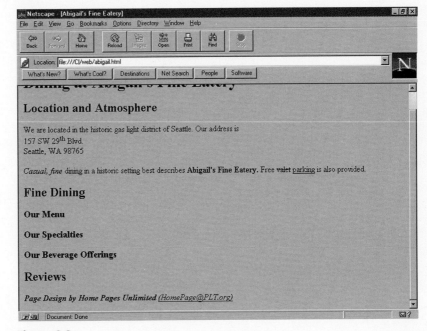

Figure 2.8

 If necessary, you can exit the editor and browser and continue this project later.

USING ATTRIBUTES WITH TAGS

You can include optional attributes with some tags; these attributes further define the tag. The attribute is entered after the command and before the final angle bracket. Some attributes appear by themselves, and other attributes can appear with a value modifier. The syntax of an attribute with a value modifier is as follows:

```
attribute=value
```

Here's an example:

In this example, the text `Computer Textbooks` will appear formatted for Heading 1 because of the `<H1>` tag and centered because the `ALIGN` attribute is assigned the value `CENTER`.

In this example, the `CENTER` value is a given value; that is, you choose one value from the available `ALIGN` values of `LEFT`, `RIGHT`, or `CENTER`. You can choose only one value. A given value doesn't need any other punctuation around it, such as quotation marks.

However, some commands allow you to include an attribute that has any value, for example, a number to define a size or a URL to define an address; these values need to be enclosed in straight quotation marks (" "). For example:

```
<IMG SCR="IMAGE.GIF">
```

The `<IMG>` tag uses the image designated between the quotation marks, placing it in the document.

CHANGING THE FONT SIZE

You can change the font size for the entire Web document, or you can change the size of a character, word, or group of words.

To change the font size for the entire document, you use the `<BASFONT>` tag. This tag has a required attribute, `SIZE=VALUE`. You can define the value using a number from 1 to 7, where 3 is the default size, or you can use relative size changes such as +1 or –1. (Relative sizes still must fall in the range 1–7.) The `<BASEFONT>` tag appears as follows:

```
<BASEFONT SIZE=4>
```

or

```
<BASEFONT SIZE=+1>
```

These two examples actually call for the same base font size.

You may find increasing the size of the base font useful for short Web documents to improve their appearance; for long Web documents, you can decrease the base font to fit more on the page.

> **Tip** You should use only one <BASEFONT> tag in an HTML document. All text after the tag will use the size designated in the SIZE attribute.

To change the size of a character, word, or group of words in the Web document, you use the <FONT> tag. This tag also has a required attribute, SIZE=*VALUE*. You can define the value using a number from 1 to 7, where 3 is the default size, or you can use relative size changes such as +1 or –1. (Relative sizes still must fall in the range 1–7.) The <FONT> tag appears as follows:

```
<FONT SIZE=5>text</FONT>
```

or

```
<FONT SIZE=+2>text</FONT>
```

Notice that the <BASEFONT> tag isn't a paired tag, but the <FONT> tag is paired. When you close the <FONT> command with the </FONT> tag, the font size returns to the base font setting.

Figure 2.9 shows the HTML source code for the base font set at 5 and the Font size ranging from 1 to 7. Figure 2.10 shows the browser representation of that source code.

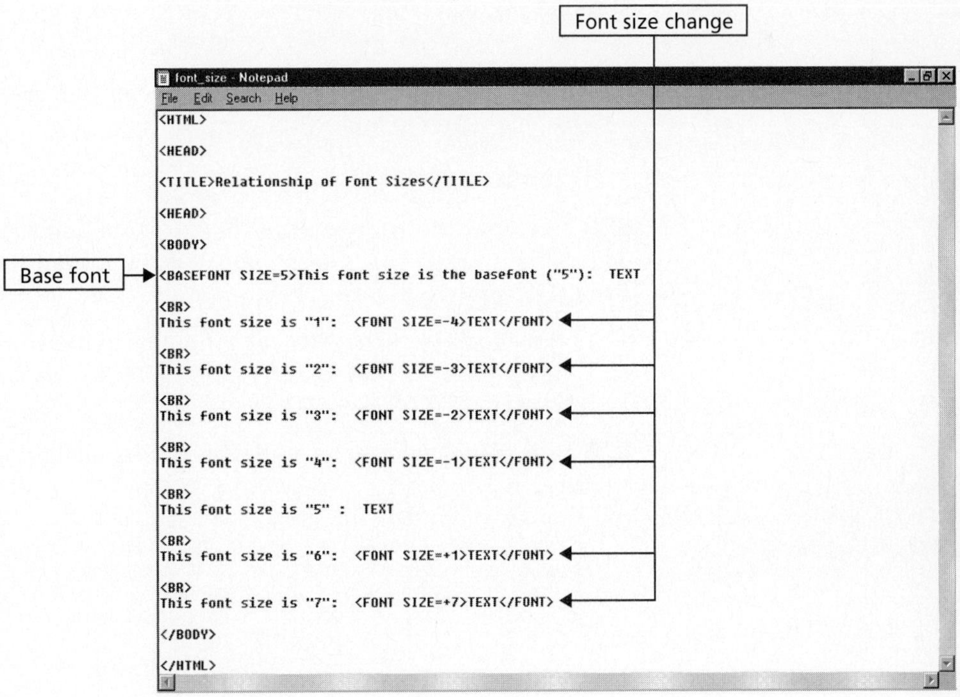

Figure 2.9

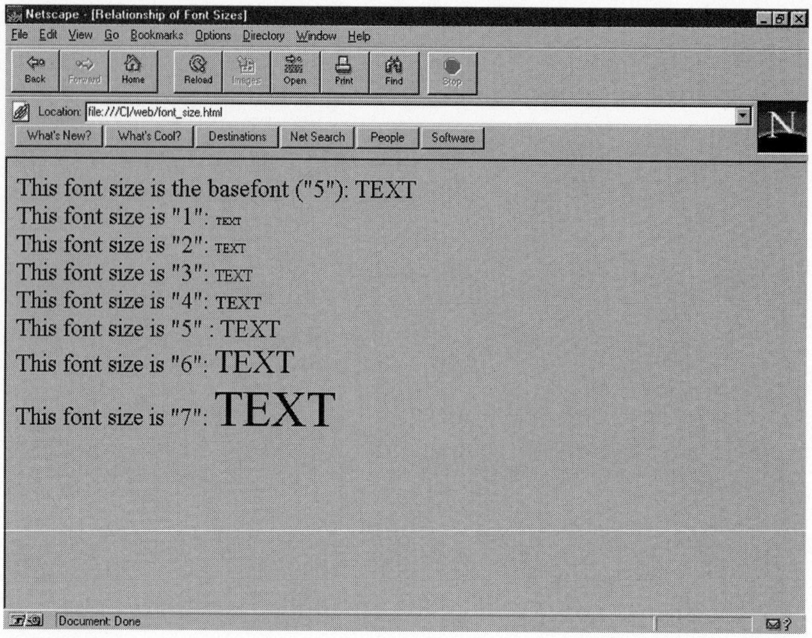

Figure 2.10

In the following steps, you modify *abigail.html* to use a base font of 4 and change some of the text to use a font size of +2.

To change font size using the <BASEFONT> and <FONT> tags:

1 At the top of the *abigail.html* document, just below the opening <BODY> tag, type the following line:

<BASEFONT SIZE=4>

2 In the second paragraph of the Location and Atmosphere section, add the tags <FONT SIZE=+2> and </FONT> around the words Abigail's Fine Eatery (see Figure 2.11):

<EM>Casual, fine</EM> dining in a historic setting best describes **<FONT SIZE=+2>**<STRONG>Abigail's Fine Eatery</STRONG>**</FONT>**.

3 Save the changes, and view the results using your browser (see Figure 2.12).

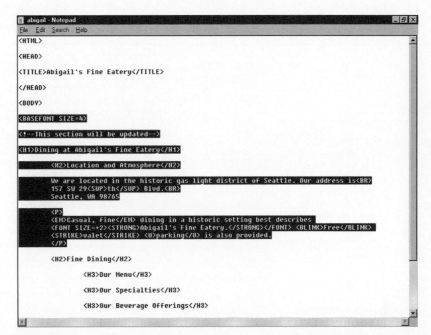

Figure 2.11

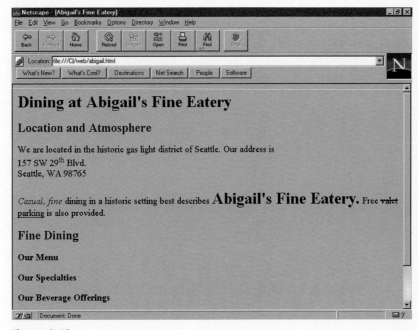

Figure 2.12

In Figure 2.12, the font increase for the words `Abigail's Fine Eatery` is obvious. However, the base font change is more subtle. Remember that the default font size is 3, so you're only increasing the base font by one size. Practice changing the base font to different numbers to see more obvious differences.

 If necessary, you can exit the editor and browser and continue this project later.

USING BLOCK QUOTES AND PREFORMATTED TEXT

If you want to include a long quotation in your text, you can use the <BLOCKQUOTE> tag. Many browsers indent the text to set it off, while other browsers may italicize or use some other method to set the text apart.

Use the <BLOCKQUOTE> tag as follows:

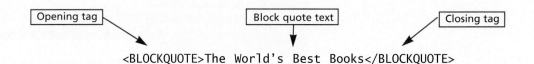

```
<BLOCKQUOTE>The World's Best Books</BLOCKQUOTE>
```

Sometimes you may not want browsers to strip out all the space you place in text, or you may want to create a table in your word processing software and cut-and-paste it into your Web page. The <PRE> tag lets you bring in preformatted text, and browsers will display the text the way you set it up, that is, browsers won't change the way the preformatted text appears. Text within the <PRE> tags is displayed in a **monospaced** (evenly spaced) **font** such as Courier, keeping text in tables aligned correctly.

> **Reminder** With this method, you can simply use the [Enter] key in your word processing software to break lines as you would for any document. However, using the [Tab] key can create problems because different browsers may use a different number of spaces between tab stops; instead, use the [space bar] to create white space. Also, keep your lines short so that they'll fit the width of any browser.

The format is as follows:

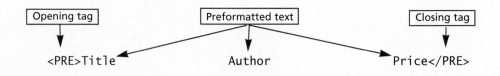

```
<PRE>Title          Author          Price</PRE>
```

To add block quotes and preformatted text:

1 In the *abigail.html* document, move the insertion point below the heading Reviews and type <BLOCKQUOTE> as the opening tag.

2 Add the following text (see Figure 2.13):

```
<P>
When it comes to fine dining, I always choose to go to
Abigail's Fine Eatery. You simply can't have a better
experience at any of the competing establishments in all of
Seattle. The service, atmosphere, and most of all the food is
wonderful—Commentary from a satisfied customer.
</P>
</BLOCKQUOTE>
```

Figure 2.13

Figure 2.14 shows the text viewed with Netscape Navigator. Notice that the block quote is indented automatically.

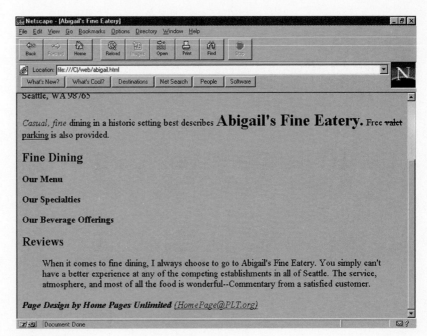

Figure 2.14

3 Move the insertion point below the heading Our Menu.

4 Type the following text, using the (SPACE BAR) to align the prices:

```
<PRE>
Roast Spring Lamb for Two          $39.95
Lobster Newburg                    $19.99
Saute Prawns                       $25.99
</PRE>
```

Figure 2.15 shows the new text.

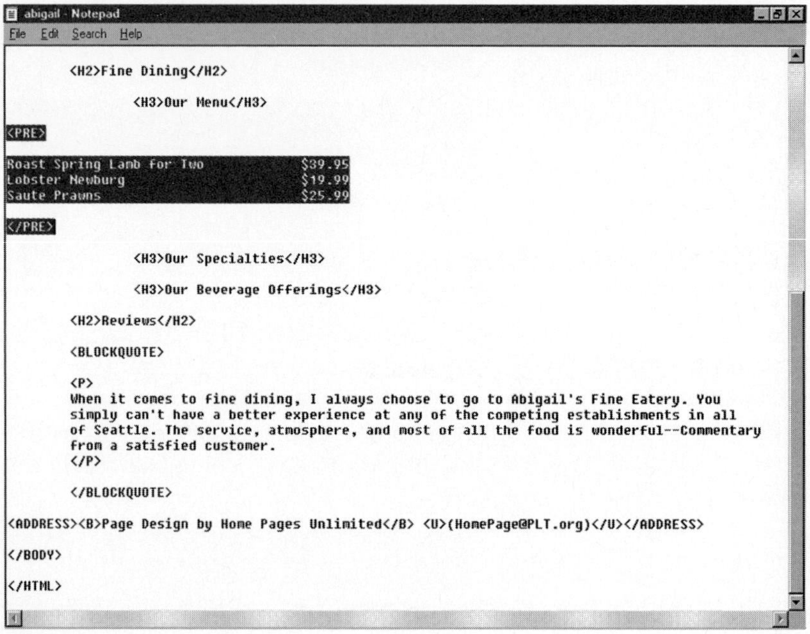

Figure 2.15

5 Check out the results in your browser; compare to Figure 2.16.

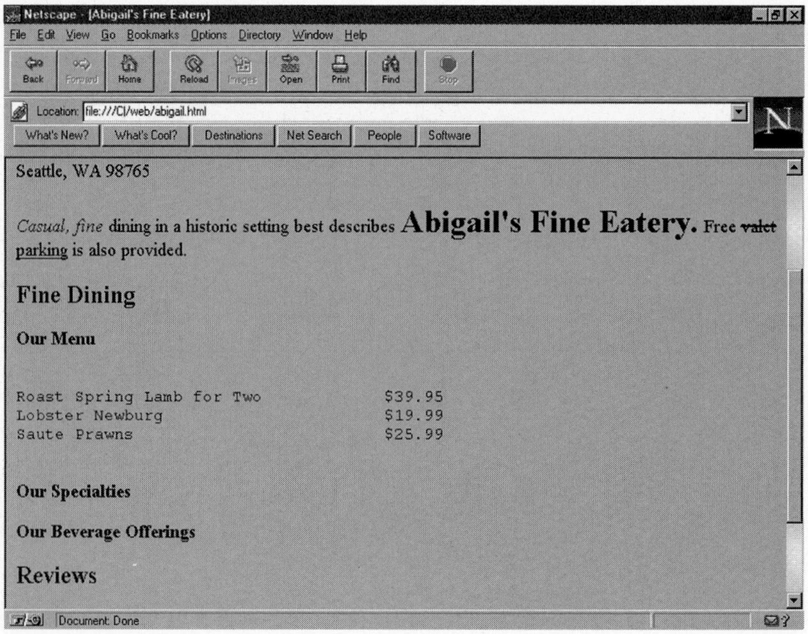

Figure 2.16

EXIT If necessary, you can exit the editor and browser and continue this project later.

CENTERING TEXT HORIZONTALLY

HTML offers two methods used to center text horizontally: the `<CENTER>` tag and the `ALIGN=CENTER` attribute. The `<CENTER>` tag is a paired tag and follows the same syntax as the formatting tags listed earlier in Table 2.1:

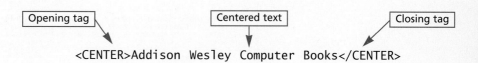

```
<CENTER>Addison Wesley Computer Books</CENTER>
```

If you use the `ALIGN` attribute to center text, more browsers will be able to center the text than if you use the `<CENTER>` tag. You always use the `ALIGN` attribute within other tags, such as heading commands or the paragraph command. Use the `ALIGN` attribute as follows:

```
<H1 ALIGN=CENTER>Software Texts</H1>
```

or

```
<P ALIGN=CENTER>Software Texts</P>
```

In these examples, all the text in the heading or the paragraph will be centered.

 To use the ALIGN attribute to center text:

1 In the *abigail.html* document, move the insertion point after the number 1 in the `<H1>` tag preceding the text `Dining at Abigail's Fine Eatery`.

2 Press the (SPACE BAR).

3 Type **ALIGN=CENTER** before the closing angle bracket (>). Your HTML code should look like that in Figure 2.17.

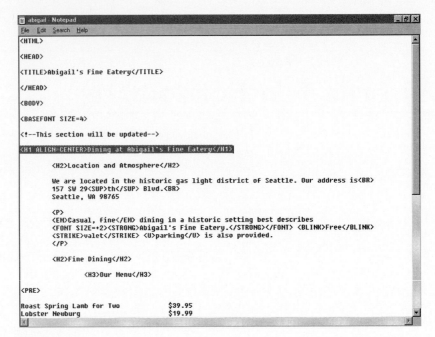

Figure 2.17

4 Check out the results in your browser. The heading in your Web page should look like that in Figure 2.18.

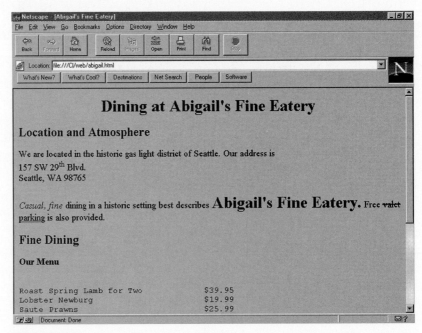

Figure 2.18

 If necessary, you can exit the editor and browser and continue this project later.

USING SPECIAL CHARACTERS

HTML documents are **ASCII text files**; that is, files based on the **American Standard Code for Information Interchange** (**ASCII**). ASCII files use only the letters, numbers, and symbols that you can type from your keyboard, which, along with some essential control characters, equal 128 characters. Just as you might include special characters not on the keyboard in a word processing document, you can also include special characters in a Web document. Most word processing software enables you to select the character in a dialog box and insert it into the document. However, to insert special characters using HTML, you need to do so manually—by typing the name or number of the special character.

HTML uses the **ISO-Latin-1** (also called the **ISO-8859-1**) **character set**. The upper characters—those above the first 128 standard characters—include accented characters such as the cedilla for use in languages other than English, and such common symbols as the copyright symbol. This system has its drawbacks, however, because some characters simply aren't available in the character set, and because some computers may not translate the characters correctly. (Appendix A lists the ISO-Latin1 Character Set.)

You can use two methods to include a character from the extended ASCII. If the special character has a name, you can use the name; otherwise, you need to use the character's number, which is designated by its location in the character set. Whether you use the character's name or number, you must start the code with the ampersand (&) and close it with a semicolon (;). The number sign appears immediately after the ampersand in codes using numbers. Table 2.2 shows the syntax for special characters.

Table 2.2

Character	Name	Code
è	è	è
È	È	È
©	©	©
<	<	<
>	>	>
&	&	&
"	"	&#34

Notice that the table includes four characters that are located on your keyboard. These four special characters present a problem in HTML because of the syntax of the language. For example, to type A<B, you need to designate the less-than sign (<) as a special character because a browser knows that the less-than sign starts a tag. The same holds true for other HTML character tags.

Notice that the first accented character in Table 2.2 is lowercase and the second is capitalized; then look at the codes for each of the characters. The first code contains a small *e* and the second a capital *E*. The codes are case-sensitive. Also if you change the initial character in the code from *e* to another vowel such as *u*, that character will appear with the accent.

To use special characters in a Web document:

1 In the *abigail.html* document, move the insertion point immediately after the word and in the heading Location and Atmosphere.

2 Replace the word and with & to change it to an ampersand (&).

3 Move the insertion point to the end of the word Saute in the Our Menu section.

4 Replace the letter e in saute with é to change saute to sauté. Your HTML code should look like that in Figure 2.19.

Figure 2.19

5 Check out the results in your browser. Your Web page should have the special characters shown in Figure 2.20.

Here's the ampersand

Here's the accented é

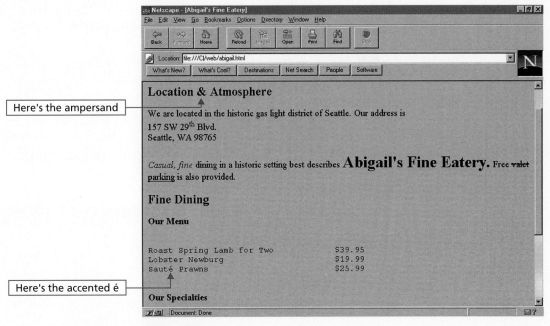

Figure 2.20

EXIT If necessary, you can exit the editor and browser and continue this project later.

USING MONOSPACED TEXT

Text produced by modern word processing software is ***proportional type***; that is, narrower characters such as the letter *i* take up less space than wide characters such as the letter *w*. The older type font produced by typewriters and old word processing software is ***monospaced***. In ***monospaced fonts***, every character takes up the same amount of space, regardless of its size. The newer proportional typefaces are easier to read, but you may have reasons for using a monospace font, such as to format tables and lists, and HTML provides several codes that allow you to do so. Table 2.3 describes the tags that apply monospacing.

Table 2.3

Code	Description
<TT>*text*</TT>	Places `text` in a typewriter font
<CODE>*text*</CODE>	Used for text such as computer codes
<SAMP>*text*</SAMP>	Sample text for the user
<KBD>*text*</KBD>	Provides an example of what the user should type

To create monospaced text with the <SAMP> tag:

1 In the *abigail.html* document, move the insertion point above the <ADDRESS> tag near the end of the document.

2 Type the following text (see Figure 2.21):

<P>
The URL of this page is
<SAMP>HTTP://www.restaurant.com/abigail</SAMP>
</P>

```
abigail - Notepad                                                          _ 8 X
File  Edit  Search  Help

<PRE>

Roast Spring Lamb for Two            $39.95
Lobster Newburg                      $19.99
Saut&eacute; Prawns                          $25.99

</PRE>

                 <H3>Our Specialties</H3>

                 <H3>Our Beverage Offerings</H3>

        <H2>Reviews</H2>

        <BLOCKQUOTE>

        <P>
        When it comes to fine dining, I always choose to go to Abigail's Fine Eatery. You
        simply can't have a better experience at any of the competing establishments in all
        of Seattle. The service, atmosphere, and most of all the food is wonderful--Commentary
        from a satisfied customer.
        </P>

        </BLOCKQUOTE>

<P>
The URL of this page is <SAMP>HTTP://www.restaurant.com/abigail</SAMP>
</P>

<ADDRESS><B>Page Design by Home Pages Unlimited</B> <U>(HomePage@PLT.org)</U></ADDRESS>

</BODY>

</HTML>
```

Figure 2.21

3 Check out the results in your browser. Your Web page should have monospaced text something like that shown in Figure 2.22.

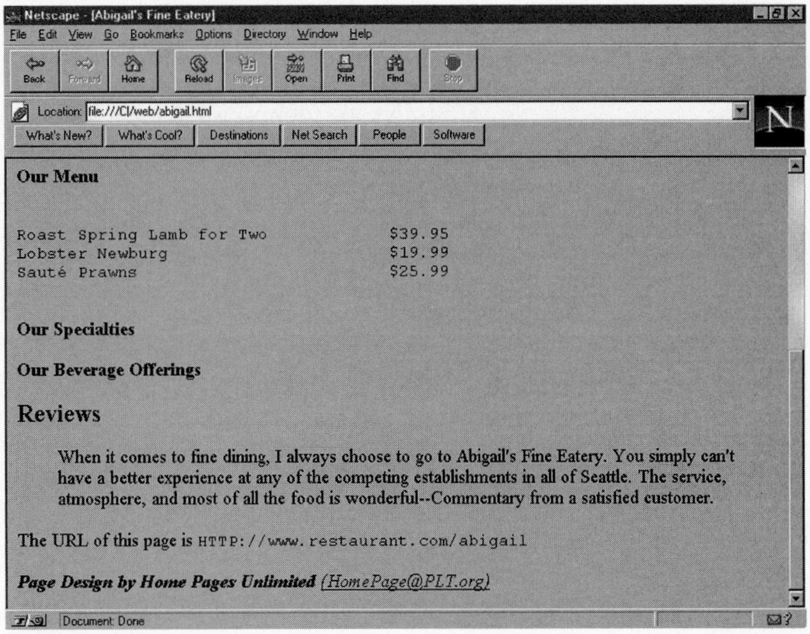

Figure 2.22

4 Save and close the Web document.

The Next Step

Practice formatting text using both physical and logical tags; then view the results in more than one browser to compare how the browsers treat the tags.

This concludes the project. You can either exit your editor and browser or go on to work the Study Questions, Review Exercises, and Assignments.

Summary and Exercises

Summary

- Use logical formatting tags when possible to provide emphasis.
- <EM></EM> and <STRONG></STRONG> are logical formatting tags that format the text between the opening and closing tags for emphasis.
- Physical tags can be used to format text, but if a browser doesn't understand the tag, no formatting will appear.
- Many HTML tags take attributes that further define the tag. Some attributes are limited to choices available; others can take any value.
- To change the font size for the entire Web document, use the <BASEFONT> tag.
- To change the font size for part of the Web document, place the text between the opening <FONT SIZE=*value*> tag and the closing </FONT> tag.
- To include preformatted text, place the text between the opening <PRE> tag and the closing </PRE> tag.

- To include long quotations, place the text between the opening <BLOCK-QUOTE> tag and the closing </BLOCKQUOTE> tag.
- To include a special character, use the character's name or number.
- To include monospace type, use one of the monospace tags.

Key Terms

ASCII   monospace type
attribute   nested tag
base font   physical formatting
block quote   preformatted text
logical formatting   proportional typeµ

Study Questions

Multiple Choice

1. Physical formatting
   a. is possible only in word processing software.
   b. varies with each browser.
   c. is better than logical formatting because it requires less memory.
   d. changes the type of graphics included in a Web page.
   e. both b and c.

2. To insert a block of text into a Web page, you use
   a. Ctrl+Paste.
   b. <QUOTE>.
   c. <BLOCK>.
   d. <INSERT>.
   e. none of the above.

3. Inserting special characters in a Web page
   a. is impossible because HTML uses only those characters on the keyboard.
   b. is dependent on the browser that views the Web page.
   c. is possible only by using the UPC codes.
   d. requires a familiarity with ASCII characters.
   e. can be accomplished by choosing Insert, Special Characters.

4. To make text both bold and italic, you use
   a. <B,I>*text*</I,B>.
   b. <HEADING=B,I>*text*</HEADING=I,B>.
   c. <B><I>*text*<B><I>.
   d. <B><I>*text*</B></I>.
   e. <B><I>*text*</I></B>.

5. Proportional type
   a. provides a standard for only 128 characters, numbers, and symbols.
   b. makes text appear raised above the line.
   c. tells the browser how the text is to be used.
   d. gives narrower characters such as the letter *i* less space than wide characters such as the letter *w*.
   e. makes text appear lowered below the line.

6. The logical formatting tag that provides emphasis is
   a. <B>.
   b. <EM>.
   c. <I>.
   d.
.
   e. all of these answers.

7. Monospaced type
   a. is easier to read.
   b. is the newer type of font.
   c. gives each character the same amount of space.
   d. gives characters space depending on their size.
   e. places special characters in your document.

8. To include spaces that won't be stripped out by a browser, you use
   a. <STRIKE>.
   b. <WHITE>.
   c. <PRE>.
   d. <STRONG>.
   e. <SPACE>.

9. Which code places marked characters above the line of text?
   a. <SUB>
   b. <SIZE>
   c. <SUP>
   d. <BLINK>
   e. <UP>

10. To increase or decrease the font size for the entire document, you use
   a. <BASEFONT SIZE=*VALUE*>.
   b. <FONT SIZE=*VALUE*>.
   c. <FSIZE>.
   d. <SIZE>.
   e. <HTML=*VALUE*>.

Short Answer

Provide the proper HTML coding for each of the following questions.

1. Emphasize the following text, using a logical tag:

```
This is important
```

2. Strongly emphasize the following text, using a logical tag:

```
This is very important
```

3. Bold the word BOLD and italicize the word ITALICS in the following text:

```
BOLD and ITALICS
```

4. Underline the following text:

```
Home Page Design
```

5. Include the special character greater-than (>) in the following text:

```
100 > 50
```

6. Include the registered trademark symbol (®) in the following text:

```
This symbol ® indicates a registered trademark
```

7. Format the text that the user should type (monospace format) in the following text:

   ```
   Please type HTTP://server.com/home.htm
   ```

8. Center the following paragraph so that it won't change from browser to browser:

   ```
   <P>
   This is a paragraph that needs to be centered.
   </P>
   ```

9. Make the following text monospaced:

   ```
   Please make certain that your phone number is correct.
   ```

10. Add the HTML tag that will superscript endings of the ordinal numbers:

    ```
    1st       2nd       3rd       4th
    ```

For Discussion

1. Compare and contrast physical and logical formatting.

2. Compare and contrast proportional and monospaced fonts.

3. Discuss formatting text to draw attention to some text elements on your Web document.

4. Discuss situations in which you may need to use special characters in a Web page.

Review Exercises

Formatting the Alphabits Bookstore Web Page

Change the format of the Alphabits Bookstore Web page, making the following changes (see Figure 2.23):

1. Superscript the th in 12th (in the address).

2. Format the e-mail address for monospace type.

3. Center the mailing address, e-mail address, and phone number.

4. Strongly emphasize the text 10-6 Monday through Saturday.

5. Italicize the text Page design by Home Pages Plus (HomePlus@net.com).

6. Increase the base font for the entire document by 1.

7. Increase the font size of the text We are open from 10-6 Monday through Saturday, but we are closed on Sunday by 1.

8. Save the file.

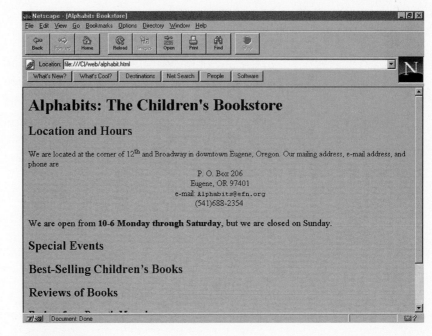

Figure 2.23a

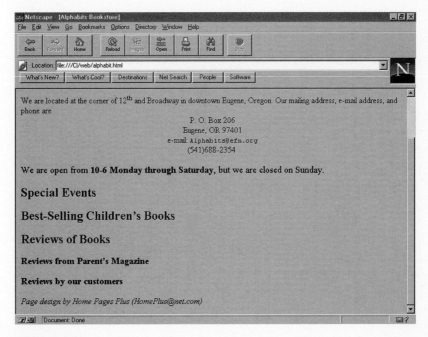

Figure 2.23b

Enhancing the Animal Web Page

Use any of the text-formatting features from this project to enhance the Web page you started in Project 1. You should include at least four different tags.

Assignments

Modifying Your Personal Web Page

Use any of the text-formatting features from this project to enhance the Web page you started in Project 1. You should include at least four different tags.

Formatting the Organization or Nonprofit Web Page

Use any of the text-formatting features from this project to enhance the Web page you started in Project 1. You should include at least four different tags.

What Is IRC? IRC (**Internet Relay Chat**) allows people on the Internet to have real-time conversations with each other. A channel is formed from a server to all clients or computers that want to take part in the conversation. Messages are sent to everyone on the channel, unless the messages are addressed to a specific client. IRC is much like using a CB radio; people use "handles" (or nicknames) instead of real names, and you really don't know who you're talking to. People who use this feature usually communicate with others who share a similar interest. The topics are as diverse as the people who communicate over the Internet.

PROJECT 3: USING LISTS AND CREATING SIMPLE LINKS

In this project, you will use lists to organize information in your Web document. You will also start to see some of the power of Web documents by creating links.

Objectives

After completing this project, you should be able to:

▶ Create unordered or bulleted lists

▶ Create ordered or numbered lists

▶ Create definition lists

▶ Nest lists

▶ Create anchors and links in the same document

CASE STUDY: CREATING A WEB PAGE

You've created a Web page and formatted the text within that page. Now you're concerned with the layout of the information on that page. What's the best way to present information to the reader of your Web page? Lists are very effective for organizing and presenting information in any document, including Web pages.

As you've seen with the Abigail's Fine Eatery Web project, a Web page can become Web page*s*; that is, the screen is too small to display all the information and text flows to another page. To make navigating through the pages of your Web document easy for your reader, you can use *links* (text that the user clicks) and *anchors* (locations to which the user jumps).

Designing the Solution

In this project, you'll create various types of lists, and create links to other locations in a document. These additions to the Abigail's Restaurant Web page are shown in Figure 3.1.

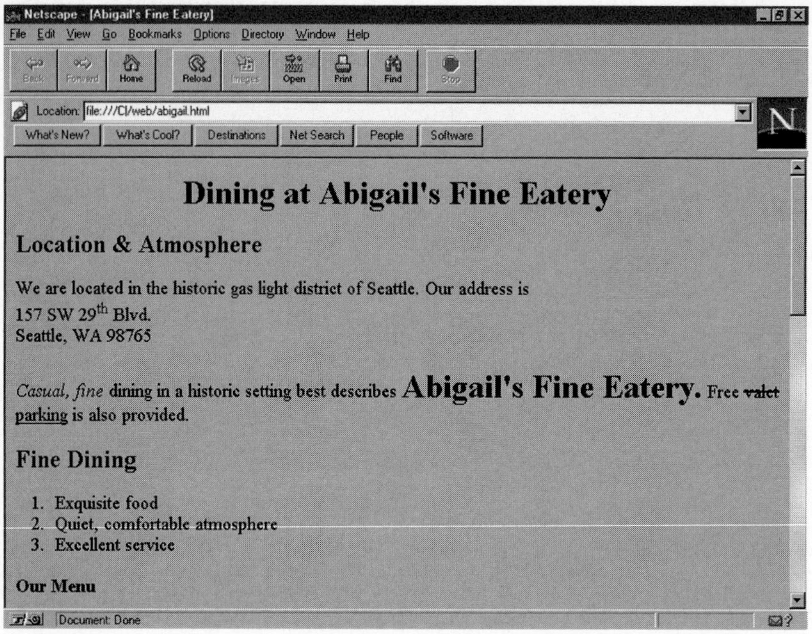

Figure 3.1a

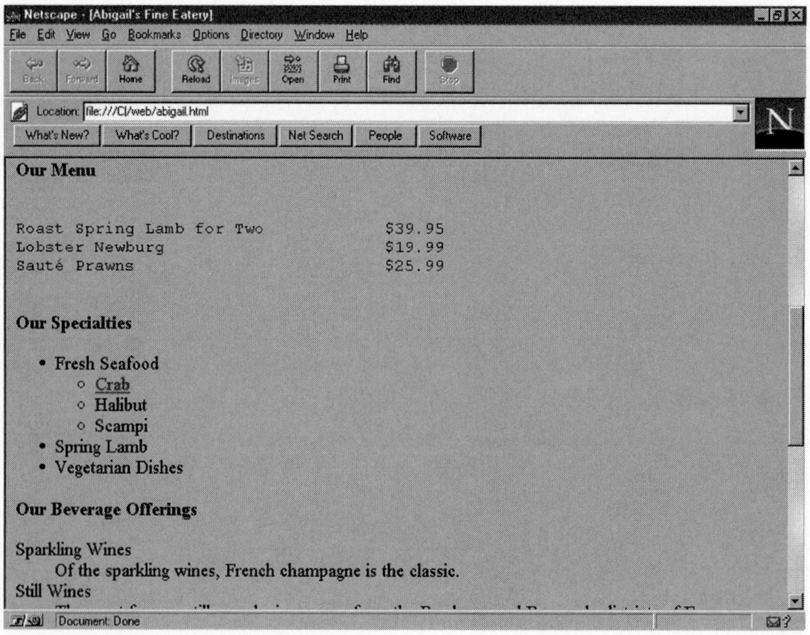

Figure 3.1b

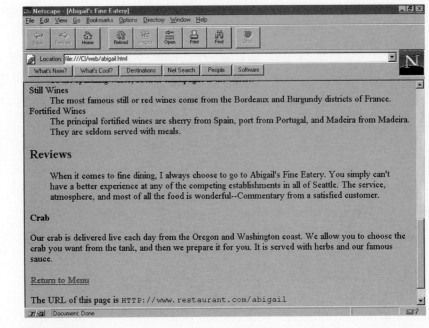

Figure 3.1c

CREATING UNORDERED OR BULLETED LISTS

The most common type of list used is the ***unordered list*** (also called ***bulleted list***). It's a short list of information that doesn't need to be presented in any particular order. The unordered list appears with ***bullets*** (special characters) before each line item. Remember these important points about unordered lists:

- Each list begins with the <UL> tag and ends with the </UL> tag.
- Each line of the list must be indicated with the <LI> tag, which is not paired.
- Each line of the unordered list appears indented and is preceded by a bullet. (Exact display varies from browser to browser.)

HTML offers three bullet types to use in unordered lists:

● Solid round bullet

○ Empty round bullet

■ Square bullet

The default bullet is the solid round bullet. Here's an example of an unordered list that uses the default bullet:

```
<UL>
        <LI>Word processing software
        <LI>Spreadsheet software
</UL>
```

To change the shape of the bullet from the default value disc, you use TYPE=*value* (with square or round as the value). To change the bullet type for an entire list, use this syntax:

```
<UL TYPE=square>
```

or

```
<UL TYPE=round>
```

To change the bullet type within a list—note that every subsequent line will use the newly defined bullet—use this format:

```
<UL>
        <LI>Word processing software
        <LI TYPE=value>Desktop publishing software
        <LI>Spreadsheet software
</UL>
```

You can use the <BR> tag to insert a line break in the list. The subsequent line will be indented but won't be preceded by a bullet.

Although you don't have to place the <UL> and </UL> tags on lines by themselves and indent them, this strategy makes it easier to see where the list begins and ends as you work with your Web document. Using the ⟨TAB⟩ key to indent bulleted lists is especially useful when organizing lists in your source code.

To create an unordered or bulleted list:

1 Open *abigail.html* and find the heading Our Specialties.

2 Add the following list directly under the heading:

```
<UL>
<LI>Fresh Seafood
<LI>Spring Lamb
<LI>Vegetarian Dishes
</UL>
```

The HTML code is shown in Figure 3.2. Notice how the extra spaces and tabs help to organize the list logically in the code.

```
abigail - Notepad
File  Edit  Search  Help

</PRE>

                <H3>Our Specialties</H3>

                <UL>
                <LI>Fresh Seafood
                <LI>Spring Lamb
                <LI>Vegetarian Dishes
                </UL>

                <H3>Our Beverage Offerings</H3>

        <H2>Reviews</H2>

        <BLOCKQUOTE>

        <P>
        When it comes to fine dining, I always choose to go to Abigail's Fine Eatery. You
        simply can't have a better experience at any of the competing establishments in all
        of Seattle. The service, atmosphere, and most of all the food is wonderful--Commentary
        from a satisfied customer.
        </P>

        </BLOCKQUOTE>

<P>
The URL of this page is <SAMP>HTTP://www.restaurant.com/abigail</SAMP>
</P>

<ADDRESS><B>Page Design by Home Pages Unlimited</B> <U>(HomePage@PLT.org)</U></ADDRESS>

</BODY>

</HTML>
```

Figure 3.2

3 Save the updates and view the document in your browser. The list should look similar to Figure 3.3.

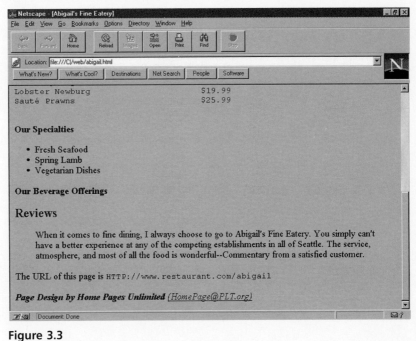

Figure 3.3

EXIT If necessary, you can exit the editor and browser and continue this project later.

CREATING ORDERED OR NUMBERED LISTS

Sometimes the information you're presenting in a list in a Web document should show a defined sequence, such as instructions for steps in a process. To create a list that shows a sequence, you use the *ordered list* (also called *numbered list*). You start the list with the <OL> tag and end the list with the </OL> tag. Within those tags, begin each line you would like numbered with the <LI> tag; the ordered list is automatically numbered for you. Following is an example of an ordered list:

```
<OL>
<LI>Create the document
<LI>Spell check the document
</OL>
```

By default, each line of the list is indented when you view it in the browser, and the first line of the list starts with the number 1.

You can change the default numbering for the entire list by using START=*value* within the <OL> tag. For example, you start the list with the number 10 as follows:

```
<OL START=10>
```

If you want to change the number of one line and have all subsequent lines increase by one, you use VALUE=*value* within the <LI> tag. Here's an example, changing a line number to 7:

```
<OL>
<LI>If your document is complete, you can jump to step 7
<LI>Edit the document
<LI VALUE=7>Save and print the document
<LI>Close the file
<LI>Exit the software
</OL>
```

In this example, the line numbering changes to 7 with the VALUE attribute, and each line after that increases starting from 7; that is, 8, 9, and so on.

If you want to change the default numbering scheme to letters or Roman numerals, you use the TYPE attribute. In most browsers, the default TYPE value is 1. See Table 3.1 for a list of available TYPE attributes.

Table 3.1

Value	Syntax/Example	Result
A	<OL TYPE=A>	Each line begins with a capital letter.
a	<OL TYPE=a>	Each line begins with a lowercase letter.
I	<OL TYPE=I>	Each line begins with a capital Roman numeral.
i	<OL TYPE=i>	Each line begins with a lowercase Roman numeral.
1	<OL TYPE=1>	The ordered list uses numbers—the default setting.

You can use the TYPE and the START attributes together. For example, to start a list with a capital *M*, here's the command:

```
<OL TYPE=A Start=M>
```

In the following steps, you will add a numbered list to *abigail.html*, under the heading Fine Dining.

To create an ordered list:

1 In the *abigail.html* document, type the following lines under the heading Fine Dining:

```
<OL>
<LI>Exquisite food
<LI>Quiet, comfortable atmosphere
<LI>Excellent service
</OL>
```

2 Save the file and view it in your browser. See Figure 3.4 for the HTML code and Figure 3.5 for the browser rendition.

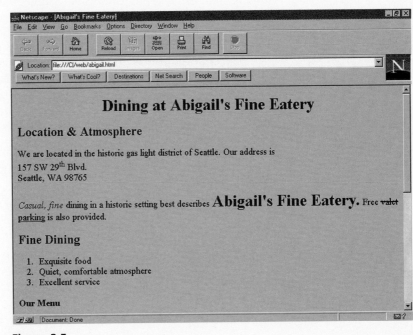

```
abigail - Notepad
File  Edit  Search  Help

<H1 ALIGN=CENTER>Dining at Abigail's Fine Eatery</H1>

        <H2>Location &amp; Atmosphere</H2>

        We are located in the historic gas light district of Seattle. Our address is<BR>
        157 SW 29<SUP>th</SUP> Blvd.<BR>
        Seattle, WA 98765

        <P>
        <EM>Casual, fine</EM> dining in a historic setting best describes
        <FONT SIZE=+2><STRONG>Abigail's Fine Eatery.</STRONG></FONT> <BLINK>Free</BLINK>
        <STRIKE>valet</STRIKE> <U>parking</U> is also provided.
        </P>

        <H2>Fine Dining</H2>

        <OL>
        <LI>Exquisite food
        <LI>Quiet, comfortable atmosphere
        <LI>Excellent service
        </OL>

               <H3>Our Menu</H3>

<PRE>

Roast Spring Lamb for Two          $39.95
Lobster Newburg                    $19.99
Saut&eacute; Prawns                        $25.99

</PRE>

               <H3>Our Specialties</H3>

               <UL>
               <LI>Fresh Seafood
```

Figure 3.4

Netscape - [Abigail's Fine Eatery]
File Edit View Go Bookmarks Options Directory Window Help

Location: file:///C|/web/abigail.html

Dining at Abigail's Fine Eatery

Location & Atmosphere

We are located in the historic gas light district of Seattle. Our address is
157 SW 29th Blvd.
Seattle, WA 98765

Casual, fine dining in a historic setting best describes **Abigail's Fine Eatery.** Free ~~valet~~ parking is also provided.

Fine Dining

1. Exquisite food
2. Quiet, comfortable atmosphere
3. Excellent service

Our Menu

Document: Done

Figure 3.5

EXIT   If necessary, you can exit the editor and browser and continue this project later.

CREATING DEFINITION OR GLOSSARY LISTS

A specialized type of list is the *definition list* or *glossary list*. This type of list pairs words or a short phrase with a definition or explanation, such as a term with its definition. You start the definition list with the <DL> tag and end it with the </DL> tag. Then you give each component its own tag; that is, the word or term to be defined starts with the <DT> tag, and the definition of the term starts with the <DD> tag. Neither of these two tags is paired. Following is an example of a typical definition list:

```
<DL>
        <DT>URL<DD>Uniform Resource Locator
        <DT>ISP<DD>Internet Service Provider
</DL>
```

When the definition list appears in a browser, the term generally appears on a line by itself and the definition is indented on a line by itself.

In the following steps, you create a definition list under the heading Our Beverage Offerings in the *abigail.html* document.

To create a definition list:

1 In your editor, open the *abigail.html* document and type the following items under the heading Our Beverage Offerings:

```
<DL>
<DT>Sparkling Wines<DD>Of the sparkling wines, French
champagne is the classic.
<DT>Still Wines<DD>The most famous still or red wines
come from the Bordeaux and Burgundy districts of France.
<DT>Fortified Wines<DD>The principal fortified wines are
sherry from Spain, port from Portugal, and Madeira from
Madeira. They are seldom served with meals.
</DL>
```

Figure 3.6 shows the HTML code. Notice that the <DT> and <DD> tags are on different lines, with tabs indenting the <DD> tags just as they will appear in the Web browser. This setup makes the resulting list a little easier for other users to visualize, without having to display it in the browser.

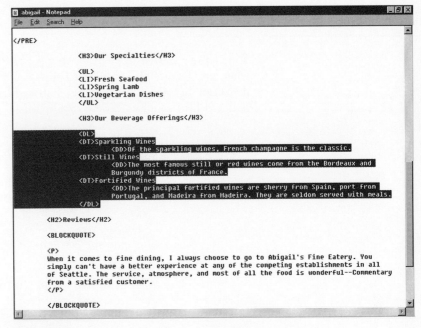

Figure 3.6

2 Save your work and view it in your browser (see Figure 3.7).

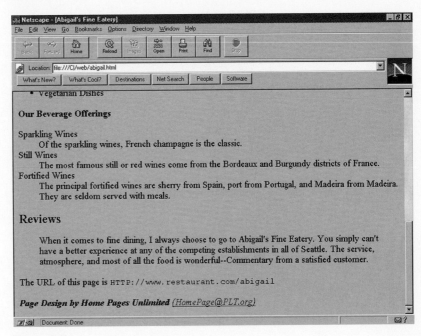

Figure 3.7

CREATING NESTED LISTS

You create a **_nested list_** when you insert a list within a list—for example, when you want a bulleted list to appear within an ordered list, within a definition list, or within another bulleted list. Following is an example of a bulleted list nested within an ordered list:

```
<OL>
        <LI>Open the file
              <UL>
              <LI>Type the document
              <LI>Edit the document
              <LI>Spell check the document
              </UL>
        <LI>Save and print the file
</OL>
```

Figure 3.8 shows this nested list in a browser.

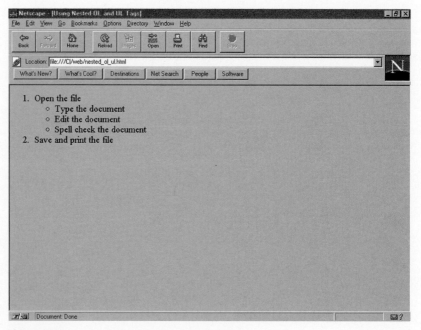

Figure 3.8

To create an outline, you can nest an ordered list within another ordered list. Here's an example:

```
<OL TYPE=I>
        <LI>The World Wide Web
                    <OL TYPE=A>
                    <LI>Using Browser Software
                            <OL TYPE=1>
                            <LI>Netscape
                            <LI>Microsoft
                            </OL>
                    <LI>Using an Editor
                    </OL>
        </OL>
```

Figure 3.9 shows this nested ordered list.

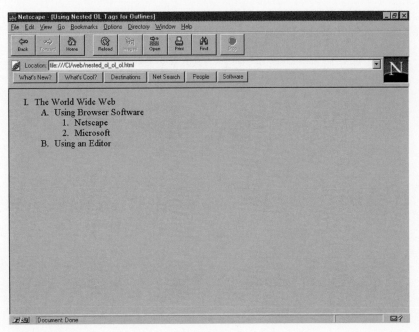

Figure 3.9

Quick Reminder As these examples show, you need to include a closing tag (</OL>) for each list when you want the list to revert to the previous level.

In the following steps, you turn the list under the Our Specialties heading in the Abigail's Web document into a nested list.

To modify an existing list to make it a nested list:

1 In the document *abigail.html*, place the cursor under the bulleted item Fresh Seafood (under the heading Our Specialties).

2 Type the following lines:

```
<UL>
<LI>Crab
<LI>Halibut
<LI>Scampi
</UL>
```

Figure 3.10 shows the HTML source code.

Quick Reminder Notice that this list you just typed is tabbed in farther than the other lists to maintain the hierarchical structure.

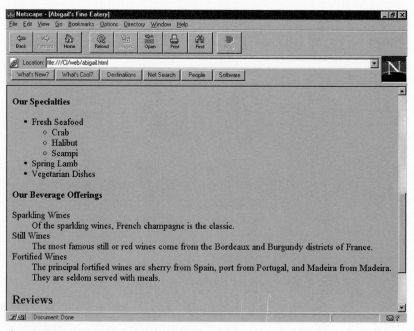

Figure 3.10

3 Save your work and view it in your browser (see Figure 3.11).

Figure 3.11

If necessary, you can exit the editor and browser and continue this project later.

CREATING LINKS AND ANCHORS IN THE SAME DOCUMENT

One of the features that make Web documents so powerful is their linking capability. A *link* provides text or an object that the user can click, and the user's display automatically "jumps" to the pre-programmed location. The link can be to a location within the same document or to a different Web document. You can make a link to any page that exists on the Web—as long as it doesn't have a security system to keep you out.

> **Tip** Although you aren't required to do so, it's common courtesy to contact the Webmaster of the site to which you would like to link and ask his or her permission.

You can create links using the *anchor* tag in two ways:

- The general method links directly to the beginning of a Web page. This is the most common way to create a link—because you most likely want your readers to start at the beginning of the document.
- The second method links to a particular point in the same Web page. This strategy is very useful for pages that include a table of contents at the top. With this type of anchor, you can list your topics at the top of the page and allow your reader to click a topic that's explained in more detail later in the same page.

> **Caution** This type of link usually works only at a site where you have complete control over the content. You not only need to create the anchor for the reader to click, but also the anchor that specifies the exact location in the Web document to which the reader will "jump" when he clicks.

Linking to other Web pages is discussed in Project 7. In this project, you create links that jump the reader from one location to another within the same document.

First, you need to go to the location in the HTML code to which you want the user to jump. To create the anchor tag that defines the location to which the reader will jump, you must insert and name an <A NAME> anchor at that location. For example, if you want the user to jump to text containing the heading Description, you place an anchor tag on the line preceding the heading or on the same line as the heading. Additionally, you must give the location a value—usually associated with the location. This is the format:

```
<A NAME="description">
<H2>Description</H2></A>
```

You also can nest the anchor tag within the heading tag:

```
<H2><A NAME="description">Description</A></H2>
```

You use the value of the NAME attribute (in this case, "description") to tell the browser where to jump. The quotation marks are required.

To create the anchor tag around the text that the reader will click, move back to that text in the HTML code. This anchor tag includes the attribute HREF, which stands for *H*ypertext *REF*erence. Usually this tag contains the URL for the location of the Web document to which you would like to link (see Project 7). In this case, however, the link is referencing a location on the same page. When you're specifically targeting a location on a page like this, the server is really looking for the location of the <A NAME> value that matches the value in your <A HREF> anchor. To tell the server that you're looking for an <A NAME>, you must precede the value of the <A HREF> with a pound sign (#). The format of the anchor tag is

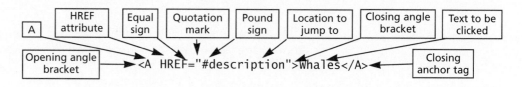

To summarize this example, when you click the word Whales, the server looks for an <A NAME> with the value description on the same Web page. You then "jump" to the Description heading that's marked with the value description by the <A NAME> anchor.

You may have seen Web pages that have phrases such as click here to indicate a link. You should avoid meaningless text and instead create links that flow with the text. The user knows to click the text without having to be told to click there, because the text has been formatted as hypertext— usually blue and underlined. You could create a link like this:

```
To read a description of mating whales, <A
HREF="#description">click here</A>
```

But wouldn't this one be better?

```
There have been many <A HREF="#description">descriptions</A>
of mating whales documented over the last hundred years.
```

In the following steps, you make a link from the nested bullet line Crab to the bottom of the page in the *abigail.html* document.

To create links and anchors in a Web document:

1 In the *abigail.html* document, place the tags <A HREF="#crab"> and </A> around the word Crab as follows:

<A HREF="#crab">Crab</A>

This action makes a link to a section in *abigail.html* that is denoted with the tag <A NAME="crab"> (you create this tag in the next step). See Figure 3.12 to view this change in the HTML code and Figure 3.13 to view the link in the browser. Notice that the word Crab now appears as an underlined link in the browser.

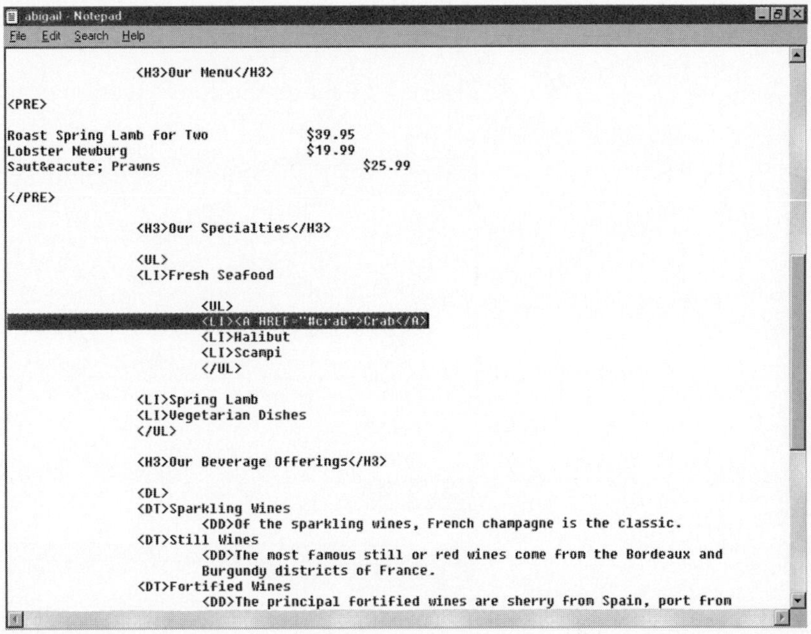

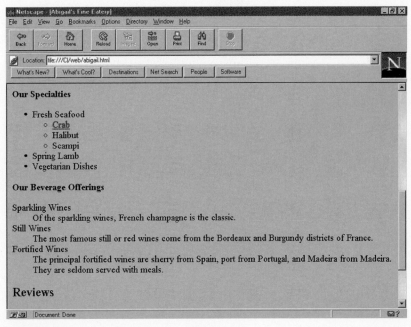

Figure 3.12

Figure 3.13

2 To create the new "crab" section for the <A HREF="#crab"> tag to reference, create a new heading near the bottom of *abigail.html*, just above the URL reference:

```
<A NAME="crab">
<H3>Crab</H3>
</A>
Our crab is delivered live each day from the Oregon and
Washington coast. We allow you to choose the crab you want
from the tank, and then we prepare it for you. It is served
with herbs and our famous sauce.
```

The <P></P> tags aren't required in this case because they're implied as part of the <H3> tag.

Figure 3.14 shows the added section in the HTML code.

Figure 3.14

3 Save your changes and view the document in your browser (see Figure 3.15).

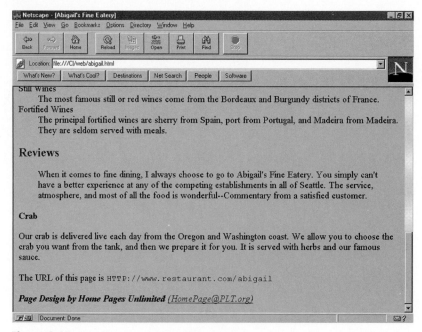

Figure 3.15

4 Click the word Crab in your browser. If you've done everything correctly, your display should "jump" to the Crab section that you created in step 2.

5 Next you need to create a link from the Crab section back to the Our Specialties heading. First you have to create a <A NAME> anchor. Find the heading Our Specialties and add a NAME anchor around it as follows:

```
<A NAME="specialties">
<H3>Our Specialties</H3>
</A>
```

Figure 3.16 shows the HTML source code with these changes.

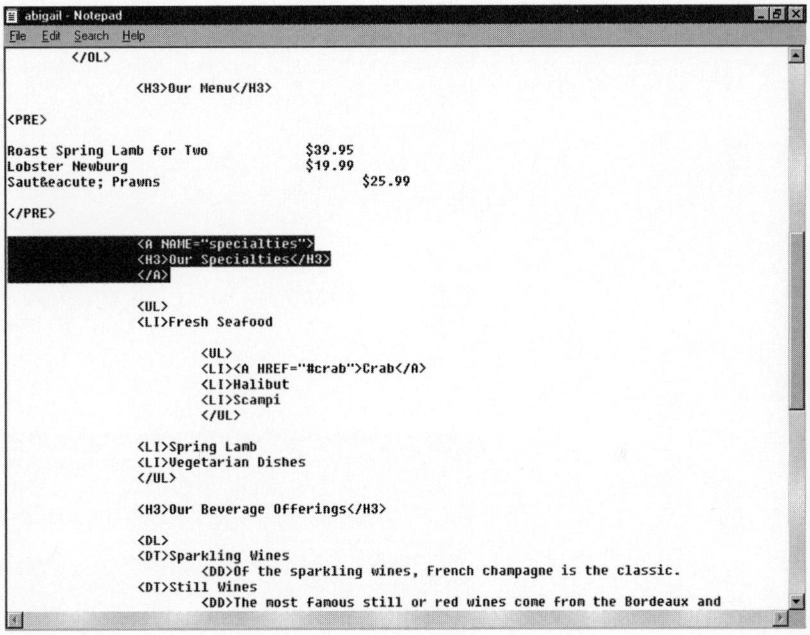

Figure 3.16

6 Now add a link back to the Our Specialties section from the Crab section at the bottom of the page. Type the following code lines after the paragraph about fresh crab delivery:

```
<P>
<A HREF="#specialties">Return to Menu</A>
</P>
```

See Figure 3.17 for the new version of the HTML code.

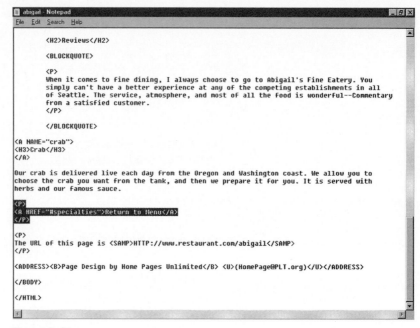

Figure 3.17

7 Save your work and view the modifications in your browser, as shown in Figure 3.18. When you click the words `Return to Menu` you should "jump" directly to the `Our Specialties` heading.

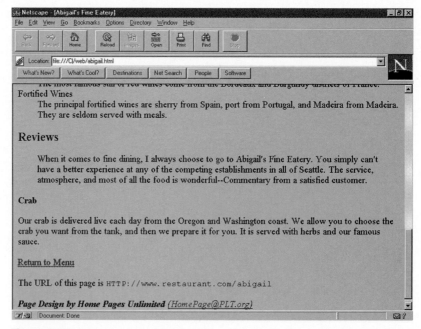

Figure 3.18

THE NEXT STEP

Practice inserting bulleted, numbered, definition, and nested lists in a sample HTML document. Use the techniques you learned in this project to add links from one section of the document to another. Remember to use a new name when you save the practice file so that you can view it with your browser. The *abigail.html* document will be used again in the next project.

This concludes the project. You can either exit your editor and browser or go on to work the Study Questions, Review Exercises, and Assignments.

SUMMARY AND EXERCISES

Summary

- To create an unordered list, use the <UL> opening tag and the </UL> closing tag.
- To create an ordered list, use the <OL> opening tag and the </OL> closing tag.
- Each line of an ordered or unordered list uses the <LI> tag.
- To create a definition list or glossary, use the <DL> opening tag and the </DL> closing tag.
- Each term in the definition list is preceded by the <DT> tag.
- Each definition in the definition list is preceded by the <DD> tag.
- To define an anchor to which a link will jump, use the <A NAME="*anchor*">text</A> code.
- To define a link that, when clicked, will jump to another location, use the <A HREF="#*location*">*text to be clicked*</A> command.

Key Terms

anchor
bullet
definition (or glossary) list
link

nested list
ordered (or numbered) list
unordered (or bulleted) list

Study Questions

Multiple Choice

1. To create a glossary, you use
   a. an ordered list.
   b. an unnumbered list.
   c. an HREF attribute.
   d. a definition list.
   e. none of the above.

2. The anchor name must always have a
   a. !
   b. #
   c. '
   d. ,
   e. . (period)

3. To display the default bullet in a bulleted list, you use
   a. `<UL TYPE=default>`.
   b. `<UL TYPE=square>`.
   c. `<UL TYPE=round>`.
   d. `<UL TYPE=none>`.
   e. `<UL>`.

4. You can change the character that begins an ordered list by using which attribute?
   a. `START`.
   b. `TYPE`.
   c. `BEGIN`.
   d. `ORDER`.
   e. `ARRANGE`.

5. To indent a definition in a definition list, you use
   a. `TAB`.
   b. `INDENT`.
   c. `ALIGN`.
   d. `#####`.
   e. none of the above.

6. Unordered lists
   a. are used for items in sequence.
   b. can change from numbers to letters.
   c. are the most common list used in Web documents.
   d. are used for lists of items that don't necessarily have a sequence.
   e. all of these answers.

7. An anchor
   a. defines the location where the user will jump.
   b. cannot be text.
   c. must always be in another document.
   d. must be placed in a heading tag.
   e. all of these answers.

8. Definition lists
   a. have a term and a definition.
   b. use the `<LI>` tag to indicate the term.
   c. use the `<DT>` and `<DD>` tags.
   d. both a and c.
   e. all of these answers.

9. Links
   a. allow the user to jump to another location.
   b. must always jump to a different document.
   c. appear unformatted in the browser.
   d. aren't a very powerful feature.
   e. all of these answers.

10. Nesting Lists
    a. can occur only with the same type of list; that is, only unordered lists can be nested within unordered lists.
    b. can occur with any type of list.
    c. can occur with any type of list, but you can't use links within nested links.
    d. are used only for definitions.
    e. all of these answers.

Short Answer

1. Make the following items into an unordered list:
   ```
   Copying Files
   Moving Files
   Deleting Files
   Editing Files
   ```

2. Change the following unordered list to use square bullets:
   ```
   Copying Files
   Moving Files
   Deleting Files
   Editing Files
   ```

3. Make the following an ordered list:
   ```
   Beat four eggs
   Add one cup of flour
   Add two tablespoons of sugar
   Add one tablespoon of salt
   ```

4. Change the first number in the following ordered list to 7:
   ```
   Beat four eggs
   Add one cup of flour
   Add two tablespoons of sugar
   Add one tablespoon of salt
   ```

5. Make the following an ordered list that uses capital Roman numerals:
   ```
   Introduction
   Objectives
   Descriptions
   Conclusion
   ```

6. Make the following a definition list:
   ```
   folder          A directory
   file            Information stored under one name
   file extension  Three letters found at the end of the file
                   name, usually placed there by the software
   ```

7. Make the following an unordered list within an ordered list:
   ```
   Learn how to use the World Wide Web
           Purchase a modem
           Sign up with an Internet provider
           Install a browser
   Learn how to create Web documents
   ```

8. Make the following an anchor to which the user can jump:
   ```
   <H3>Explanation</H3>
   ```

9. Make the following the link that jumps to the anchor you defined in Question 8:
   ```
   Edible Mushrooms
   ```

10. Make the following return to an anchor called Outline:
    ```
    Return to Menu
    ```

For Discussion

1. When would you use an unordered, an ordered, or a definition list?

2. Why should you enable your Web page visitor to jump back to the original location of the link?

3. Give an example of a time when you might need to use a nested list in a Web page.

4. How can you (and why should you) avoid using the phrase `Click here` in your Web page?

5. Describe the design considerations that arise with using links on Web pages.

Review Exercises

Adding Lists to the Alphabits Bookstore Web Page

1. Add the following list as an ordered list under the heading `Best-Selling Children's Books`:
   `The Cat in the Hat`
   `Winnie-The-Pooh`
   `The Wind in the Willows`
   `The Secret Garden`

2. Include the following books as an unordered list under the heading `Special Events`:
   `Visit from Pooh Bear`
   `Free Books`
   `Puppet Shows`

3. Add the following text to the bottom of the body section:
   `Every time your child purchases and reads 25 books from Alphabits Bookstore, she will receive a free book.`

4. Make the text you added to the bottom of the document an anchor to which the user can jump. Use the anchor name `free`.

5. Make the heading `Free Books` the link to the anchor `free`.

6. Complete the link by adding an anchor and link that returns the user to the top of the document.

Figure 3.19 shows the changes in the document.

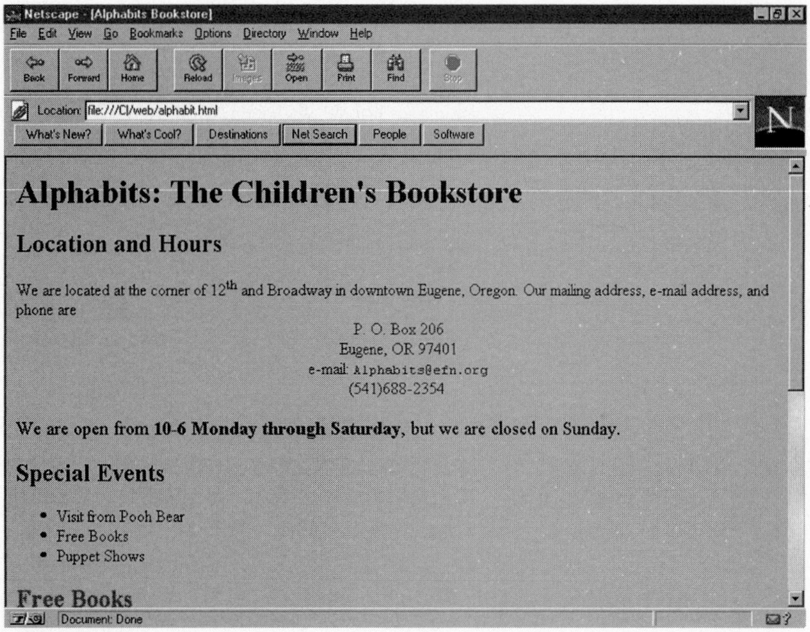

Figure 3.19a

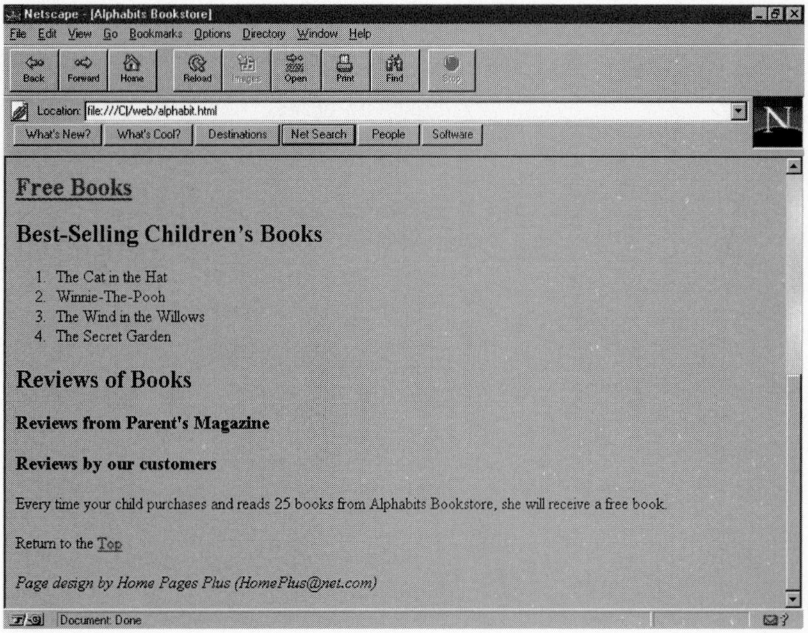

Figure 3.19b

Adding Lists to the Animal Web Page

1. Make use of two types of lists on your animal Web page.

2. Add a link from one of the lists to further information about a certain breed of animal.

Assignments

Linking Your Résumé to Your Personal Web Page

Use the `Work Experience` heading on your personal Web document to create a link to your résumé. Type your résumé at the end of the document. Create a second anchor and link so that the reader can return to the top of your Web document.

Adding Lists and Links in the Organization or Nonprofit Web Page

In the organization Web document, add a nested list. Create a link and anchor to provide the reader with more information about some aspect of the organization. For example, use the `Bylaws` heading to jump the reader to a section that includes the organization's bylaws. Create a second anchor and link so that the reader can return to the top of your Web document.

What Is a Firewall? When most businesses and institutions maintained a private network, it was much harder for hackers to gain access to their information. But as more and more of these businesses want to provide information and even do business on the Web, security is becoming more of an issue. Businesses and institutions are installing *firewall* systems. These are computers that work like a wall to stop "fires" by limiting access to the private network of the business, and thus to its sensitive and confidential files. Some businesses are placing their Web servers outside the firewall so that the general public can access their Web pages but not their internal documents.

PROJECT 4: INCLUDING IMAGES ON A HOME PAGE

In this project, you will learn how to use images in Web documents. You will also learn about the image formats that are used on the World Wide Web.

Reminder All images in this project were downloaded from the Net~User's Web Art Library at `http://www.net-user.com/graphics/`.

Objectives

After completing this project, you should be able to:

▶ Use inline images

▶ Include alternative text

▶ Arrange images and text

▶ Align images

▶ Use images as links

CASE STUDY: ADDING GRAPHICS TO THE WEB PAGE

So far you have placed only text on the Abigail's Fine Eatery Web page. Now you add graphic images, which are an important part of Web documents. Much of the popularity of the World Wide Web can be attributed to its capability of including images in Web documents. For example, the home pages of most businesses or organizations include at least a logo. As the Web becomes increasingly commercial, vendors sell their wares by displaying pictures of the products they offer. Even many personal home pages include a photograph of the page owner. The possibilities are endless.

Designing the Solution

To include a logo or photograph in a Web page, you need to have the image scanned or converted into a format that allows it to be viewed by browser programs. If you don't own or have access to a scanner, you can have a copy shop provide this service. If you need to convert an existing graphics file, you can use a graphics program such as PaintShop Pro, Adobe Photoshop, or one of many other graphics packages available commercially or on the Web. You can also purchase graphics commercially or find graphics on the Web that are free for use.

Caution Not all graphics on the Web are free to be used; many are the work of artists who copyright those images. Be cautious and courteous; always contact the Webmaster of the site before you use any artwork from it.

The two main formats widely used for Web graphics are .GIF and .JPEG (pronounced *jiff* and *J-peg*). The .GIF standard, short for *Graphics Interchange Format*, was developed by CompuServe, and sometimes is referred to as the *CompuServe format*. This format uses *LZW compression*, which looks at an image, finds large blocks of the same color in the image, and compresses those blocks, thereby reducing the size of the file considerably.

The .GIF format also uses what's called an *indexed color scheme*; that is, .GIF devises a custom palette for each image, using only 256 colors of the 16 million colors that are available. When the image appears on-screen, the index codes each color used in the image. In this way, .GIF images can be compressed and then displayed without any loss in quality. When you save an image in .GIF format using a graphics package, you can usually make a file smaller by manually choosing the picture to use less than 256 colors for faster loading. For most pictures, especially icons used on the Web, this strategy is useful.

The term .JPEG stands for *Joint Photographic Expert Group*. This standard was developed by a committee for use with photographs because the image can contain millions of colors. The .JPEG format is known as a *lossy type compression* because, when the image is compressed, it permanently loses some of its quality. Let's say you have a picture of a grassy field with red and yellow flowers peppered through it. The .JPEG format "looks" through this picture for similar green colors and replaces them all with one green. So, rather than having 1000 different shades of green in your picture, you may have 500 shades. When you convert an image to .JPEG, the graphics software available allows you to control the amount of data lost by controlling the ratio between data loss and how much the image is compressed; for example, 20:1 or 50:1. .JPEG does a very good job of choosing what colors to "lose" so that the image usually doesn't look much different from the original. Additionally, the human eye can't distinguish between all those millions of colors, so losing 500 shades of thousands of greens usually doesn't make much of a difference to us visually.

When you are ready to scan or convert images, you must decide between the two formats, .GIF and .JPEG. If your image is small, has blocks of the same color, or has few colors, the best format for the image is .GIF because you can manually limit the number of colors in the picture. If your image is large, has no blocks of color but instead has subtle tones, or has many colors, the best format for the image is .JPEG.

Most graphic file types (including .GIF files) save the color information of pictures line by line, starting from the top of the picture and logically stepping through the lines until they reach the bottom. Therefore, the viewer immediately gets the full detail of the picture as each line is loaded, but may not know exactly what the picture contains until it's fully loaded and every line is in place. Unlike most other file types, .GIF files also give you the option of saving a file in an *interlaced format*. This means that the color information is saved starting from the top of the picture, but it skips to every eighth line as it saves. So it saves lines 1, 8, 16, 24, 32, and so on; when it gets to the bottom of the image, it goes back and saves lines 2, 9,

17, 25, 33, and so on, until every line in the picture has been saved. When the picture is displayed, the viewer sees it load each line in this pattern. Therefore, the entire picture is outlined immediately and becomes more detailed as the second through seventh lines fill in. With this method, the viewer gets an immediate sense of what the picture contains, which usually conveys the feeling that an interlaced picture is loading more "quickly" than a normal picture.

> **Tip** If you are trying to make the image available to the most browsers, .GIF is the safest format; not all browsers support .JPEG.

Another consideration when including images in your Web document is the time required for a user to display the image. As everyone who uses the Web discovers, some pages just take too long to load, so you stop them before they can finish. If you want people to view your Web documents, keep the size of the images small, about a total of 30K for the entire page, so that people will be willing to visit your site often.

In the next section, you will add a graphic image to the Abigail's Fine Eatery Web page (see Figure 4.1). This image will help convey the message that this is an elegant place to dine.

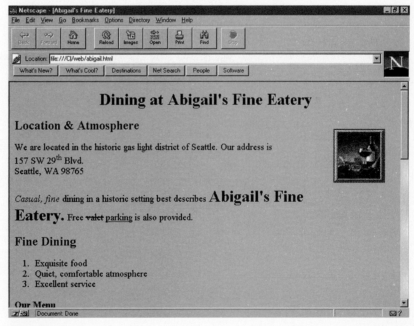

Figure 4.1

USING INLINE IMAGES

The term *inline image* means that an image can be included in a line of text. Inline images are internal to the Web document; that is, they are loaded as the page is loaded and appear automatically (if the user has image loading turned on). *External images* are loaded only at the user's request, and can be in other file formats that the user wants to download.

To include an inline image on your Web document, place the insertion point where you want the image to appear and use the <IMG> tag. The tag includes the SRC="*path/filename*" variable.

You can use two different formats for the command:

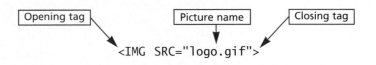

```
<IMG SRC="logo.gif">
```

or

```
<IMG SRC="http://www.aw.com/~user/images/logo.gif">
```

The <IMG> tag is not a paired tag.

> **Reminder** The path and file name are case sensitive, so be careful of spelling and case when typing a long path.

 To add an inline image to a Web document:

1 Open the *abigail.html* document.

2 Find the heading Dining at Abigail's Fine Eatery and type the following text below it:

<IMG SRC="images/tasten2.gif">

This line tells HTML that the image file is called *tasten2.gif* and is in a folder called *images*, located within the folder where *abigail.html* is stored. Check with your instructor to see where the graphic files are located on your system.

Figure 4.2 shows the HTML source code.

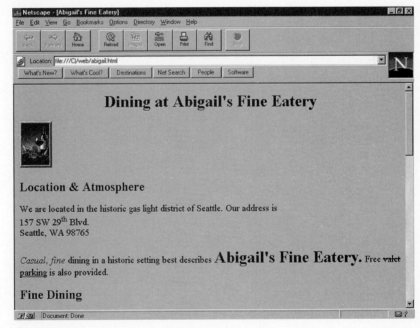

```
abigail - Notepad

File   Edit   Search   Help

<HTML>

<HEAD>

<TITLE>Abigail's Fine Eatery</TITLE>

</HEAD>

<BODY>

<BASEFONT SIZE=4>

<!--This section will be updated-->

<H1 ALIGN=CENTER>Dining at Abigail's Fine Eatery</H1>

<IMG SRC="images/tasten2.gif">

        <H2>Location &amp; Atmosphere</H2>

        We are located in the historic gas light district of Seattle. Our address is<BR>
        157 SW 29<SUP>th</SUP> Blvd.<BR>
        Seattle, WA 98765

        <P>
        <EM>Casual, fine</EM> dining in a historic setting best describes
        <FONT SIZE=+2><STRONG>Abigail's Fine Eatery.</STRONG></FONT> <BLINK>Free</BLINK>
        <STRIKE>valet</STRIKE> <U>parking</U> is also provided.
        </P>

        <H2>Fine Dining</H2>

        <OL>
        <LI>Exquisite food
        <LI>Quiet, comfortable atmosphere
        <LI>Excellent service
```

Figure 4.2

3 Save your work and then check out the results in your browser. The inline graphic is inserted, as shown in Figure 4.3.

Figure 4.3

EXIT   If necessary, you can exit the editor and browser and continue this project later.

INCLUDING ALTERNATIVE TEXT

Not every graphic you place on a page will achieve the effect you intended. Some older browsers don't display graphics at all, and some newer browsers don't display .JPEG files. When a browser doesn't display a graphic, your Web page visitor may feel she has missed something if she can't tell what appears in the image. On the other hand, some visitors who have older modems want to see pages more quickly, so they choose not to load graphics automatically, and then they decide, based on the content of your page, whether they want to take the time to display the individual images.

You can help all these visitors by adding alternative text. *Alternative text* describes the image for visitors who can't or have chosen not to view images. Rather than having just the word IMAGE displayed on the screen when a graphic doesn't appear, you can present a description of the contents of the missing graphic image.

To include alternative text, you add the ALT attribute to the <IMG> tag. The alternative text must be contained in straight quotation marks. Here's an example:

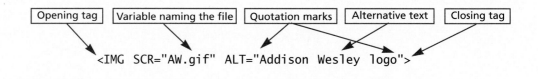

 ## To add alternative text to an image:

1 In the *abigail.html* document, find this line in your source code:

```
<IMG SRC="images/tasten2.gif">
```

2 After the quotation mark at the end of the file name, type the following alternative text:

```
<IMG SRC="images/tasten2.gif" ALT="Abigail's Restaurant
Logo">
```

Figure 4.4 shows the source code.

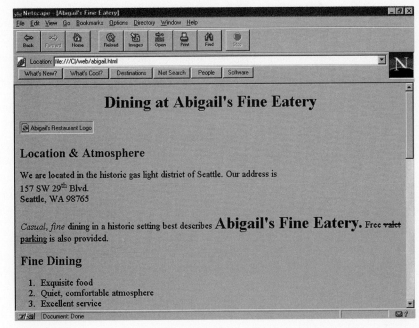

```
abigail - Notepad
File  Edit  Search  Help

<HTML>

<HEAD>

<TITLE>Abigail's Fine Eatery</TITLE>

</HEAD>

<BODY>

<BASEFONT SIZE=4>

<!--This section will be updated-->

<H1 ALIGN=CENTER>Dining at Abigail's Fine Eatery</H1>

<IMG SRC="images/tasten2.gif" ALT="Abigail's Restaurant Logo">

        <H2>Location &amp; Atmosphere</H2>

        We are located in the historic gas light district of Seattle. Our address is<BR>
        157 SW 29<SUP>th</SUP> Blvd.<BR>
        Seattle, WA 98765

        <P>
        <EM>Casual, fine</EM> dining in a historic setting best describes
        <FONT SIZE=+2><STRONG>Abigail's Fine Eatery.</STRONG></FONT> <BLINK>Free</BLINK>
        <STRIKE>valet</STRIKE> <U>parking</U> is also provided.
        </P>

        <H2>Fine Dining</H2>

        <OL>
        <LI>Exquisite food
        <LI>Quiet, comfortable atmosphere
        <LI>Excellent service
```

Figure 4.4

3 Save your work and view it in your browser. Turn off image display in the browser and reload the Abigail's page to see the alternative text (see Figure 4.5). The words Abigail's Restaurant Logo should replace the image.

```
Netscape - [Abigail's Fine Eatery]
File  Edit  View  Go  Bookmarks  Options  Directory  Window  Help

Back  Forward  Home  Reload  Images  Open  Print  Find  Stop

Location: file:///C|/web/abigail.html                                    N

What's New?  What's Cool?  Destinations  Net Search  People  Software
```

Dining at Abigail's Fine Eatery

Abigail's Restaurant Logo

Location & Atmosphere

We are located in the historic gas light district of Seattle. Our address is
157 SW 29th Blvd.
Seattle, WA 98765

Casual, fine dining in a historic setting best describes **Abigail's Fine Eatery.** Free ~~valet~~ parking is also provided.

Fine Dining

1. Exquisite food
2. Quiet, comfortable atmosphere
3. Excellent service

```
Document: Done
```

Figure 4.5

If necessary, you can exit the editor and browser and continue this project later.

ARRANGING IMAGES AND TEXT

Sometimes you'll want to include images in lines of text rather than always on a line by themselves; that's why the images are referred to as *inline*. To place an image on a line, you include the <IMG> tag at the location where you want the image to appear in the line of text. For example, if you want the company logo for the publisher Internet Books Inc. to appear in a heading between the words Internet and Books, you use this command:

```
<H1>Internet <IMG SRC="images/book.gif"> Books Inc.</H1>
```

Figure 4.6 shows the results of the command.

Figure 4.6

In addition to including the image in the line of text, you can control where on the line the image appears. By default, the image aligns with the bottom of the text. You can change the alignment so that the image aligns with the middle or top of the line of text by adding the ALIGN=*variable* attribute to the IMG command, using the following format:

```
<IMG SRC="image.gif" ALIGN=TOP>
```

Table 4.1 describes the variable options available.

Table 4.1

Variable	Image Alignment
TOP	At the top of the line–the top of the text or the top of another image
TEXTTOP	At the top of the text
MIDDLE	Centered vertically in the middle of the line
ABSMIDDLE	Aligned with the middle of the largest element on the line
BOTTOM	At the bottom of the line–the bottom of the text or the bottom of another image
ABSBOTTOM	Aligned with the bottom of the largest element

Figure 4.7 shows the various alignments. Note that the picture of the book is stationary and doesn't use any of the ALIGN attributes. It is present so that you can view the effect of the ALIGN attribute on the steaming cup of coffee. Notice how the cup is positioned relative to the text and the book in each example.

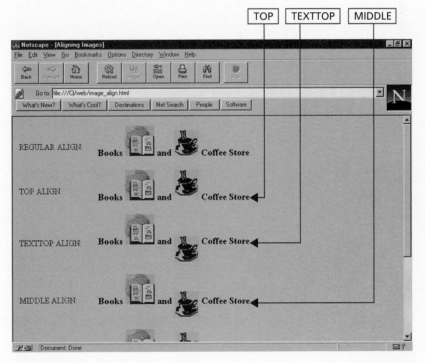

Figure 4.7a

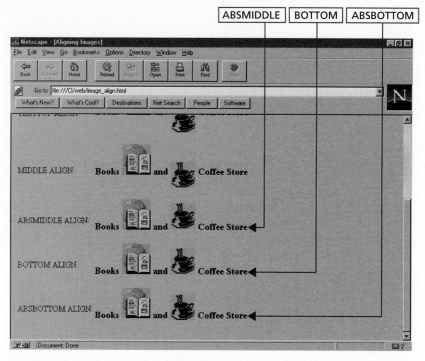

Figure 4.7b

When you include an image in a line of text, you may need to include more space around the image so that the image stands out and the text can be read easily. You can add space horizontally to the right and left side of an image by including the HSPACE=*value* attribute. The value following the equal sign (=) is the number of ***pixels***–dots of color–to add on to each side of the image.

You can add space vertically to the top and the bottom of the image by including the VSPACE=*value* attribute. The value following the equal sign is the number of pixels to add to the top and the bottom of the image. You can use these attributes together or separately; however, the limitation is that HSPACE adds the space to both sides, and VSPACE adds the space to both the top and bottom of the image. Here's an example:

```
<IMG SRC="images/tasten2.gif" HSPACE=10 VSPACE=5>
```

Figure 4.8 shows the results.

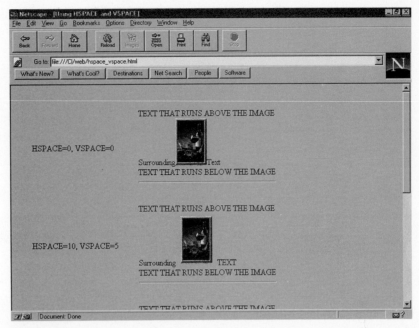

Figure 4.8a

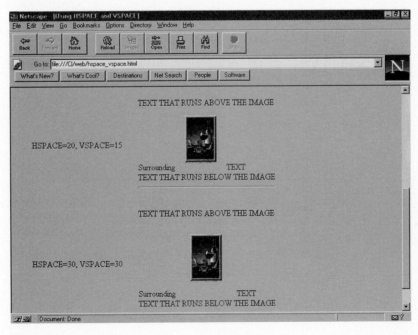

Figure 4.8b

At times, you may want to *scale* the image; that is, change the height and width of the image. Keep the following points in mind when scaling an image:

- Scaling down a large image doesn't reduce its file size. To have an image that loads quickly, create one that's smaller in file size.
- Scaling up an image doesn't increase its file size. You can use scaling to make your small image appear larger on the screen.
- The more you scale an image, the more grainy it becomes; it may even become blurry.
- To increase the speed at which an image loads, specify the exact dimensions of the image. The browser doesn't have to do any computations but can simply load the image at the specified dimensions.

To scale an image, you include the WIDTH=*value* and HEIGHT=*value* attributes with the <IMG> tag. The *value* setting is the number of pixels for the width and height.

Caution If you specify numbers that aren't proportional, the image will appear out of proportion.

Following is an example of how you use these attributes:

```
<IMG SRC="image.gif" WIDTH=100 HEIGHT=100>
```

In the following steps, you will add the alignment, size, and spatial attributes to the image tasten2.gif.

To fine-tune an image:

1 In the *abigail.html* document, add the following attributes and values to the IMG tag for the image tasten2.gif:

```
ALIGN=TOP
WIDTH=100
HEIGHT=100
HSPACE=20
VSPACE=20
```

You should still have an ALT attribute in the image.

Your additions should make the tag look like this:

```
<IMG SRC="images/tasten2.gif" ALIGN=TOP WIDTH=100
HEIGHT=100 HSPACE=20 VSPACE=20 ALT="Abigail's Restaurant
Logo">
```

Look at Figure 4.9 to see the changes in the HTML source code. In the figure, notice that part of this tag is indented. This technique helps to point out the fact that, although the tag continues on another line, it's still part of the same tag.

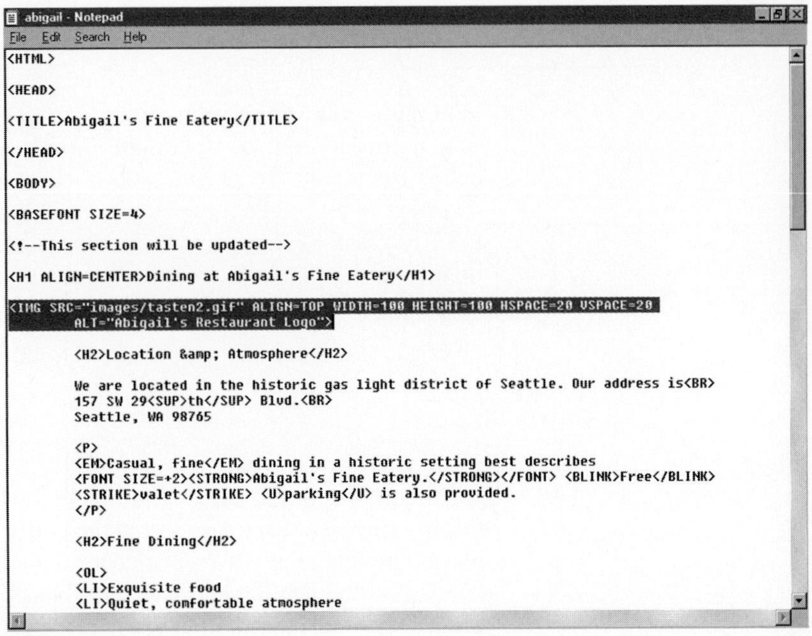

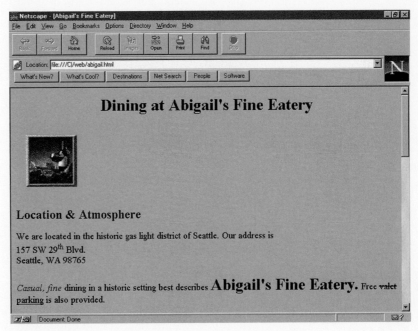

Figure 4.9

2 Save your work and view it in your browser (see Figure 4.10). Do you see any difference?

Figure 4.10

EXIT If necessary, you can exit the editor and browser and continue this project later.

ALIGNING IMAGES

When you include an inline image in a Web page, by default only one line of text appears next to the image. Any subsequent lines of text appear below the image. To create Web documents with more than one line of text next to an image, you use the ALIGN attribute with either the value LEFT to place the image at the left and lines of text at the right of the image, or the value RIGHT to place the image at the right and lines of text at the left of the image. You use the ALIGN attribute this way:

```
<IMG SRC="cupicon.gif" ALIGN=LEFT>
```

or

```
<IMG SRC="cupicon.gif" ALIGN=RIGHT>
```

The first example places the image at the left margin, and any text that follows the image appears to the right of the image. The second example places the image at the right margin, and any text that follows the image appears to the left of the image, as shown in Figure 4.11. Notice that the picture on the second line aligns itself with the right side of the *screen*–not with the right side of the text.

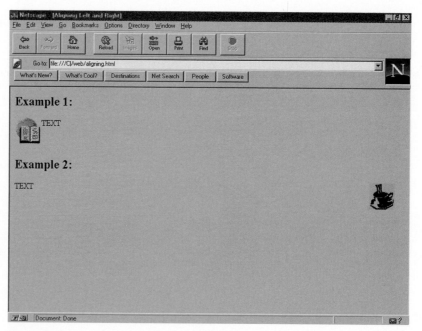

Figure 4.11

You may want to create an effect with two images and text flowing between the two images. To create this arrangement, you align one image to the left and the other to the right; the text that follows flows between the two images. This is how it's done:

```
<IMG SRC="image1.gif" ALIGN=LEFT>
<IMG SRC="image2.gif" ALIGN=RIGHT>
Text
```

Figure 4.12 shows the results.

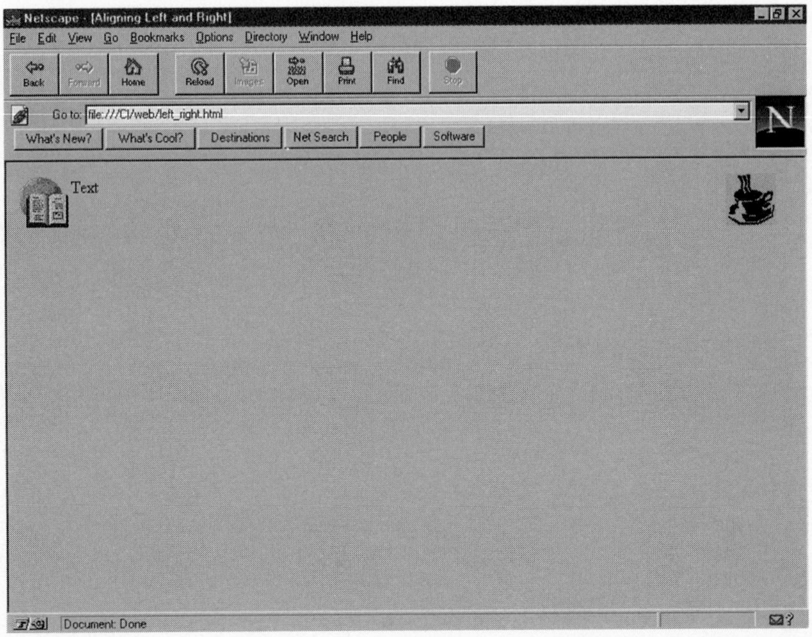

Figure 4.12

In the following steps, you will change the alignment of the *tasten2.gif* image in the Web page for Abigail's Fine Eatery.

To wrap text next to an image:

1 In the *abigail.html* document, move the insertion point to the line containing the image reference. It currently looks like this:

<IMG SRC="images/tasten2.gif" ALIGN=TOP WIDTH=100 HEIGHT=100 HSPACE=20 VSPACE=20 ALT="Abigail's Restaurant Logo">

2 Change the alignment from ALIGN=TOP to ALIGN=RIGHT (see Figure 4.13).

3 Save the file and check out the results in your browser. The text appears next to the image, as shown in Figure 4.14.

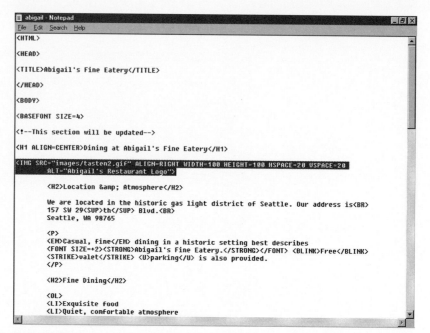

Figure 4.13

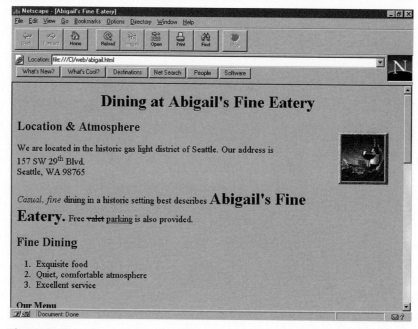

Figure 4.14

 If necessary, you can exit the editor and browser and continue this project later.

USING IMAGES AS LINKS

In Project 3, you learned about using text as links to other locations in a document. You can also use images as links to other locations. This powerful feature enables you to include icons that the user clicks to jump to another location. For example, you might include small inline images that allow the user to click to see more information, or include a small version of the image that loads quickly, allowing the user to click and see a larger version of the image.

To make an image into a link, you include the <IMG> tag inside the link tag. This is the format:

```
<A HREF="#location"><IMG SRC="image.gif"></A>
```

When the user clicks the image, the browser jumps to the *location* designated in HREF="#*location*".

If you want to make the image and the surrounding text into a link, you include both the image and the text in the link tag, like this:

```
<HREF="#location"><IMG SCR="image.gif">text</A>
```

To make an image into a link to another location:

1 In the *abigail.html* document, move the insertion point to the line containing the image. It currently looks like this:

```
<IMG SRC="images/tasten2.gif" ALIGN=RIGHT WIDTH=100
HEIGHT=100 HSPACE=20 VSPACE=20 ALT="Abigail's Restaurant
Logo">
```

2 Place the insertion point before the beginning of the <IMG> tag.

3 Type **<A HREF="#crab">** as the beginning of the anchor tag.

4 Move the insertion point after the closing angle bracket (>) of the <IMG> command.

5 Type **</A>** to close the anchor tag (see Figure 4.15).

```
abigail - Notepad
File  Edit  Search  Help
<HTML>

<HEAD>

<TITLE>Abigail's Fine Eatery</TITLE>

</HEAD>

<BODY>

<BASEFONT SIZE=4>

<!--This section will be updated-->

<H1 ALIGN=CENTER>Dining at Abigail's Fine Eatery</H1>

<A HREF="#crab">
<IMG SRC="images/tasten2.gif" ALIGN=RIGHT WIDTH=100 HEIGHT=100 HSPACE=20 VSPACE=20
     ALT="Abigail's Restaurant Logo">
</A>

         <H2>Location &amp; Atmosphere</H2>

         We are located in the historic gas light district of Seattle. Our address is<BR>
         157 SW 29<SUP>th</SUP> Blvd.<BR>
         Seattle, WA 98765

         <P>
         <EM>Casual, fine</EM> dining in a historic setting best describes
         <FONT SIZE=+2><STRONG>Abigail's Fine Eatery.</STRONG></FONT> <BLINK>Free</BLINK>
         <STRIKE>valet</STRIKE> <U>parking</U> is also provided.
         </P>

         <H2>Fine Dining</H2>

         <OL>
```

Figure 4.15

6 Save the file and test the results in your browser (see Figure 4.16). When clicked, the link will jump to the location named Crab from Project 3. In Figure 4.16, notice that the mouse pointer is positioned over the *tasten2.gif* image, and the link for that image is visible in the status bar at the bottom of the screen.

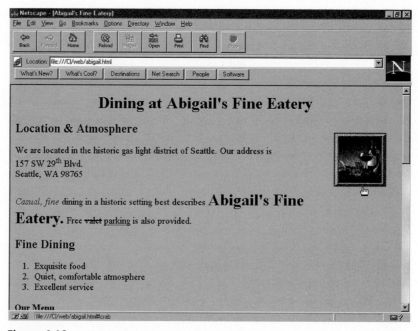

Figure 4.16

THE NEXT STEP

Now that you have had some practice in inserting images into the Web page, try working with other images supplied by your instructor or downloaded from the Web. Use the techniques you learned in this project to reposition the images in different places on the page, adding links to other parts of the page to practice working with the anchor tags. Insert alternative text for each image. Remember to use a new name when you save the practice file so that you can view it with your browser. The *abigail.html* document will be used again in the next project.

This concludes the project. You can either exit your editor and browser or go on to work the Study Questions, Review Exercises, and Assignments.

SUMMARY AND EXERCISES

Summary

- The two most common graphic formats used on the World Wide Web are .GIF and .JPEG.
- To include an image on a Web page, use the <IMG SRC="*image*.gif"> tag, where the name of the graphic image appears in quotation marks.
- To include alternative text, use the ALT attribute and include the text that you want to appear when an image doesn't display, like this: <IMG SRC="*image*.gif" ALT="*text to display*">.
- Images can be included in a line of text by placing the <IMG SRC="*image*.gif"> tag in the exact location where you want the image to appear.
- Images appear aligned with the bottom of a line of text. To change the alignment, use the ALIGN=*value* attribute, like this: <IMG SRC="*image*.gif" ALIGN=TOP>.
- To add more white space to the right and left of the image, use the HSPACE=*value* attribute, where *value* is the number of pixels to add: <IMG SRC="*image*.gif" HSPACE=10>.
- To add more white space to the top and bottom of the image, use the VSPACE=*value* attribute, where *value* is the number of pixels to add: <IMG SRC="*image*.gif" VSPACE=20>.
- To create Web documents with more than one line of text next to an image, use the ALIGN attribute with the value LEFT to place the image at the left and lines of text at the right, or the value RIGHT to place the image at the right and lines of text at the left: <IMG SRC="*image*.gif" ALIGN=RIGHT>
- To make an image into a link, include the <IMG> tag inside the link tag: <A HREF="#*location*"><IMG SRC="*image*.gif"></A>.

Key Terms

alternative text
external image
GIF
indexed color scheme
inline image

JPEG
lossy type compression
LZW compression
pixel

Study Questions

Multiple Choice

1. When you scale down an image, you
   a. reduce the file size.
   b. must also change the VSPACE attribute.
   c. must also change the HSPACE attribute.
   d. make no impact on the file size.
   e. may permanently damage the file.

2. To increase the speed at which an image loads,
   a. specify the exact location of the file.
   b. specify the exact colors in the image.
   c. create an index.
   d. specify the exact size of the file.
   e. specify the exact dimensions of the file.

3. Interlaced .GIF files
   a. are saved one line at a time, starting at the top of the image.
   b. are displayed one line at a time, starting at the top of the image.
   c. are displayed first faintly and then more clearly as they are filled in.
   d. are displayed one line at a time, starting at the bottom of the image.
   e. are displayed left to right.

4. Images can be
   a. internal; that is, located in the same document.
   b. external; that is, located in a different location.
   c. used as links.
   d. drawings or photographs.
   e. all these answers.

5. Alternative text
   a. replaces text that some visitors may consider offensive.
   b. tells the visitor that an image is missing.
   c. gives the visitor the ability to make choices.
   d. lets the visitor determine what color to make the text.
   e. describes an image.

6. The .GIF format
   a. was developed by CompuServe.
   b. explains what appears in the image.
   c. loads images when the page is loaded.
   d. changes the size of the image.
   e. was developed for photographs.

7. The .GIF format
    a. can be compressed and then displayed without any loss in quality.
    b. uses "lossy" compression.
    c. is used for images with subtle tones of color.
    d. is the format developed by a committee.
    e. all of these answers.

8. The .JPEG format
    a is used if the image is small.
    b. is used if the image has blocks of the same color.
    c. is used if the image has many varying colors.
    d. is the format created by CompuServe.
    e. all of these answers.

9. The code <IMG SRC="image.gif" ALIGN=TEXTTOP> aligns the image
    a. at the top of the document.
    b. with the top of the text.
    c. with the top of the largest element on the line.
    d. in the center of the line.
    e. all of these answers.

10. To include more space to the left and right of the image, you use the attribute
    a. CELLPADDING.
    b. HSPACE.
    c. VSPACE.
    d. LEFT.
    e. RIGHT.

Short Answer

Supply the appropriate HTML code to achieve the following instructions.

1. Include an image called `map.gif`.

2. Include the alternative text `map of the world`.

3. Include an image called `icon.gif` at the beginning of the following heading:

    `<H1>Map of the World</H1>`

4. Include an image called `icon.gif` at the end of the following heading:

    `<H1>Map of the World</H1>`

5. Link the image `map.gif` to a location in the same document and name the location `World`.

6. Include the image `map.gif` and align it at the left margin, with text flowing on the right side of the image.

7. Include the image `map.gif` and add 20 pixels of space around the image.

8. Include the image `map.gif` and make it 200 by 200 pixels.

9. Include the image `icon.gif` and align it with the middle of the line of text.

10. Include the image `logo.gif` and the alternative text `Company Logo`.

For Discussion

1. Compare and contrast the .GIF and .JPEG formats.

2. Discuss the ethics involved in copying elements from an existing Web page and using it on your own page without the author's permission.

3. Describe a situation in which you would want to have two graphics with text between them.

4. Describe the process involved in using images as links.

Review Exercises

Adding a Graphic to the Alphabits Bookstore Web Page

Include the image *alpha.gif* on the Web page. Place it at the top left with text flowing to the right. Use any attributes necessary to create a nice design (see Figure 4.17).

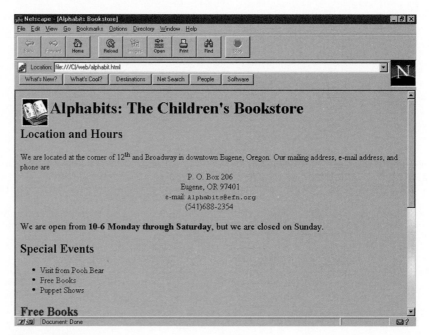

Figure 4.17

Adding an Image to the Animal Web Page

Include an image of one of the animals described in your Web document. Use the image as a link to further information about the animal. Use any attributes necessary to create a nice design.

Assignments

Adding an Icon to Your Personal Web Page

Add a small icon to your page that you can use to create a link to another location. For example, you could include a small mailbox to link to your complete address. Use any attributes necessary to create a nice design.

Adding a Graphic to the Organization or Nonprofit Web Page

Include the logo for the organization. If the logo isn't available in GIF format, you can have it scanned at a copy shop. Use any of the attributes to make the logo fit the overall page design.

What Is VRML? Virtual Reality Modeling Language (VRML) is a programming language used to create virtual reality sites on the Web. Virtual reality sites allow you to navigate through virtual worlds by moving not just up and down or back and forth as you do in two dimensions, but also in and out of three dimensions. This modeling language uses mathematical expressions to describe the virtual worlds.

PROJECT 5: ENHANCING THE HOME PAGE

In this project, you will learn how to change the background and text color, use an image file as a background, create a banner, and include rules in your Web document.

Objectives

After completing this project, you should be able to:

► Use background color

► Change the text color

► Use images as a background

► Create a banner

► Include horizontal rules

CASE STUDY: IMPROVING THE APPEARANCE OF A WEB PAGE

So far, you have placed text and graphics on the Abigail's Fine Eatery home page. In this project, you will change the background by changing the color or using a simple image. You will create a banner that can help unify your home pages, and add rules to the document, which can help divide sections of the document. You will also change text color for emphasis.

Designing the Solution

To give your Web document a unifying element, you can use a color background or use a graphic as a background. Colored text is handy to set off important ideas. Including a banner on each page of the Web document can make your Web pages look more uniform. Finally, rules (lines) are helpful to divide sections of the Web document for clarity. Figure 5.1 shows how these special features give the Abigail's Fine Eatery document a more professional look.

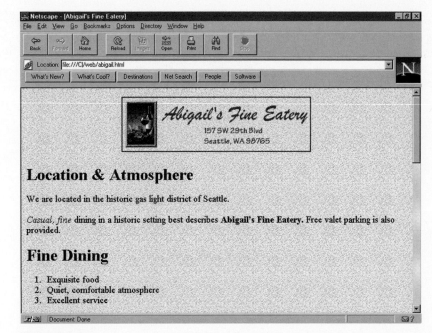

Figure 5.1a

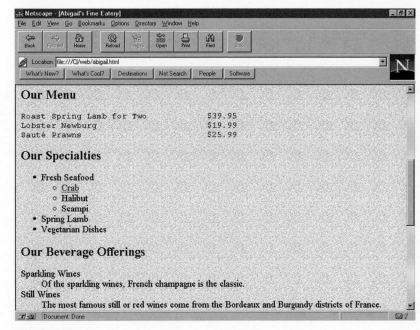

Figure 5.1b

Netscape - [Abigail's Fine Eatery]

File Edit View Go Bookmarks Options Directory Window Help

Back Forward Home Reload Images Open Print Find Stop

Location: file:///C|/web/abigail.html

What's New? What's Cool? Destinations Net Search People Software

Reviews

When it comes to fine dining, I always choose to go to Abigail's Fine Eatery. You simply can't have a better experience at any of the competing establishments in all of Seattle. The service, atmosphere, and most of all the food is wonderful--Commentary from a satisfied customer.

Crab

Our crab is delivered live each day from the Oregon and Washington coast. We allow you to choose the crab you want from the tank, and then we prepare it for you. It is served with herbs and our famous sauce.

Return to Menu

The URL of this page is HTTP://www.restaurant.com/abigail

Page Design by Home Pages Unlimited (HomePage@PLT.org)

Document: Done

Figure 5.1c

USING BACKGROUND COLOR

When you started your Web document, you defined the body of the document with the <BODY> tag and closed it with the </BODY> tag. If you want to change the background color of your Web document from the standard gray, you do so by adding the BGCOLOR attribute to the opening body tag. For example, if you want to have a blue background, here's how you do it:

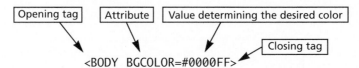

In this example, #0000FF is the RGB (Red, Green, Blue) value of blue; that is, its red, green, and blue values. The first two digits in this number designate the red value; the second two digits, the green value; and the last two digits, the blue value. To specify these RGB values for the color you want, you must know or look up the hexadecimal equivalent that represents the color. (Appendix B contains a list of common colors you might want to use on your Web documents, with their hexadecimal equivalents.)

Hexadecimal (or *hex*) is a numbering system that uses base 16 rather than base 10. The hex system uses the numbers 0–9, along with the letters A–F. This numbering system enables you to represent all numbers up to 256 with only two digits, and has been used extensively with computers for that reason. If you aren't used to working in hex, don't be confused by the mixture of letters and numbers; just remember that letters represent numbers greater than 9, with F being the highest.

The color equivalents range from 00 to 255. (Because you start counting with 0, 255 is the highest number, for a total of 256 numbers.) This range of numbers represents colors on the spectrum from black through white. That is, 000000, the lowest value, represents black, and FFFFFF, the highest value, represents white. Other color numbers fall in the range between these two.

If you would like a dark red, for example, choose a hex value closer to 0 for the red RGB value. #330000 would be a dark red. #FF0000 represents a bright red. You can also combine the color values to create colors of your choice. For instance, to create a dark purple, combine a dark value of red (33) and a slightly lighter value of blue (55) like #330055. Also try varying the different values of red to see the differences (33 versus 3C versus 2A).

Caution Colors will look different on different types of computers.

In the following steps, you will change the background of the Web page for Abigail's Fine Eatery from the standard gray to yellow.

To change the background of a Web page:

1 Open the *abigail.html* Web document.

2 Find the <BODY> tag and add the attribute **BGCOLOR=#FFFF00** to it so it looks like this:

    <BODY BGCOLOR=#FFFF00>

Figure 5.2 shows this change in the HTML source code.

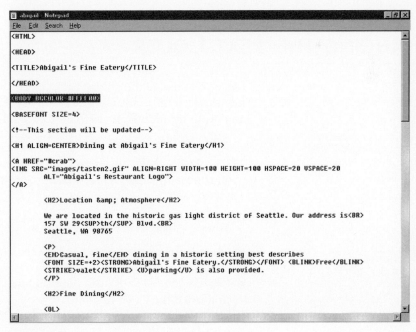

Figure 5.2

3 Save your changes and check out the results in your browser (see Figure 5.3). The Web page appears with the yellow background.

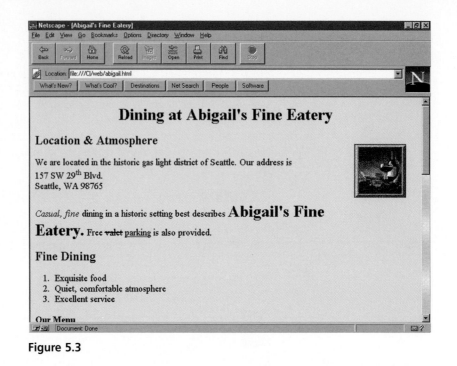

Figure 5.3

 If necessary, you can exit the editor and browser and continue this project later.

CHANGING THE TEXT COLOR

Once you change the color of the background of a Web document, you might also want to change the color of the text that appears on the page. You do so by adding an attribute to the opening <BODY> tag.

> **Tip** Always view your page with a browser to make sure that the color you choose for text will stand out from the colored background and is easy to read.

You can change the color of four different types of text:

- Change the normal text that appears in your document with the TEXT attribute.
- Change the color of links (text the user clicks to jump to another location) with the LINK attribute.
- Change the color of visited links (links that the user has already clicked) with the VLINK attribute.
- Change the color of active links with the ALINK attribute. This attribute designates the color of the link as you click it.

You use the same RGB hexadecimal equivalents described for the background colors to designate the desired colors of text. For normal text in red, for example, this is the command:

```
<BODY TEXT=#FF0000>
```

When you use the TEXT attribute to designate red text with the BGCOLOR attribute of blue, it looks like this:

```
<BODY BGCOLOR=#0000FF TEXT=#FF0000>
```

This command designates the LINK value as pink, VLINK as green, and ALINK as tan:

```
<BODY BGCOLOR=#0000FF TEXT=#FF0000 LINK=#F33E96 VLINK=#00FF7F ALINK=#DEB887>
```

> **Caution** Because many users are accustomed to the default colors for links and visited links, you should avoid changing these settings. Instead, use the default colors for links and change only the color of non-linked text.

In the following steps, you will change the color of the text in the Web document for Abigail's to red from the standard black.

To change the color of the text in a Web document:

1 In the *abigail.html* document, locate the <BODY> tag. Type **TEXT=#550044** immediately after the BGCOLOR attribute, as follows:

```
<BODY BGCOLOR=#FFFF00 TEXT=#550044>
```

Figure 5.4 shows the HTML source code change.

```
abigail - Notepad
File  Edit  Search  Help
<HTML>

<HEAD>

<TITLE>Abigail's Fine Eatery</TITLE>

</HEAD>

<BODY BGCOLOR=#FFFF00 TEXT=#550044>

<BASEFONT SIZE=4>

<!--This section will be updated-->

<H1 ALIGN=CENTER>Dining at Abigail's Fine Eatery</H1>

<A HREF="#crab">
<IMG SRC="images/tasten2.gif" ALIGN=RIGHT WIDTH=100 HEIGHT=100 HSPACE=20 VSPACE=20
        ALT="Abigail's Restaurant Logo">
</A>

        <H2>Location &amp; Atmosphere</H2>

        We are located in the historic gas light district of Seattle. Our address is<BR>
        157 SW 29<SUP>th</SUP> Blvd.<BR>
        Seattle, WA 98765

        <P>
        <EM>Casual, fine</EM> dining in a historic setting best describes
        <FONT SIZE=+2><STRONG>Abigail's Fine Eatery.</STRONG></FONT> <BLINK>Free</BLINK>
        <STRIKE>valet</STRIKE> <U>parking</U> is also provided.
        </P>

        <H2>Fine Dining</H2>

        <OL>
```

Figure 5.4

2 Check out the results in your browser (see Figure 5.5). The text color changes to a dark maroon. (The contrast in color between the black text in Figure 5.3 and the dark maroon text in Figure 5.5 is fairly subtle. You may not be able to distinguish the change without looking closely at the two figures.)

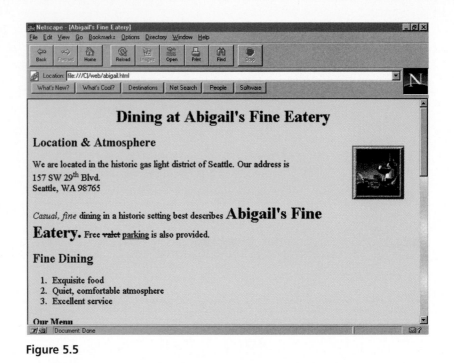

Figure 5.5

 If necessary, you can exit the editor and browser and continue this project later.

USING IMAGES AS A BACKGROUND

In addition to changing the background color, you can use an image as the background, such as the company's or organization's logo.

> **Reminder** Be careful to use an image that doesn't make the page difficult to read, and, as you learned in Project 4, make sure that the image file size isn't so large that it makes the Web document very slow to load.

To add an image to the background of your Web document, you use the BACKGROUND attribute in the opening <BODY> tag. The format of the BACKGROUND attribute is

    <BODY BACKGROUND="image.gif">

or

    <BODY BACKGROUND="logo.gif">

Notice that the name of the graphic image appears in quotation marks.

To add an image to the background of a Web document:

1 In the *abigail.html* document, find the <BODY> tag.

2 After the BGCOLOR and TEXT attributes, type this command:

BACKGROUND="images/oyster.gif"

Here's how the complete <BODY> tag should look at this point:

```
<BODY BGCOLOR=#FFFF00 TEXT=#550044 BACKGROUND="images/oyster.gif">
```

Your HTML source code should look like Figure 5.6.

```
abigail - Notepad                                                    _ 回 X
File  Edit  Search  Help
<HTML>

<HEAD>

<TITLE>Abigail's Fine Eatery</TITLE>

</HEAD>

<BODY BGCOLOR=#FFFF00 TEXT=#550044 BACKGROUND="images/oyster.gif">

<BASEFONT SIZE=4>

<!--This section will be updated-->

<H1 ALIGN=CENTER>Dining at Abigail's Fine Eatery</H1>

<A HREF="#crab">
<IMG SRC="images/tasten2.gif" ALIGN=RIGHT WIDTH=100 HEIGHT=100 HSPACE=20 VSPACE=20
        ALT="Abigail's Restaurant Logo">
</A>

        <H2>Location &amp; Atmosphere</H2>

        We are located in the historic gas light district of Seattle. Our address is<BR>
        157 SW 29<SUP>th</SUP> Blvd.<BR>
        Seattle, WA 98765

        <P>
        <EM>Casual, fine</EM> dining in a historic setting best describes
        <FONT SIZE=+2><STRONG>Abigail's Fine Eatery.</STRONG></FONT> <BLINK>Free</BLINK>
        <STRIKE>valet</STRIKE> <U>parking</U> is also provided.
        </P>

        <H2>Fine Dining</H2>

        <OL>
```

Figure 5.6

Although both the BGCOLOR attribute and the BACKGROUND attribute are present in the <BODY> tag, the BGCOLOR will show only around the edges.

3 Save your work and view it in your browser. (See Figure 5.7.)

Note that if the image you use for the background is small, it will appear ***tiled***; that is, repeated to fill the screen. That's what happened to the little mottled pattern (*oyster.gif*) in this example.

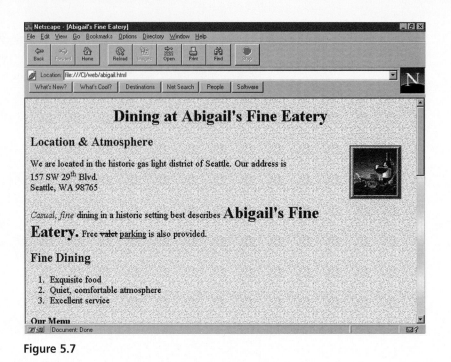

Figure 5.7

 If necessary, you can exit the editor and browser and continue this project later.

CREATING A BANNER

A *banner* is a graphic that extends the width of the screen, much like what you'd see in a newsletter or newspaper. The banner identifies the company or organization and can be used on all the Web pages associated with a company. Each link that the user clicks displays the same banner. Using a banner on every page really doesn't slow down loading the document because each page uses the same image file, which is already in memory. You can use your graphics package to create the banner.

> **Caution** Keep the banner size about 450 pixels wide by 100 pixels high. If you make the banner wider, some browsers may cut off important text.

After creating your banner file, you simply use the <IMG> tag you learned about in Project 4 to include the banner in your Web page. You place the <IMG> tag at the top of the Web document and then copy the tag to all subsequent pages. It's also a good idea to include alternative text for users who can't or don't view images, just as you would for any image.

Because the banner will be introduced on top of the textured background in the *abigail.html* document, integrating it seamlessly with the background may be a problem. However, in addition to its interlacing feature, the .GIF format also includes a feature that can help–the capacity to save certain areas of an image as transparent. In a *transparent image*, you designate certain colors to be transparent, so that you can see through them to the background. For instance, in Figure 5.8, notice the fluorescent green background in the graphic called `banner.gif`. Compare this to the gray background in `bannert.gif` in Figure 5.9. Using an image processing program, the green background was coded to be transparent, and therefore appears gray here. However, as you will see in the following steps, it won't appear either green or gray in the Web page–you can see through it to the background.

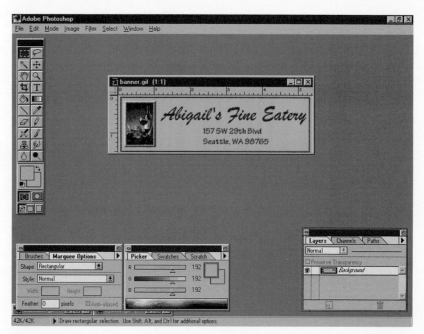

Figure 5.8

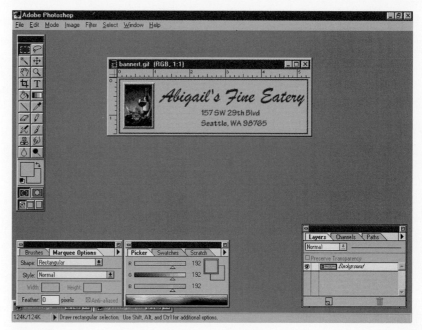

Figure 5.9

In the following steps, you will add a centered banner to the top of the page in the *abigail.html* document.

To include a banner in a Web document:

1 In *abigail.html*, type the following command, placing it after the <BASEFONT> command as shown in Figure 5.10:

<CENTER>

<IMG SRC="images/bannert.gif" ALT="Banner for Abigail's Fine Eatery">

</CENTER>

Notice that alternate text is included for users who don't have graphics capabilities or who have graphics turned off. Also note that the <CENTER> tag may not work with all browsers.

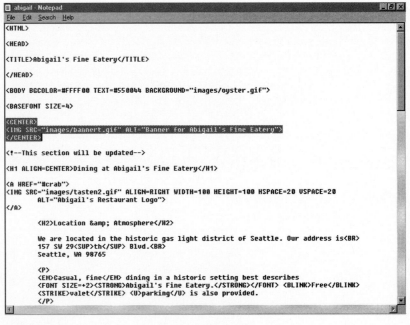

Figure 5.10

2 Save your changes and view them in your browser (see Figure 5.11).

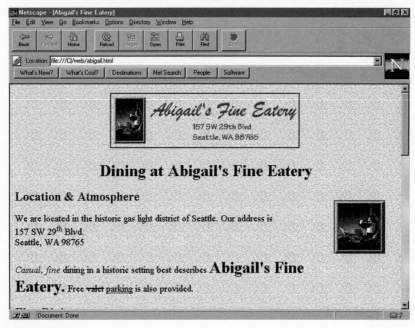

Figure 5.11

 EXIT If necessary, you can exit the editor and browser and continue this project later.

MAKING YOUR WEB PAGE LOOK MORE PROFESSIONAL

As Figure 5.11 shows, some elements are no longer needed in the Abigail's Web page. For instance, because you have inserted the banner, you can delete the first heading and the *tasten2.gif* image—they just repeat what's in the banner. Also, to achieve a more professional and consistent page, you should delete some elements that were included in Projects 1–4 to introduce you to certain HTML tags, and are no longer needed.

 ### To update abigail.html:

1 First remove the heading `Dining at Abigail's Fine Eatery`. In the HTML document, it looks like this:

```
<H1 ALIGN=CENTER>Dining at Abigail's Fine Eatery</H1>
```

2 Logically, the <H2> headings should line up with left margin because they are now the top-level headings, and the <H3> headings should become <H2> headings. Reformat your HTML code by removing the first tab from each line. Although updating heading levels may seem tedious or a waste of time, updating keeps your code cleaner and more accurate.

3 Remove the image `tasten2.gif` and its alternative text. Here's how it looks in the code:

```
<A HREF="#crab">

<IMG SRC="images/tasten2.gif" ALIGN=RIGHT WIDTH=100
HEIGHT=100 HSPACE=20 VSPACE=20 ALT="Abigail's Restaurant
Logo">

</A>
```

4 Remove the following comment:

```
<!-This section will be updated->
```

5 Now remove the reference to the address from the first paragraph following the heading `Location & Atmosphere`:

```
We are located in the historic gas light district of
Seattle. Our address is<BR>

157 SW 29<SUP>th</SUP> Blvd.<BR>

Seattle, WA 98765
```

The sentence now should just read like this:

```
We are located in the historic gas light district of
Seattle.
```

6 Finally, remove some elements in the second paragraph following the heading `Location & Atmosphere` that detract from the aesthetic quality of the page. Currently, the paragraph should look something like this:

```
<EM>Casual, fine</EM> dining in a historic setting best
describes <FONT SIZE=+2><STRONG>Abigail's Fine
Eatery.</STRONG></FONT> <BLINK>Free</BLINK>
<STRIKE>valet</STRIKE> <U>parking</U> is also provided.
```

Remove the `<FONT>` change around the words `Abigail's Fine Eatery`, the `<BLINK>` tag around the word `Free`, the `<STRIKE>` tag around the word `valet`, and the `<U>` tag around the word `parking`. The paragraph should now read this way:

```
<EM>Casual, fine</EM> dining in a historic setting best
describes <STRONG>Abigail's Fine Eatery.</STRONG> Free
valet parking is also provided.
```

7 Remove the extra lines in the preformatted table section of the document. The code currently looks like this:

```
<PRE>

Roast Spring Lamb for Two                    $39.95
Lobster Newburg                              $19.99
Saut&eacute; Prawns                          $25.99

</PRE>
```

Remember that blank lines and extra spaces usually don't affect the output in the Web page, but they *do* have an effect in preformatted text.

Removing the extra lines collapses the code to even the spacing in the Web document:

```
<PRE>

Roast Spring Lamb for Two                   $39.95
Lobster Newburg                             $19.99
Saut&eacute; Prawns                         $25.99

</PRE>
```

Figure 5.12 shows how the HTML source code should look.

```
abigail - Notepad
File  Edit  Search  Help
<HTML>

<HEAD>

<TITLE>Abigail's Fine Eatery</TITLE>

</HEAD>

<BODY BGCOLOR=#FFFF00 TEXT=#550044 BACKGROUND="images/oyster.gif">

<BASEFONT SIZE=4>

<CENTER>
<IMG SRC="images/bannert.gif" ALT="Banner for Abigail's Fine Eatery">
</CENTER>

<H1>Location &amp; Atmosphere</H1>

We are located in the historic gas light district of Seattle.

<P>
<EM>Casual, fine</EM> dining in a historic setting best describes
<STRONG>Abigail's Fine Eatery.</STRONG> Free valet parking is also provided.
</P>

<H1>Fine Dining</H1>

<OL>
<LI>Exquisite food
<LI>Quiet, comfortable atmosphere
<LI>Excellent service
</OL>

        <H2>Our Menu</H2>

<PRE>
```

Figure 5.12a

```
abigail - Notepad
File  Edit  Search  Help
<PRE>
Roast Spring Lamb for Two       $39.95
Lobster Newburg                 $19.99
Saut&eacute; Prawns                      $25.99
</PRE>

        <A NAME="specialties">
        <H2>Our Specialties</H2>
        </A>

        <UL>
        <LI>Fresh Seafood

                <UL>
                <LI><A HREF="#crab">Crab</A>
                <LI>Halibut
                <LI>Scampi
                </UL>

        <LI>Spring Lamb
        <LI>Vegetarian Dishes
        </UL>

        <H2>Our Beverage Offerings</H2>

        <DL>
        <DT>Sparkling Wines
                <DD>Of the sparkling wines, French champagne is the classic.
        <DT>Still Wines
                <DD>The most famous still or red wines come from the Bordeaux and
                Burgundy districts of France.
        <DT>Fortified Wines
                <DD>The principal fortified wines are sherry from Spain, port from
                Portugal, and Madeira from Madeira. They are seldom served with meals.
        </DL>
```

Figure 5.12b

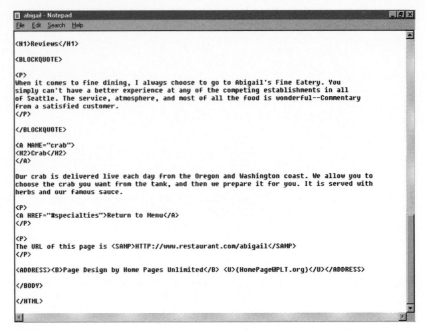

Figure 5.12c

8 Save your work and view the results in your browser (see Figure 5.13).

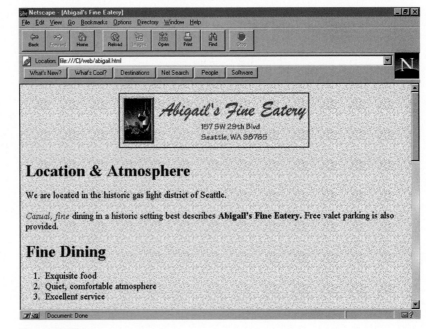

Figure 5.13a

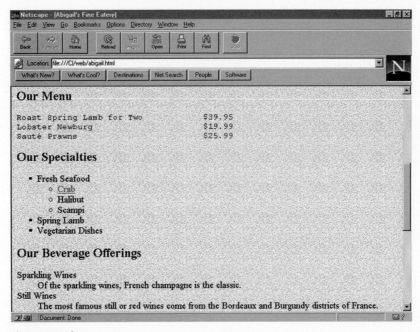

Figure 5.13b

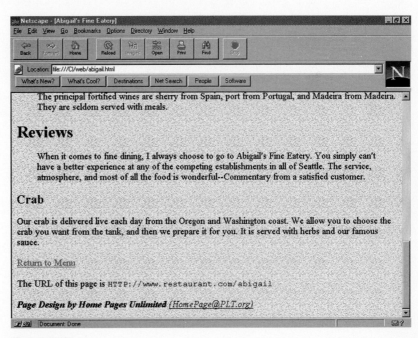

Figure 5.13c

If necessary, you can exit the editor and browser and continue this project later.

Including Horizontal Rules

Horizontal rules are divider lines that you can include in your Web document. The <HR> tag, which is not paired, places a line across the screen. By default, horizontal rules are centered on the page. If you want to control the appearance of the line, you use attributes with the <HR> tag.

To control the thickness of the line, use the SIZE attribute. You designate the size in pixels. To change the thickness of a line from the default 2 pixels to 8 pixels, for example, here's the command:

```
<HR SIZE=8>
```

To control the width of the line, use the WIDTH attribute. You can designate the width of the rule in pixels or by the percentage of the width of the screen:

```
<HR WIDTH=400>
```

or

```
<HR WIDTH=50%>
```

Figure 5.14 shows lines of various thicknesses and widths.

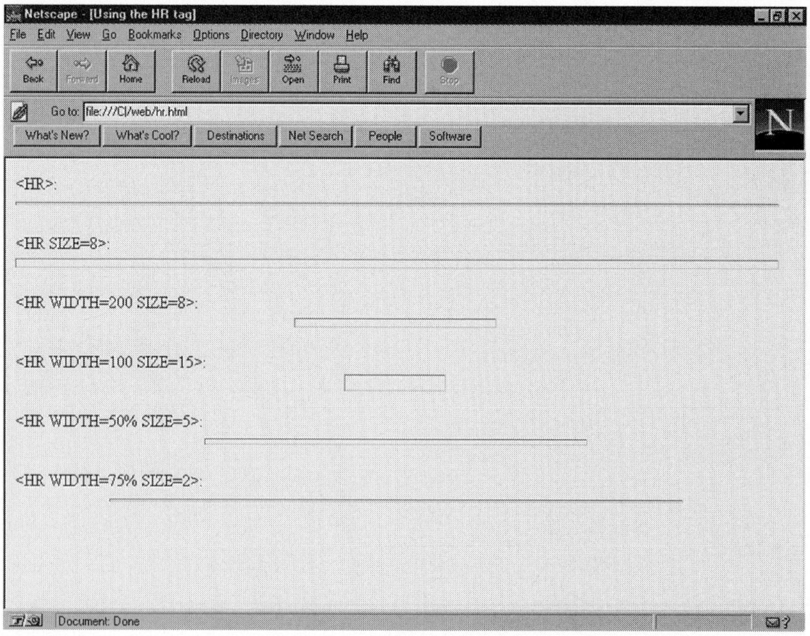

Figure 5.14

If the line is less than 100 percent of the width of the screen, you can specify an alignment for the line. To control the alignment, use the ALIGN attribute with the values LEFT, RIGHT, and CENTER. For example, to center a rule that extends across 50 percent of the screen, you use the following command:

```
<HR WIDTH=50% ALIGN=CENTER>
```

You can use the WIDTH and ALIGN attributes together to create patterns of various length lines, as shown in Figure 5.15.

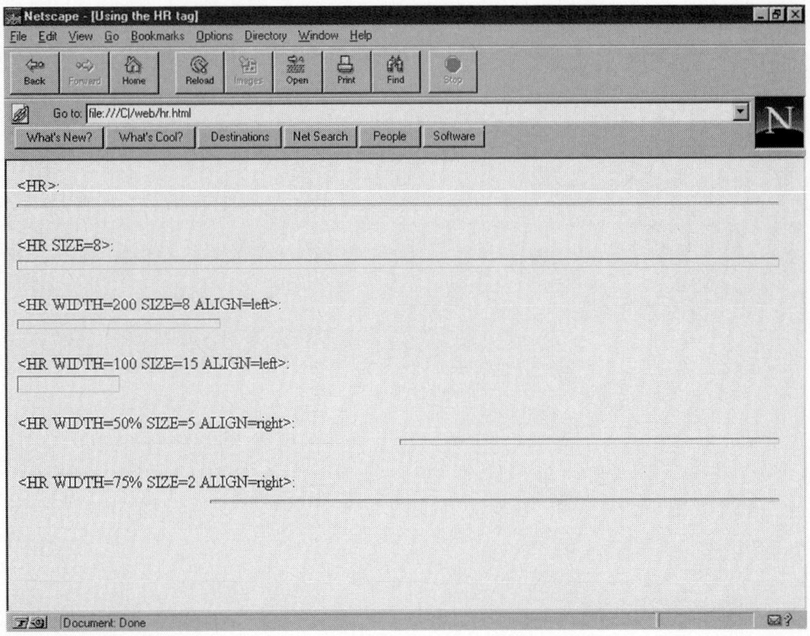

Figure 5.15

By default, the rules appear with three-dimensional shading. If you want to change the line to a solid bar, use the NOSHADE attribute. The syntax is as follows:

```
<HR  NOSHADE>
```

Figure 5.16 shows the result of the NOSHADE attribute.

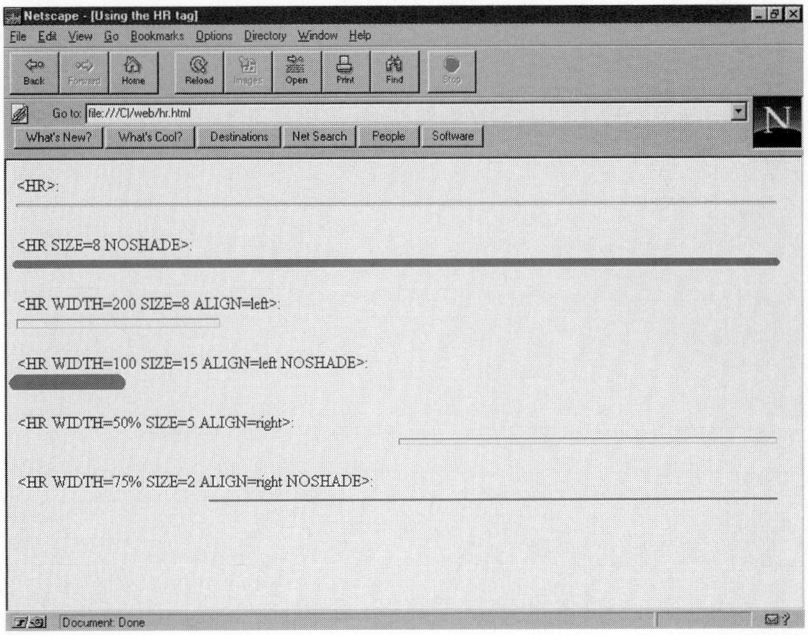

Figure 5.16

To add a rule to the Web document:

1 In the *abigail.html* document, find the URL listing at the end of the
code. Above it, type this line:

```
<HR SIZE=6 WIDTH=85% ALIGN=CENTER>
```

You can view the code change in Figure 5.17.

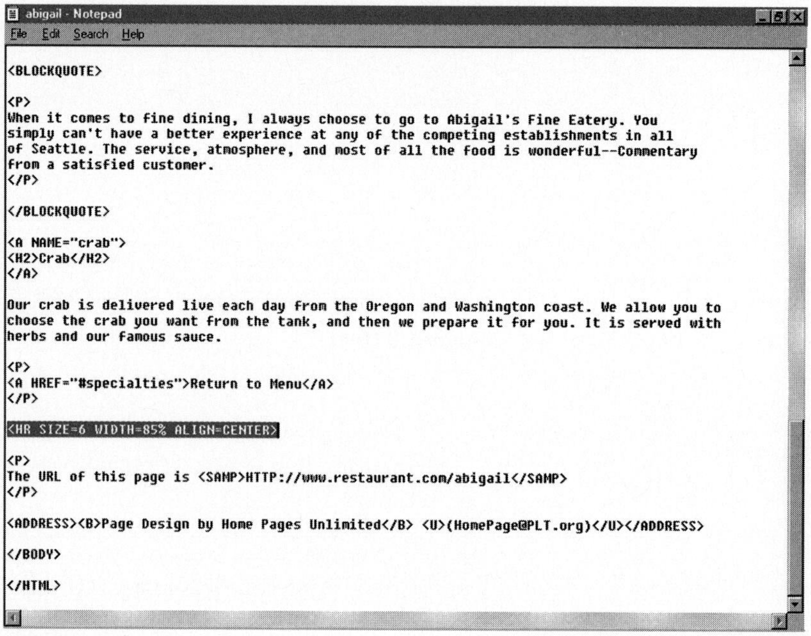

```
abigail - Notepad
File  Edit  Search  Help

<BLOCKQUOTE>

<P>
When it comes to fine dining, I always choose to go to Abigail's Fine Eatery. You
simply can't have a better experience at any of the competing establishments in all
of Seattle. The service, atmosphere, and most of all the food is wonderful--Commentary
from a satisfied customer.
</P>

</BLOCKQUOTE>

<A NAME="crab">
<H2>Crab</H2>
</A>

Our crab is delivered live each day from the Oregon and Washington coast. We allow you to
choose the crab you want from the tank, and then we prepare it for you. It is served with
herbs and our famous sauce.

<P>
<A HREF="#specialties">Return to Menu</A>
</P>

<HR SIZE=6 WIDTH=85% ALIGN=CENTER>

<P>
The URL of this page is <SAMP>HTTP://www.restaurant.com/abigail</SAMP>
</P>

<ADDRESS><B>Page Design by Home Pages Unlimited</B> <U>(HomePage@PLT.org)</U></ADDRESS>

</BODY>

</HTML>
```

Figure 5.17

2 Save your work and check out the results in your browser (see Figure
5.18).

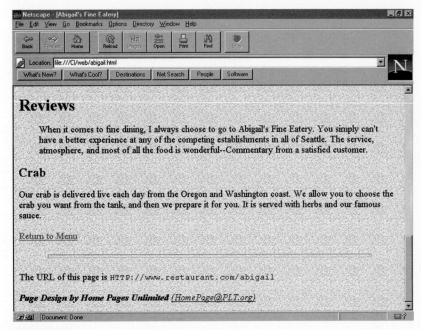

Figure 5.18

THE NEXT STEP

Spend some time searching for libraries of backgrounds. Many .GIF backgrounds are available in all sorts of patterns. When you find some you like, try them out on the pages you're creating.

This concludes the project. You can either exit your editor and browser or go on to work the Study Questions, Review Exercises, and Assignments.

SUMMARY AND EXERCISES

Summary

- To change the background color of your Web document, add the BGCOLOR attribute and the hexadecimal color number to the opening <BODY> tag.
- To change the color of the normal text that appears in a document, add the TEXT attribute and the hexadecimal color number to the opening <BODY> tag.
- HTML provides attributes for changing the colors of links and visited links, but it isn't standard practice to change these colors.
- To add an image to the background of your Web document, add the BACKGROUND attribute and the name of the image file to the opening <BODY> tag.
- A *banner* is a graphic image that you include at the top of every page in a Web document.
- Use the <HR> tag to include a horizontal line in a document.
- Use the SIZE, WIDTH, and ALIGN attributes with the <HR> tag to control the thickness, width, and alignment of a line.

Key Terms

banner
hexadecimal (or hex)
horizontal rule

tiled image
transparent image

Study Questions

Multiple Choice

1. RGB color values
   a. designate two numbers for red.
   b. designate two numbers for green.
   c. designate two numbers for blue.
   d. use hexadecimal number values.
   e. all these answers.

2. To unify a Web document, you could
   a. include a banner on every page.
   b. use the same background image on all pages.
   c. use the same background color on all pages.
   d. use the same text color on all pages.
   e. all these answers.

3. To change the thickness of a rule, you use
   a. the THICKNESS attribute.
   b. the SIZE attribute.
   c. the WIDTH attribute.
   d. the ALIGN attribute.
   e. all these answers.

4. A banner
   a. is a graphic that extends the width of the screen.
   b. identifies the company or organization.
   c. can be repeated on all pages associated with a company.
   d. unifies a Web document.
   e. all these answers.

5. Hexadecimal
   a. is used to designate text size.
   b. is used to designate colors.
   c. is base 8.
   d. is base 10.
   e. all these answers.

6. You can change the color of
   a. the normal text that appears in your document.
   b. links.
   c. visited links.
   d. active links.
   e. all these answers.

7. BACKGROUND
   a. is an attribute of the <BODY> tag.
   b. allows you to add an image to the background of the Web page.
   c. can be tiled if it's small.
   d. is handy for company logos.
   e. all these answers.

8. BGCOLOR
   a. is a tag.
   b. is an attribute of the <BODY> tag.
   c. changes the text color of visited links.
   d. changes the background color.
   e. both b and d.

9. A horizontal rule
   a. is defined with the <BR> tag.
   b. is an attribute of the <BODY> tag.
   c. is a line.
   d. changes the background color.
   e. all these answers.

10. The width of a rule
    a. can be defined as a percentage of the screen.
    b. can be defined in pixels.
    c. is an attribute of the <HR> tag.
    d. can be only one size.
    e. all these answers.

Short Answer

Supply the correct HTML coding for each of the following conditions.

1. Change the background color to red:

   ```
   <BODY
   ```

2. Change the text color for the entire document to green:

   ```
   <BODY
   ```

3. Change the color of links to purple and visited links to orange:

   ```
   <BODY
   ```

4. Change the color of the background to light blue and the text to red:

   ```
   <BODY
   ```

5. Add the image *design.gif* to the background:

   ```
   <BODY
   ```

6. Include a horizontal line in the document:

   ```
   <BODY>
   </BODY>
   ```

7. Include a horizontal line that only extends across one third of the screen:

   ```
   <BODY>
   </BODY>
   ```

8. Center the horizontal line that extends across one third of the screen:

   ```
   <BODY>
   </BODY>
   ```

9. Include a horizontal line that's a solid bar:

   ```
   <BODY>
   </BODY>
   ```

10. Include a horizontal line that's 16 pixels in thickness:

```
<BODY>
</BODY>
```

For Discussion

1. When might a company want to use a banner?

2. Explain how you could unify a Web document.

3. Why might you not want to change the color of links?

4. Explain the hexadecimal numbering system.

5. What are rules and how can they be used?

Review Exercises

Changing the Format of the Alphabits Bookstore Web Page

Include the following on the Web page for Alphabits Bookstore (*alphabit.html*):

- A light yellow background
- Dark blue text
- Red text for links
- Green text for visited links
- A horizontal rule under the first heading that is 75 percent of the width of the page and is centered
  Save the file and view it in your browser (see Figure 5.19).

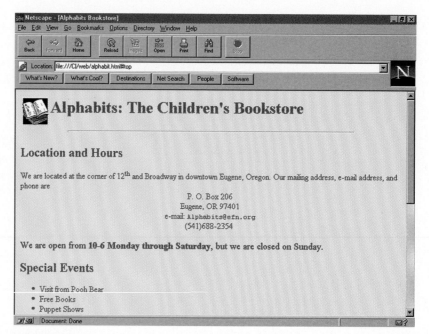

Figure 5.19a

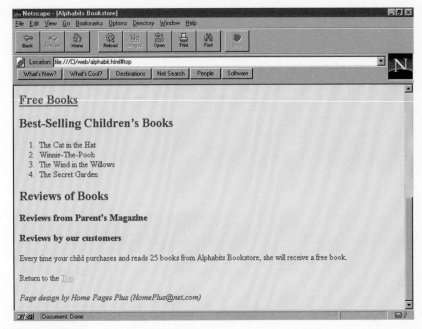

Figure 5.19b

Adding a Banner to the Animal Web Page

Create a banner for the Animal Web document and repeat it on all subsequent pages. Delete any images that need to be deleted.

Assignments

Modifying Your Personal Web Page

Change the color of the background for your personal Web page and then change the color of the text. Make sure that the document can still be read easily. Include at least one horizontal rule to separate sections of your document.

Adding a Background Image to the Organization or Nonprofit Web Page

Include the logo of the organization as a background image. Make sure that the document can still be read easily. If a logo was already included on the Web page, delete the image.

What Is FTP? **FTP** stands for **File Transfer Protocol**. This is the oldest protocol for transferring files from one computer to another. If you don't have a password to a particular system but are allowed to log on anyway with limited access to files, this is known as Anonymous FTP.

You can use FTP to download software as well as text files. Many software developers are placing their products or add-ins to their products on the Internet, so that they can be downloaded and tested. The idea is to entice you to buy the full package after trying a part of the software.

PROJECT 6: INCLUDING TABLES IN A HOME PAGE

In this project, you will learn how to include tables in a home page to help organize data. You will also learn how to enhance your tables.

Objectives

After completing this project, you should be able to:

► Create a table

► Add a caption to a table

► Control line breaks in cells and include empty cells in tables

► Span headings across columns and rows

► Add a table border and include spacing and padding in cells

► Align cell contents

► Modify the width and height of the table and individual cells

CASE STUDY: ORGANIZING DATA INTO TABLE FORMAT

So far you have placed text and graphics on your Web page. Sometimes the text you want to present to the user needs to be organized into columns and rows to make it understandable. One of the most common techniques for organizing data is to place it in a table. HTML provides codes that allow you to create and enhance tables.

In this project, you will use the HTML table tags to place menu items in a table for the Abigail's Fine Eatery home page (see Figure 6.1).

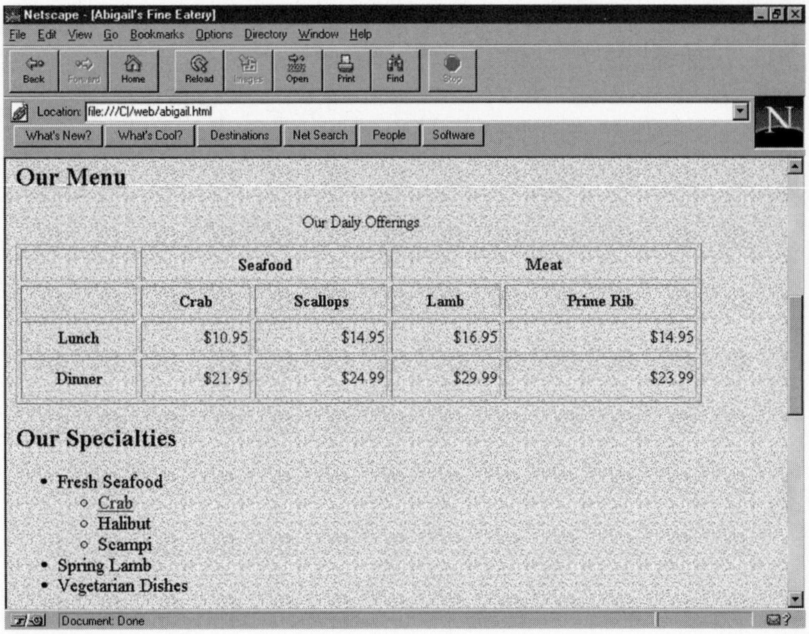

Figure 6.1

If you have ever used a spreadsheet program or the table feature in a word processing program, you're familiar with tables. Tables are useful for organizing large bodies of information so that the reader can quickly see the overall picture. Because of the power of tables, they are a widely used feature in Web pages today.

Tables are made up of data arranged in *columns* (vertically) and *rows* (horizontally). The intersection of a column and row is known as a *cell*; data is placed in cells. The top row of the table and often the first column usually contain headings (also called *labels*) that explain the data contained in the cells. A *title* is helpful for the reader to know what information the table contains.

> **Tip** Older browsers don't support the HTML table tags. In the near future, most browsers probably will support the table features. To avoid any problems users have in displaying tables in older browsers, you can use the preformatted text feature of HTML, which you learned about in Project 2.

You can even include links in tables so that the user can click a cell to jump to another location to see more information about that item. (You learn more about this process in Project 7.) You can also include graphics in tables, allowing you to *show* what you're describing, such as products you're selling.

Designing the Solution

If you want to include a table on a Web document, you should carefully plan how the table will look before you begin creating it because the table-creation process can be tedious. You should create the table on paper or in the table feature of a word processing or spreadsheet program, and then work from your model as you do the HTML coding.

CREATING A TABLE

To create a table in a Web page, you use the opening and closing <TABLE> tags. The syntax is

```
<TABLE>
        entire table
</TABLE>
```

After placing the table tags, you define the table row by row; that is, you define the contents of the first row and then the contents of each subsequent row. You start each row with the <TR> tag, which stands for table row, and end it with </TR>. Everything between those two tags will appear in one row of the table. The syntax is

```
<TABLE>
<TR>
        text of first row
</TR>
<TR>
        text of second row
</TR>
<TR>
        text of third row
</TR>
</TABLE>
```

You then define the contents of each cell in each row:

- If a cell contains a heading, you use the table heading tag <TH>, type the heading, and close the heading cell with </TH>. Table headings appear in bold in most browsers.
- If a cell contains data, you use the table data tag <TD>, type the data, and close the data cell with </TD>. Data cells appear in the normal text format in most browsers.

For example, if the first row of a three-column, three-row table contains headings and the rest of the table is all data, this is how the coding looks (see Figure 6.2):

```
<TABLE>

<TR>
        <TH>heading one</TH>
        <TH>heading two</TH>
        <TH>heading three</TH>
</TR>

<TR>
        <TD>data</TD>
        <TD>data</TD>
        <TD>data</TD>
</TR>
```

```
<TR>
      <TD>data</TD>
      <TD>data</TD>
      <TD>data</TD>
</TR>

</TABLE>
```

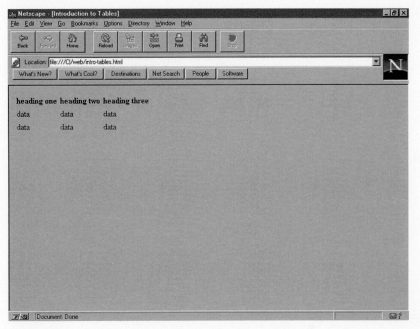

Figure 6.2

If the same table also contains headings in the far left column, the syntax is as follows (see Figure 6.3):

```
<TABLE>
<TR>
      <TH>heading one</TH>
      <TH>heading two</TH>
      <TH>heading three</TH>
</TR>

<TR>
      <TH>heading</TH>
      <TD>data</TD>
      <TD>data</TD>
</TR>

<TR>
      <TH>heading</TH>
      <TD>data</TD>
      <TD>data</TD>
</TR>
</TABLE>
```

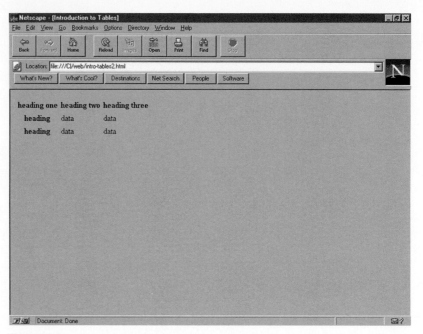

Figure 6.3

Tip Notice that tabs and extra lines in the code help you see more easily what will appear on each line. This strategy becomes even more helpful as your tables become more complex.

To start creating a simple table for use in a Web document:

1 Open the *abigail.html* Web document.

2 Find the **<PRE>** section under the heading **Our Menu** and delete the entire section. You will replace this preformatted text, using the table tags.

3 Type the following code lines:

```
<TABLE>

<TR>
        <TH>empty</TH>
        <TH>Crab</TH>
        <TH>Scallops</TH>
        <TH>Lamb</TH>
        <TH>Prime Rib</TH>
</TR>

<TR>
        <TH>Lunch</TH>
        <TD>$10.95</TD>
        <TD>$14.95</TD>
        <TD>$16.95</TD>
        <TD>$14.95</TD>
</TR>
```

```
<TR>
        <TH>Dinner</TH>
        <TD>$21.95</TD>
        <TD>$24.99</TD>
        <TD>$29.99</TD>
        <TD>$23.99</TD>
</TR>

</TABLE>
```

Figure 6.4 shows how the code should look. We'll come back to the cell that includes the word **empty** in a later task.

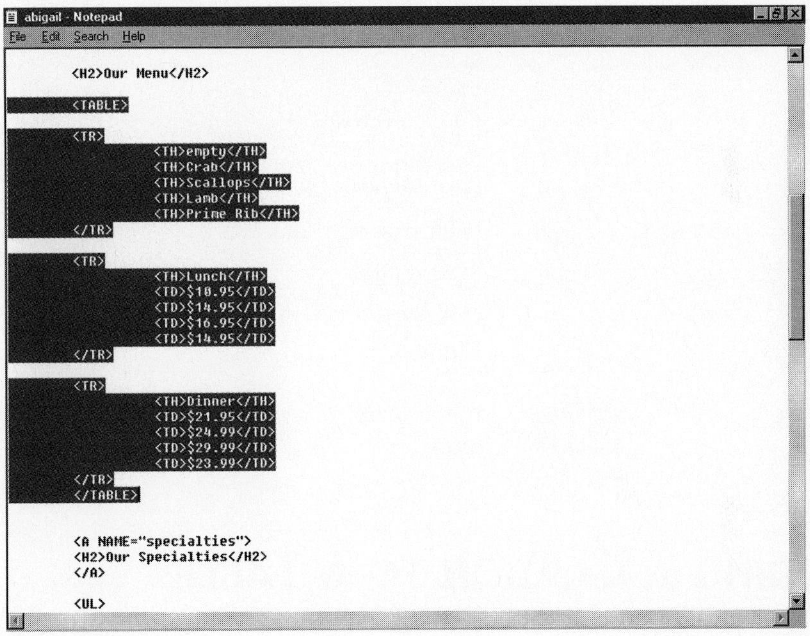

Figure 6.4

4 Save your work and check out the results in your browser (see Figure 6.5).

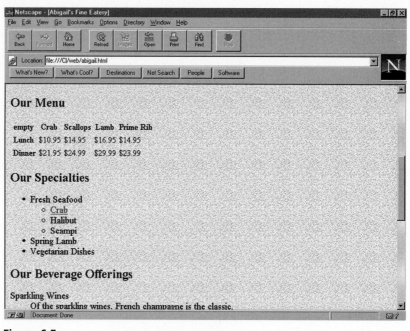

Figure 6.5

 If necessary, you can exit the editor and browser and continue this project later.

ADDING A CAPTION TO A TABLE

So that the user will know what the table contains, you should always include a title for a table. HTML calls a title on a table a *caption* and uses the <CAPTION> tag. By default, the caption appears centered above the table; however, the caption tag must appear between the opening and closing <TABLE> tags. If you want the caption to appear below the table, include the attribute ALIGN=BOTTOM. Here's an example of a caption tag:

```
<TABLE>
        <CAPTION>Killer Whale Sightings</CAPTION>
</TABLE>
```

 To add a caption to the table:

1 In the *abigail.html* document, find the opening **<TABLE>** tag and type the following caption below it:

<CAPTION>Our Daily Offerings</CAPTION>

See Figure 6.6 for the HTML source code.

```
abigail - Notepad
File  Edit  Search  Help
</P>

<H1>Fine Dining</H1>

<OL>
<LI>Exquisite food
<LI>Quiet, comfortable atmosphere
<LI>Excellent service
</OL>

        <H2>Our Menu</H2>

        <TABLE>

        <CAPTION>Our Daily Offerings</CAPTION>

        <TR>
                <TH>empty</TH>
                <TH>Crab</TH>
                <TH>Scallops</TH>
                <TH>Lamb</TH>
                <TH>Prime Rib</TH>
        </TR>

        <TR>
                <TH>Lunch</TH>
                <TD>$10.95</TD>
                <TD>$14.95</TD>
                <TD>$16.95</TD>
                <TD>$14.95</TD>
        </TR>

        <TR>
                <TH>Dinner</TH>
                <TD>$21.95</TD>
                <TD>$24.99</TD>
```

Figure 6.6

2 Save your work and check out the results in your browser (see Figure 6.7). The caption is added to the table.

```
Netscape - [Abigail's Fine Eatery]
File  Edit  View  Go  Bookmarks  Options  Directory  Window  Help
 Back  Forward  Home   Reload  Images  Open  Print  Find   Stop
Location: file:///C|/web/abigail.html
What's New?  What's Cool?  Destinations  Net Search  People  Software
```

> 2. Quiet, comfortable atmosphere
> 3. Excellent service
>
> ## Our Menu
>
>   Our Daily Offerings
>
> | empty | Crab | Scallops | Lamb | Prime Rib |
> |-------|------|----------|------|-----------|
> | Lunch | $10.95 | $14.95 | $16.95 | $14.95 |
> | Dinner | $21.95 | $24.99 | $29.99 | $23.99 |
>
> ## Our Specialties
>
> - Fresh Seafood
>   - Crab
>   - Halibut
>   - Scampi
> - Spring Lamb
> - Vegetarian Dishes
>
> ## Our Beverage Offerings

```
Document: Done
```

Figure 6.7

EXIT If necessary, you can exit the editor and browser and continue this project later.

CONTROLLING LINE BREAKS IN CELLS AND INCLUDING EMPTY CELLS IN TABLES

Various browsers may display tables differently, wrapping data in cells or extending cells beyond what looks acceptable for a table. When you create a table, you can include HTML codes that control the way the data is displayed in the viewer's browser.

Sometimes you might have a table that includes varying amounts of data in the cells, and you might want to control how the lines break–or even keep them from breaking. HTML includes codes you can use to control both of these situations.

If you want to have a cell that has more than one line of text or data, you can't use the Enter key to break the lines because browsers ignore it. (Remember, this is why adding extra carriage returns and tabs in your HTML source code doesn't affect your Web page.) You can break a line by inserting the <BR> code in the data. For example, if you have a long line of text, simply decide where you want the line to break and insert the code. This is how you do it:

```
<TD>This line of text<BR> is too long for one cell</TD>
```

With this strategy, the text would appear on two lines in the same cell. If you want even more lines to appear in the cell, insert <BR> at every place where you want the line to break.

If you have text in a cell that shouldn't be broken into more than one line, you want the opposite effect–that is, for the line not to *wrap* to the next line. You use the NOWRAP attribute with the opening table heading or table data tag. Insert the attribute immediately after either the opening <TH> or <TD> tag. The syntax is

```
<TH NOWRAP>text</TH>
```

or

```
<TD NOWRAP>text</TD>
```

The text then appears on one line, regardless of the way the table is displayed in the browser.

If you want a cell to appear as empty, you can't simply place a space between the table heading or table data tags because browsers ignore spaces. The easiest method to use to create a blank cell is to use the <BR> tag between the opening and closing tags. The syntax for a blank cell in a header is

```
<TH><BR></TH>
```

or

```
<TD><BR></TD>
```

The result in the browser will be an empty cell.

 To control word wrap in a cell and to create an empty cell:

1 In the *abigail.html* document, find the cell containing the text Prime Rib and add the **NOWRAP** command so the tag looks like this:

```
<TH NOWRAP>
```

2 Find the cell containing the word empty and delete that text. Replace it with the **
** tag so it now reads like this:

<TH>
</TH>

Figure 6.8 shows the changes in the HTML source code.

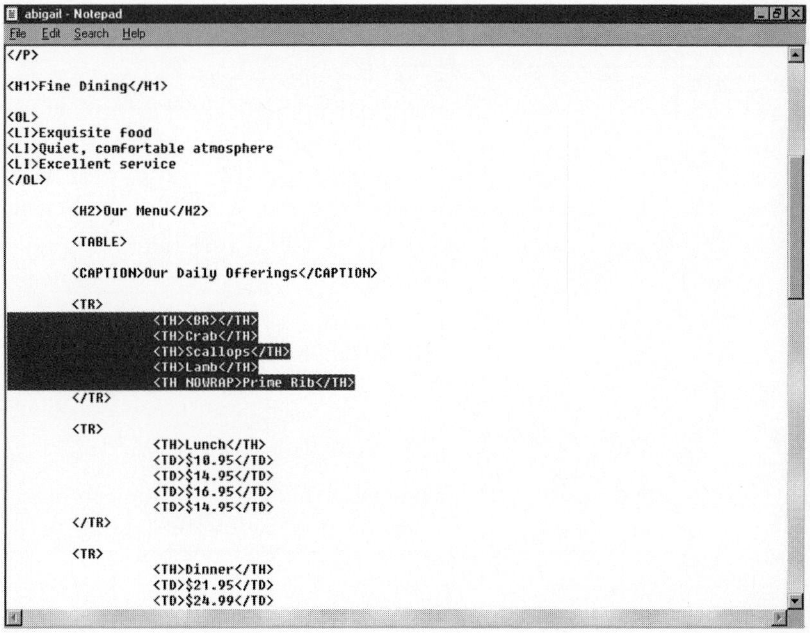

Figure 6.8

3 Save your work and view the results in your browser (see Figure 6.9). The cell that originally said empty now actually is empty; the words Prime Rib will appear on one line in their cell regardless of how the browser displays table cells.

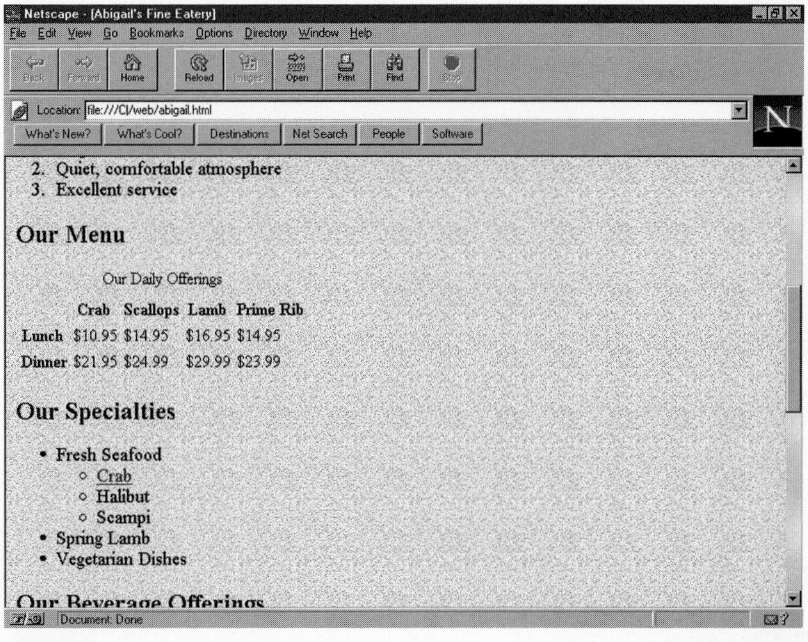

Figure 6.9

If necessary, you can exit the editor and browser and continue this project later.

SPANNING HEADINGS OR DATA ACROSS COLUMNS AND ROWS

Sometimes you might want to display data so that it extends over more than one column or more than one row. This is called *spanning* more than one column or row. You can include the attribute COLSPAN or ROWSPAN with either the <TH> or <TD> tags. You simply type the attribute name, an equal sign (=), and the number of columns or rows that you want to span. For example, if you want a heading or data to span four columns, do it like this:

<TH COLSPAN=4>*heading*</TH>

or

<TD COLSPAN=4>*data*</TD>

The cell extends across four columns.

If you want a heading or data to span down three rows, this is the command:

<TH ROWSPAN=3>*heading*</TH>

or

<TD ROWSPAN=3>*data*</TD>

The cell extends down three rows.

 ### To insert a new row and span a heading across two columns:

1 To add a new row at the top of the table in the Abigail's Web page, including two columns that span two columns each, type the following code after the line containing the caption:

```
<TR>
        <TH><BR></TH>
        <TH COLSPAN=2>Seafood</TH>
        <TH COLSPAN=2>Meat</TH>
</TR>
```

Your HTML code should look like that in Figure 6.10. Notice that we've taken into account the column that includes the empty cell.

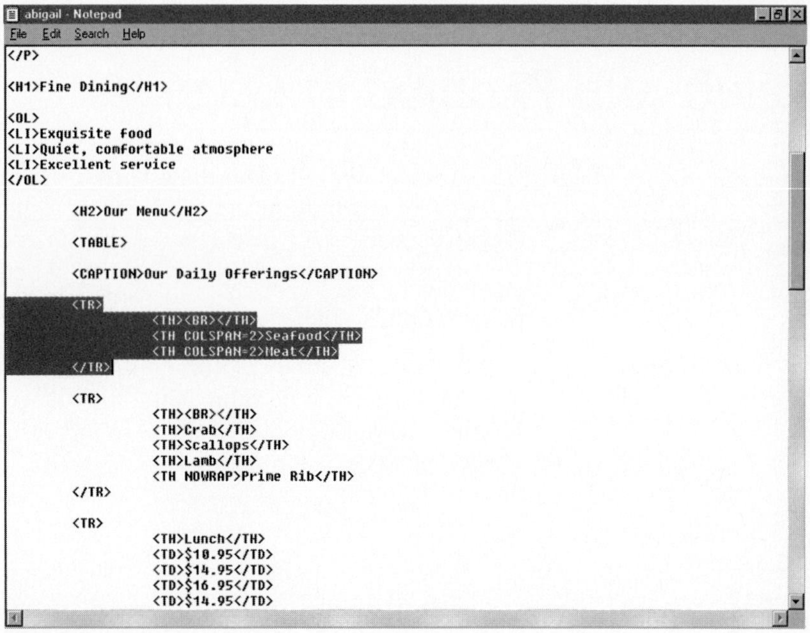

Figure 6.10

2 Save your work and check out the results in your browser (see Figure 6.11). The headings span two columns.

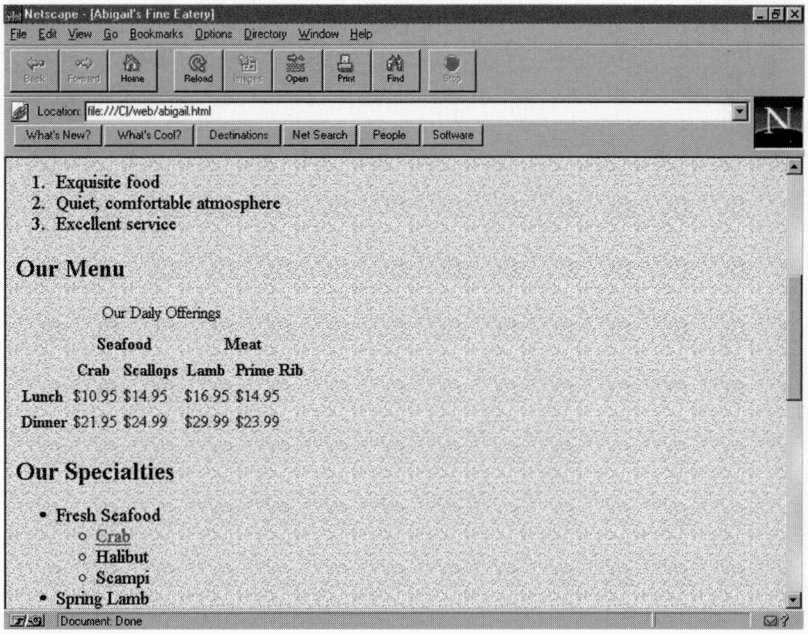

Figure 6.11

EXIT If necessary, you can exit the editor and browser and continue this project later.

ADDING A TABLE BORDER AND INCLUDING SPACING AND PADDING IN CELLS

To set a table off from the rest of the Web document, you can add the BORDER attribute to the <TABLE> tag. The BORDER attribute places a border with a width of 1 pixel around the outside edge of the table and also places borders around each individual cell. The syntax for the BORDER attribute is

```
<TABLE BORDER>
```

To change the width of the outside border, you can add a value to the BORDER attribute. The value is the number of pixels that will appear around the outside edge of the table. To increase the border to a width of 4 pixels, for example, use this format:

```
<TABLE BORDER=4>
```

Tip The value change has no effect on the borders around the individual cells.

To change the spacing between cells so that the data is easier to read, you can add the CELLSPACING attribute to the <TABLE> tag, along with a value in pixels. The default cell spacing is 2 pixels. The following command assigns a value of 4 pixels:

```
<TABLE CELLSPACING=4>
```

To add space around the cell contents, you can use the CELLPADDING attribute along with a value in pixels. The default cell padding is 1 pixel. This command sets the cell padding at 2 pixels:

```
<TABLE CELLPADDING=2>
```

You can add a border, cell spacing, and cell padding to a table simultaneously. The following command sets cell spacing at 4 pixels and cell padding at 2 pixels:

```
<TABLE BORDER CELLSPACING=4 CELLPADDING=2>
```

 To enhance a table with a border, cell spacing, and cell padding:

1 In the *abigail.html* document, replace the <TABLE> tag with the following command:

```
<TABLE BORDER CELLSPACING=4 CELLPADDING=2>
```

Your HTML code should look like that in Figure 6.12.

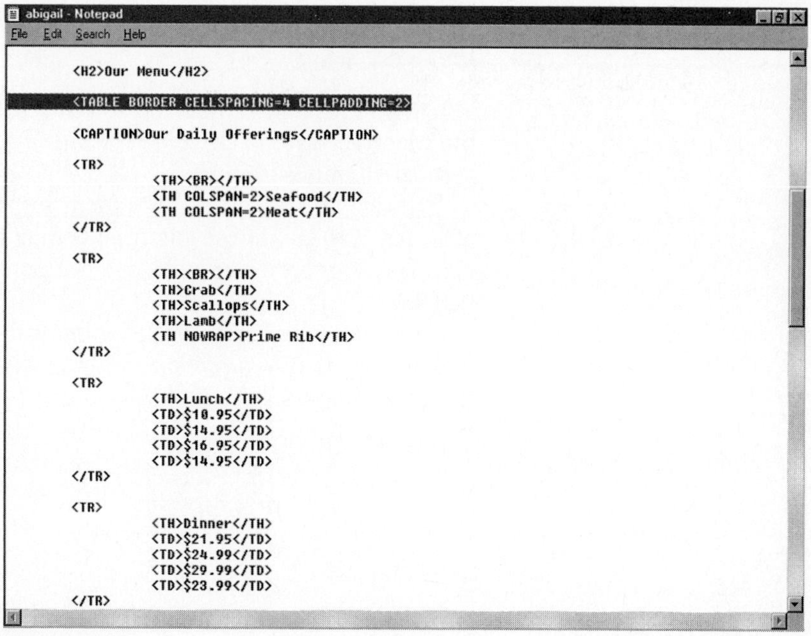


```
<H2>Our Menu</H2>

<TABLE BORDER CELLSPACING=4 CELLPADDING=2>

<CAPTION>Our Daily Offerings</CAPTION>

<TR>
        <TH><BR></TH>
        <TH COLSPAN=2>Seafood</TH>
        <TH COLSPAN=2>Meat</TH>
</TR>

<TR>
        <TH><BR></TH>
        <TH>Crab</TH>
        <TH>Scallops</TH>
        <TH>Lamb</TH>
        <TH NOWRAP>Prime Rib</TH>
</TR>

<TR>
        <TH>Lunch</TH>
        <TD>$10.95</TD>
        <TD>$14.95</TD>
        <TD>$16.95</TD>
        <TD>$14.95</TD>
</TR>

<TR>
        <TH>Dinner</TH>
        <TD>$21.95</TD>
        <TD>$24.99</TD>
        <TD>$29.99</TD>
        <TD>$23.99</TD>
</TR>
```

Figure 6.12

2 Save your work and check out the results in your browser (see Figure 6.13). The border, cell spacing, and cell padding are added to the table. Try using different values for the attributes to see what results you get.

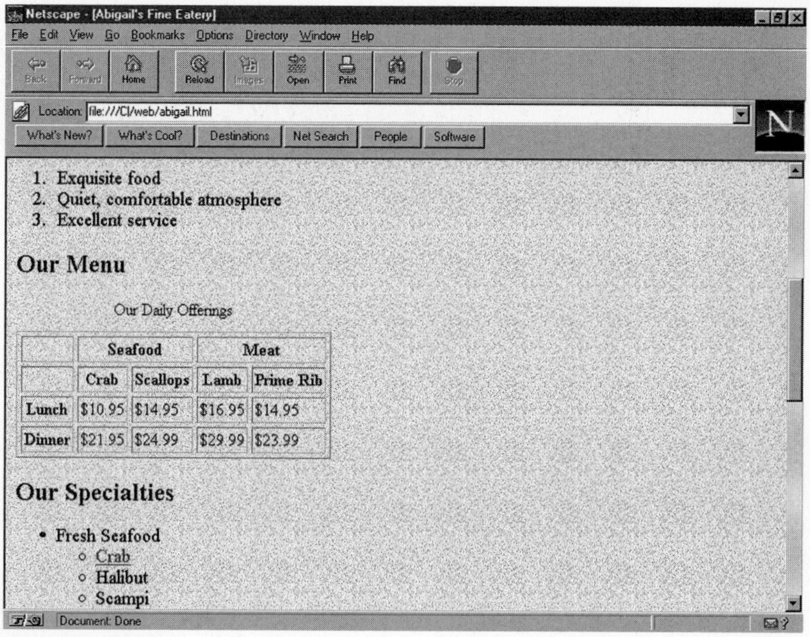

Figure 6.13

EXIT If necessary, you can exit the editor and browser and continue this project later.

ALIGNING CELL CONTENTS

When you place data in cells, you might want to have some control over the way the contents are viewed. In HTML, you can set the horizontal and vertical alignment of cells.

The default horizontal alignment for data cells is LEFT; for heading cells, it's CENTER. These alignments may meet your needs for much of your data; however, you can make the horizontal alignment LEFT, RIGHT, or CENTER.

To change the horizontal alignment for all the cells in an entire row, you use the ALIGN=*direction* attribute with the row tag (<TR>). The following example uses a centered alignment for the data in each cell in the row:

```
<TR ALIGN=CENTER>
        <TD>data</TD>
        <TD>data</TD>
        <TD>data</TD>
</TR>
```

To set the alignment for individual cells, use the ALIGN attribute with the <TH> or <TD> tag. In the following example, the first cell will be aligned at the right; the second cell will be centered, and the third cell will be aligned at the left:

```
<TR>
      <TD ALIGN=RIGHT>data</TD>
      <TD ALIGN=CENTER>data</TD>
      <TD>data</TD>
</TR>
```

To set the alignment for an entire row and then change it for individual cells, you specify the alignment for the entire row and then change it within the individual cells. In the following table, all the data in the row will be aligned at the right except for the first cell, which will be aligned at the left:

```
<TR ALIGN=RIGHT>
      <TD ALIGN=LEFT>data
      <TD>data
      <TD>data
</TR>
```

Caution If you have added cell padding to the table, the ALIGN attribute considers the inner edge of the padding as the edge of the cell, so the alignment is actually based from the inside of the cell padding.

By default, both data and heading cells are centered vertically–from the top to the bottom of the cell. If you want to change the vertical alignment for a cell, you use the VALIGN=direction attribute. The direction can be TOP, BOTTOM, or MIDDLE.

Caution Many older browsers don't recognize the VALIGN attribute.

The format for VALIGN is

`<TR VALIGN=BOTTOM>`

or

`<TD VALIGN=TOP>`

To use both the ALIGN and VALIGN attributes, this is the structure:

`<TR ALIGN=CENTER VALIGN=BOTTOM>`

or

`<TD ALIGN=CENTER VALIGN=BOTTOM>`

In the following steps, you will change the alignment for all the currency values in the table in the Web page for Abigail's Fine Eatery.

To change the horizontal alignment of cells:

1 In the table in *abigail.html*, add the attribute **ALIGN=RIGHT** to all the data cells, so that each cell reads something like this:

`<TD ALIGN=RIGHT>$10.95</TD>`

Your HTML code should look like that in Figure 6.14.

```
abigail - Notepad
File  Edit  Search  Help

    <H2>Our Menu</H2>

    <TABLE BORDER CELLSPACING=4 CELLPADDING=2>

    <CAPTION>Our Daily Offerings</CAPTION>

    <TR>
            <TH><BR></TH>
            <TH COLSPAN=2>Seafood</TH>
            <TH COLSPAN=2>Meat</TH>
    </TR>

    <TR>
            <TH><BR></TH>
            <TH>Crab</TH>
            <TH>Scallops</TH>
            <TH>Lamb</TH>
            <TH NOWRAP>Prime Rib</TH>
    </TR>

    <TR>
            <TH>Lunch</TH>
            <TD ALIGN=RIGHT>$10.95</TD>
            <TD ALIGN=RIGHT>$14.95</TD>
            <TD ALIGN=RIGHT>$16.95</TD>
            <TD ALIGN=RIGHT>$14.95</TD>
    </TR>

    <TR>
            <TH>Dinner</TH>
            <TD ALIGN=RIGHT>$21.95</TD>
            <TD ALIGN=RIGHT>$24.99</TD>
            <TD ALIGN=RIGHT>$29.99</TD>
            <TD ALIGN=RIGHT>$23.99</TD>
    </TR>
```

Figure 6.14

2 Save your work and check out the results in your browser (see Figure 6.15). The currency values are aligned to the right in each cell.

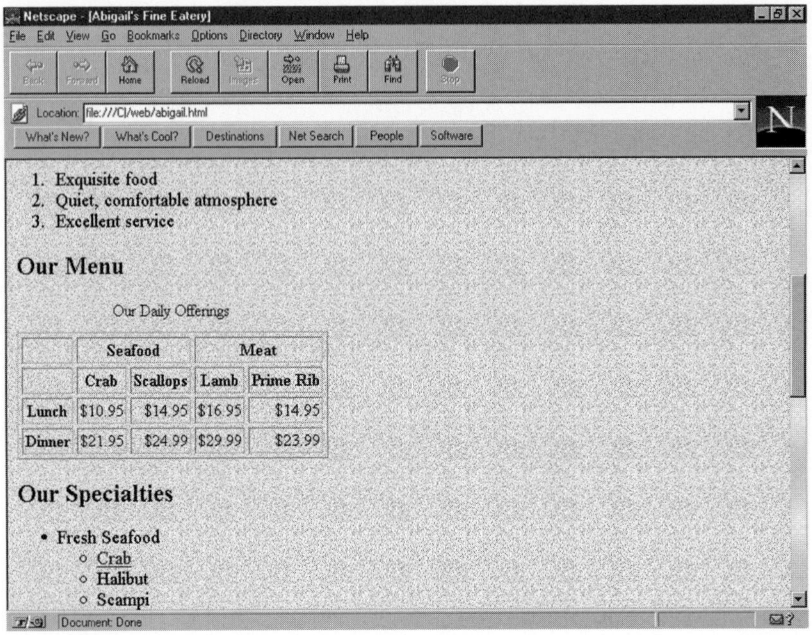

Figure 6.15

EXIT   If necessary, you can exit the editor and browser and continue this project later.

MODIFYING THE WIDTH AND HEIGHT OF THE TABLE AND INDIVIDUAL CELLS

You can control the width and height of a table and of individual cells in the table. To control the width or height of the table, add the WIDTH=size attribute or the HEIGHT=size attribute to the <TABLE> tag. You can define size as an exact width or height in pixels, or as a percentage of the window. If the user stretches or shrinks the window, a table size that's defined as a percentage will stretch or shrink to fit the window. On the other hand, if you define the width or height of the window as a certain size in pixels, the table may wrap if the user shrinks the window. Use the WIDTH attribute like this:

```
<TABLE WIDTH=50%>
```

or

```
<TABLE WIDTH=400>
```

The HEIGHT attribute works in much the same way:

```
<TABLE HEIGHT=50%>
```

or

```
<TABLE HEIGHT=200>
```

You can use both attributes together to define both the width and the height of the entire table. When viewed in a browser, the table in the following example will take up 80 percent of the width of the window and 50 percent of the height of the window:

```
<TABLE WIDTH=80% HEIGHT=50%>
```

You can also change the width and height of individual cells in the table by adding the WIDTH=*size* or HEIGHT=*size* attribute to the <TH> or <TD> tags. The size attribute can be defined as a specific number of pixels or as a percentage of the entire table:

```
<TH WIDTH=100 HEIGHT=100>
```

or

```
<TD WIDTH=100 HEIGHT=100>
```

or

```
<TH WIDTH=2% HEIGHT=2%>
```

In the last example, the cell would display as 2 percent of the width and 2 percent of the height of the entire table.

To define the overall size of the table as a percentage of the viewing window:

1 Find the <TABLE> tag in *abigail.html* and replace it with the following command:

<TABLE BORDER CELLSPACING=4 CELLPADDING=2 WIDTH=90% HEIGHT=40%>

Figure 6.16 shows the HTML source code.

```
abigail - Notepad
File  Edit  Search  Help

        <H2>Our Menu</H2>

                <TABLE BORDER CELLSPACING=4 CELLPADDING=2 WIDTH=90% HEIGHT=40%>

        <CAPTION>Our Daily Offerings</CAPTION>

        <TR>
                <TH><BR></TH>
                <TH COLSPAN=2>Seafood</TH>
                <TH COLSPAN=2>Meat</TH>
        </TR>

        <TR>
                <TH><BR></TH>
                <TH>Crab</TH>
                <TH>Scallops</TH>
                <TH>Lamb</TH>
                <TH NOWRAP>Prime Rib</TH>
        </TR>

        <TR>
                <TH>Lunch</TH>
                <TD ALIGN=RIGHT>$10.95</TD>
                <TD ALIGN=RIGHT>$14.95</TD>
                <TD ALIGN=RIGHT>$16.95</TD>
                <TD ALIGN=RIGHT>$14.95</TD>
        </TR>

        <TR>
                <TH>Dinner</TH>
                <TD ALIGN=RIGHT>$21.95</TD>
                <TD ALIGN=RIGHT>$24.99</TD>
                <TD ALIGN=RIGHT>$29.99</TD>
                <TD ALIGN=RIGHT>$23.99</TD>
        </TR>
```

Figure 6.16

2 Save the file and check out the results in your browser. The table stretches to 90 percent of the width of the window and 40 percent of the height of the window, as shown in Figure 6.17. Now you can better see all the alignment changes made earlier.

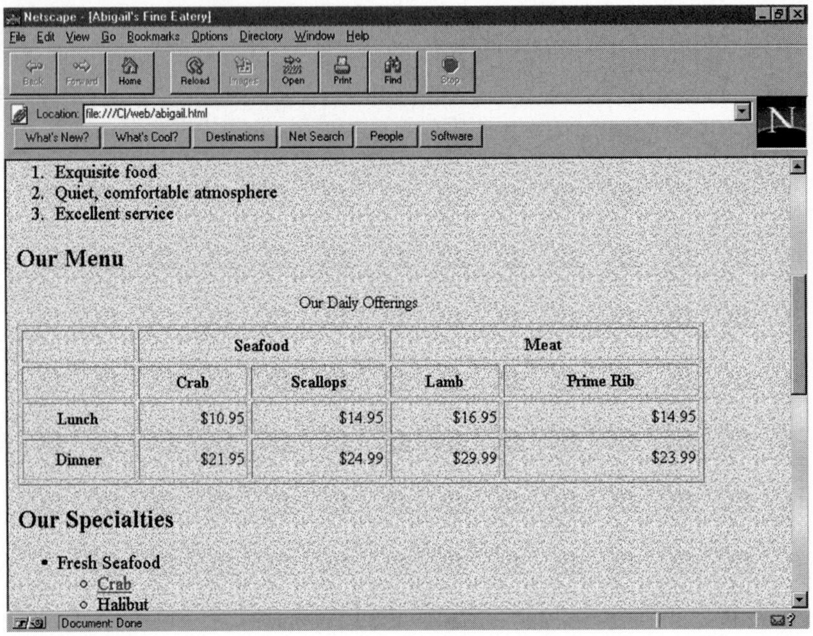

Figure 6.17

THE NEXT STEP

Spend some time browsing various home pages to see how other businesses and individuals are using tables.

This concludes the project. You can either exit your editor and browser or go on to work the Study Questions, Review Exercises, and Assignments.

SUMMARY AND EXERCISES

Summary

- You enclose the entire table between the opening <TABLE> tag and the closing </TABLE tag.
- You enclose every row of the table between an opening <TR> tag and a closing </TR> tag.
- You enclose a heading cell between an opening <TH> tag and a closing </TH> tag.
- You enclose a data cell between an opening <TD> tag and a closing </TD> tag.
- You enclose the title for the table between the opening <CAPTION> and the closing </CAPTION> tag.

- Place the <BR> tag in text where you want the text to wrap to the next line of the cell.
- Place the NOWRAP attribute within the opening <TD> or <TH> tag to keep text from wrapping in the cell.
- If you want to create an empty cell, include the <BR> tag between the opening and closing cell tags; for example, <TD>
</TD>.
- Use the COLSPAN attribute within the opening <TD> or <TH> tag to span the data over more than one column; type an equal sign and the number of columns you want to span.
- Use the ROWSPAN attribute within the opening <TD> or <TH> tag to span the data over more than one row; type an equal sign and the number of rows you want to span.
- Use the BORDER attribute within the opening <TABLE> tag to place a border around the table and the individual cells in the table.
- To change the outside border from the default setting of 1 pixel, place an equal sign after the BORDER attribute and type the number of pixels you want for the border.
- Use the CELLSPACING attribute within the opening <TABLE> tag to add more space between all the cells of the table; type an equal sign and the number of pixels you want. The default cell spacing is 2 pixels.
- Use the CELLPADDING attribute within the opening <TABLE> tag to add space around the cell contents. Type an equal sign and the number of pixels you want. The default cell padding is 1 pixel.
- Use the ALIGN attribute with the opening <TR> tag to change the horizontal alignment of the contents of an entire row; type an equal sign followed by RIGHT, LEFT, or CENTER.
- Use the ALIGN attribute with the opening <TD> or <TH> tag to change the horizontal alignment of the contents of an individual cell; type an equal sign followed by RIGHT, LEFT, or CENTER.
- Use the VALIGN attribute with the opening <TR> tag to change the vertical alignment of the contents of an entire row; type an equal sign followed by TOP, MIDDLE, or BOTTOM.
- Use the VALIGN attribute with the opening <TD> or <TH> tag to change the vertical alignment of the contents of an individual cell; type an equal sign followed by TOP, MIDDLE, or BOTTOM.

Key Terms

caption	row
cell	spanning
cell padding	table
column	title
label	wrap

Study Questions

Multiple Choice

1. To define a table row, use
    a. <TABLE>.
    b. <TH>.
    c. <TD>.
    d. <TR>.
    e. <ROW>.

2. A cell
   a. is the intersection of a column and row.
   b. can contain data.
   c. can contain a heading.
   d. can contain a link.
   e. all these answers.

3. To define data for a cell, use
   a. <TD>.
   b. <TH>.
   c. <TR>.
   d. <DATA>.
   e. <ROW>.

4. A table is made up of
   a. columns and rows.
   b. cells.
   c. data.
   d. headings.
   e. all of these answers.

5. A table is defined in HTML
   a. column by column.
   b. row by row.
   c. side by side.
   d. bottom to top.
   e. all these answers.

6. To define a heading, you use
   a. <TR>.
   b. <TD>.
   c. <TH>.
   d. <HEADER>.
   e. <TABLE>.

7. You can define the width and height of a table as
   a. an exact number of bytes.
   b. an exact number of pixels.
   c. a percentage of the viewing window.
   d. an exact number of rows.
   e. both b and c.

8. To stretch a cell over more than one column, use
   a. CELLPADDING.
   b. COLSPAN.
   c. WIDTH.
   d. CELLSPACING.
   e. STRETCH.

9. The caption
   a. is placed above the table by default.
   b. is used to explain the contents of the table.
   c. can be placed below the table.
   d. is usually regarded as a title.
   e. all these answers.

10. If you want the cell contents to appear on one line, you use
    a. NOWRAP.
    b. DOWRAP.
    c. WIDTH.
    d.
.
    e. CELLSPAN.

Short Answer

1. Define a table with a border.

2. Define a table that extends 100 percent of the width of the viewing window.

3. Create a table and add the caption Members by State.

4.–10. Write all the tags and attributes to create the following table:

Sales by Region

	North	South	East	West
Computer Sales	$130,000	$200,000	$500,000	$190,000
Computer Rentals	$90,000	$100,000	$200,000	$120,000

For Discussion

1. Describe the type of data that would best be included in a table.

2. Describe the type of data that shouldn't be included in a table.

3. Describe the difference between the <TH> and <TD> tags.

4. Describe the difference between CELLPADDING and CELLSPACING.

5. Describe how to define a table in HTML.

Review Exercises

Adding a Table to the Alphabits Bookstore Web Page

Replace the ordered list of best-selling children's books in *alphabit.html* with the following table (see Figure 6.18):

Best Selling Children's Books

	Name of Book	*Number of Books Sold*
1	The Cat in the Hat	$10,000,000
2	Winnie-the-Pooh	$9,000,000
3	The Secret Garden	$6,000,000
4	The Wind in the Willows	$4,000,000

Save the file under the same name.

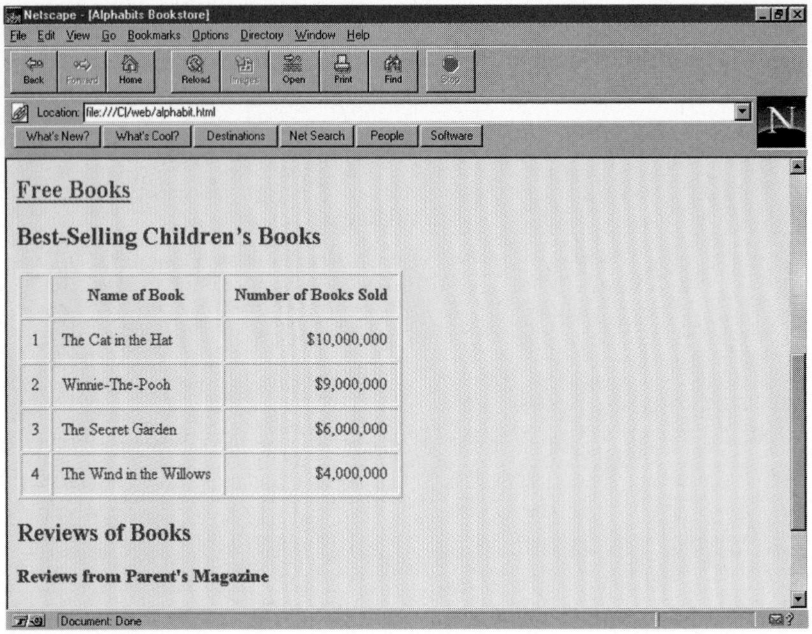

Figure 6.18

Adding a Table to the Animal Web Page

Create a table for the animal Web page. Include types of animals, animal sales, or whatever is appropriate for your document. Include at least three of the table features covered in this project.

Assignments

Adding a Table to Your Personal Web Page

Place some of the information on your personal Web document in a table. You could use this as a way to organize your work experience or special interests. Include at least three of the table features covered in this project.

Using Tables in the Organization or Nonprofit Web Page

Use the table features in the Web page you're creating for an organization. You can include a list of members, the services provided, a schedule of events, and so on. Include at least three of the table features covered in this project.

> **What Is Java?** Java is a programming language that was designed by Sun Microsystems especially for use on the World Wide Web. It is a more powerful language than HTML. Java is used for Web animation, sound, movies, and for 3-D effects. Java programs, known as *applets*, are small and travel the Internet quickly. Many applets can be used together to produce complex programs, and Java programs aren't specific to any environment; that is, they can be used by someone on a PC, a Mac, or on a UNIX system.

In this project, you will learn how to link text and images to locations that aren't in the same document–that is, the locations are *external* to the document. These documents are separate files that can be on the same server or on a different server in some other physical location. Some **external elements** are files that can't be read by your browser without the aid of helper programs, which your browser will load.

Objectives

After completing this project, you should be able to:

▶ Link to other local documents

▶ Link to documents in other locations

▶ Link to external images

▶ Link to sound and video

CASE STUDY: LINKING TO OTHER WEB DOCUMENTS

In Project 3, you linked *text* to a location in the same document. In Project 4, you linked an *image* to a location in the same document. This type of linking provides great benefits for Web document design, allowing the visitor to see more information if desired. However, one of the most powerful features of Web documents is their ability to link to *other* Web documents. These documents can be other documents located on the same server, or they can be located on a server anyplace in the world.

Designing the Solution

In this project, you will create a second document and link the Abigail's Fine Eatery home page to that document, link to a document on a different server, link from a small image to a larger image, and link to a sound file.

To send a letter to someone far away, you would need to know the correct address for the letter to reach its destination. The same concept applies on the Web. You can create a link to send your reader to another document by including the correct address of the file to which he will link. Then, when the visitor clicks the hot spot, he is transported via the Web to another location. The address of a file is its URL (Uniform Resource Locator), and each file has a unique address or URL.

Figure 7.1 shows one of the new links in the Abigail's Fine Eatery home page that you will add in this project.

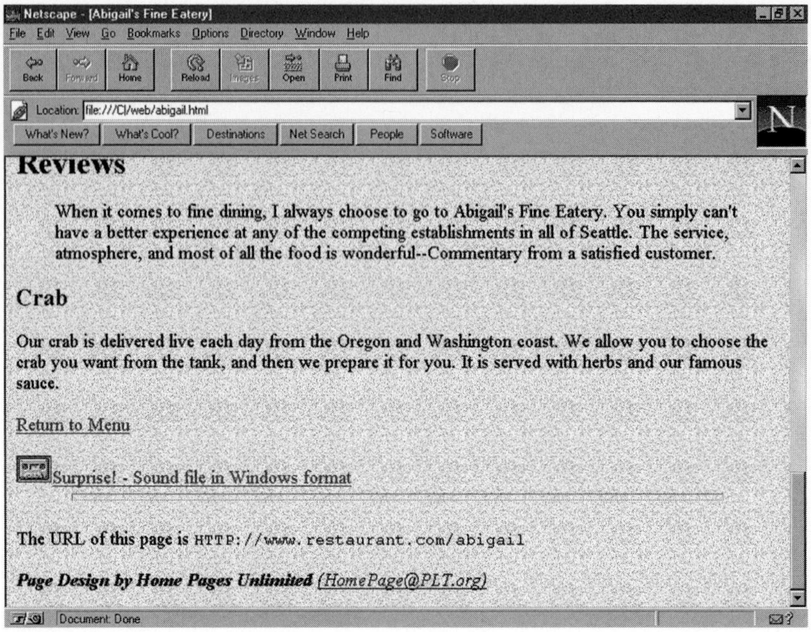

Figure 7.1

LINKING TO OTHER LOCAL DOCUMENTS

To create a link for the user to click, you include the address of the document in the link tag and place it in quotation marks. One word of warning: remember that filenames are case sensitive. The syntax is as follows:

`<A HREF="`*filename*`.html">`*text to click*`</A>`

In this example, *filename*`.html` represents the name of the document that will appear on the screen when the user clicks the accompanying text.

HTML has two ways of specifying the address for a document to link to when you place the address in a link tag: using an absolute address or using a relative address. An ***absolute address*** shows the entire path to the file. A ***relative address*** specifies the address of a file in relationship to the current document and should be used to link to documents located on the same server.

Absolute addresses always start with a forward slash (/) and are placed in quotation marks. Table 7.1 shows some absolute addresses.

Table 7.1

Absolute Address	Description
`<A HREF="/graphics/logo.gif">`	The document, *logo.gif,* is located in the *graphics* folder or directory.
`<A HREF="/html/graphics/logo.gif">`	The document, *logo.gif,* is located in the *graphics* folder, which is under the *html* folder.

If you think of your current document as home base, in a relative address you provide directions to the file to link to from your home base. It's like giving several people in different parts of town directions to one location—but from your house, rather than from their own individual homes. One major advantage of using a relative path is that it allows you to move files without destroying the links, because the links are created from the base document, regardless of its location.

Relative addresses use UNIX syntax; that is, directories or folders are separated by forward slashes (/), and the directory above the current directory is referenced by two periods (..). Table 7.2 shows some relative addresses.

Table 7.2

Relative Address	Description
`<A HREF="logo.gif">`	The document, *logo.gif*, is located in the same directory as the current document.
`<A HREF="graphics/logo.gif">`	The document, *logo.gif*, is located in a directory called *graphics*, which is under the current directory.
`<A HREF="../logo.gif">`	The document, *logo.gif*, is located in the directory above the current directory.

When you use relative addresses to reference documents and someone downloads your page or posts it at another site, sometimes the links can get disconnected. To avoid this problem, you can include the ***base address*** of your file in the head section of the document. That way, browsers know where to look for any documents referenced by relative addresses. Including the base address would be like including your home address in the directions to various people, so that they know where to start.

The <BASE> tag must appear after the opening <HEAD> tag and before the closing </HEAD> tag, and the address of your Web document is contained in quotation marks. The syntax is

```
<HEAD>
<BASE HREF="http://Web.site.com/path/filename.html">
</HEAD>
```

Any browsers reading this document use this address as the base and reference all relative addresses from it.

 To link to another document located in the same directory as your base document:

1 Create a new Web document by typing the following HTML code lines on a blank page in your editor (see Figure 7.2):

```
<HTML>
<HEAD>
<TITLE>Spring Lamb</TITLE>
</HEAD>
<BODY BGCOLOR=#FFFF00 TEXT=#550044
BACKGROUND="images/oyster.gif">
<H1>How Our Lamb Is Prepared</H1>
Our lamb is simmered in mangoes, tamarind, berber (an
African aromatic spice and chile mixture), onion, garlic, and
white wine. Our chef then removes the lamb when it has
reached the proper tenderness.
<P>
```

Return to Menu
</P>

<HR SIZE=6 WIDTH=85% ALIGN=CENTER>

<P>
The URL of this page is
<SAMP>HTTP://www.restaurant.com/abigail</SAMP>
</P>
<ADDRESS><B>Page Design by Home Pages Unlimited</B>
(HomePage@PLT.org)</ADDRESS>
</BODY>
</HTML>

As usual, insert extra lines, tabs, and so on to make the code as readable and clear as possible.

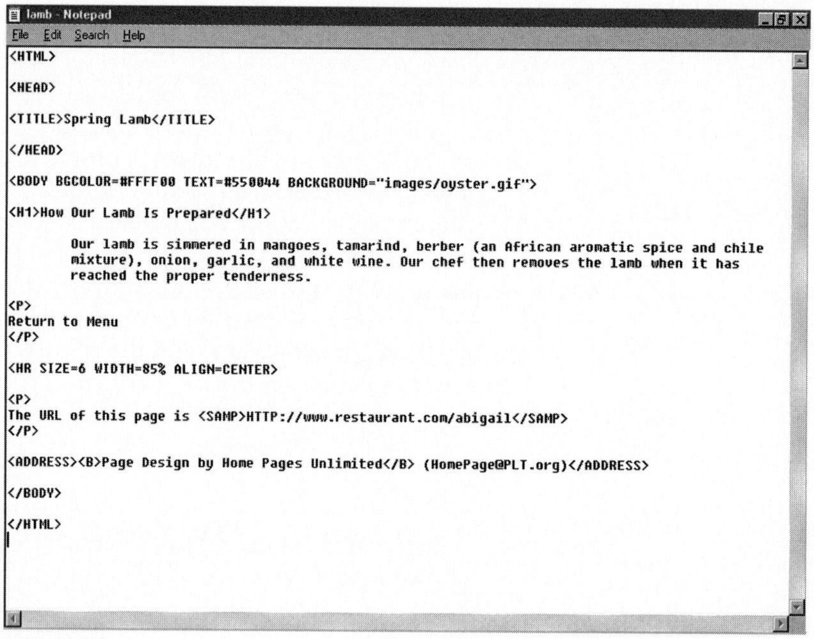

```
lamb - Notepad
File  Edit  Search  Help
<HTML>

<HEAD>

<TITLE>Spring Lamb</TITLE>

</HEAD>

<BODY BGCOLOR=#FFFF00 TEXT=#550044 BACKGROUND="images/oyster.gif">

<H1>How Our Lamb Is Prepared</H1>

        Our lamb is simmered in mangoes, tamarind, berber (an African aromatic spice and chile
        mixture), onion, garlic, and white wine. Our chef then removes the lamb when it has
        reached the proper tenderness.

<P>
Return to Menu
</P>

<HR SIZE=6 WIDTH=85% ALIGN=CENTER>

<P>
The URL of this page is <SAMP>HTTP://www.restaurant.com/abigail</SAMP>
</P>

<ADDRESS><B>Page Design by Home Pages Unlimited</B> (HomePage@PLT.org)</ADDRESS>

</BODY>

</HTML>
```

Figure 7.2

2 Save the file on the same disk and in the same directory as your *abigail.html* file. Name the file *lamb.html* and view it in your browser (see Figure 7.3). Notice how using the same background and address information in the *lamb.html* document as in the *abigail.html* document lends a feeling of consistency to the two documents.

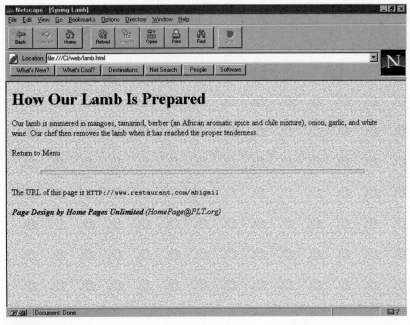

Figure 7.3

3 Close the *lamb.html* file.

4 Open the *abigail.html* file.

5 Find the bullet Spring Lamb under the heading Our Specialties.

6 Make the word Lamb a link by adding the **<A HREF="lamb.html">** and **</A>** tags around it as follows (see Figure 7.4):

```
<A HREF="lamb.html">Lamb</A>
```

The text is now a link.

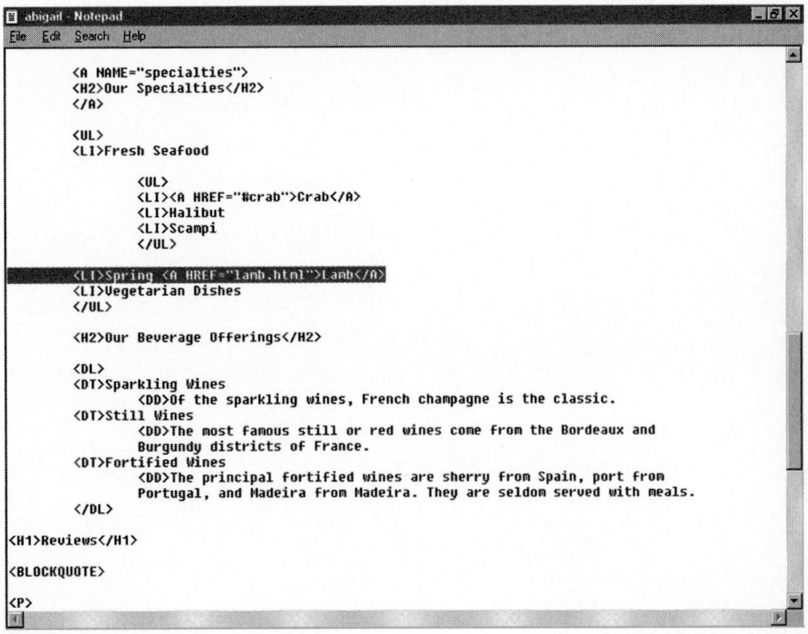

Figure 7.4

7 Save *abigail.html* and check out the results in your browser by clicking the text Lamb (see Figure 7.5). You should jump to the *lamb.html* document shown earlier (in Figure 7.3). If you didn't link to the *lamb.html* document, check your spelling and the case of the address you typed. Remember that filenames are case sensitive. If you have previously viewed the *lamb.html* document, the link may look like a visited link rather than a regular link.

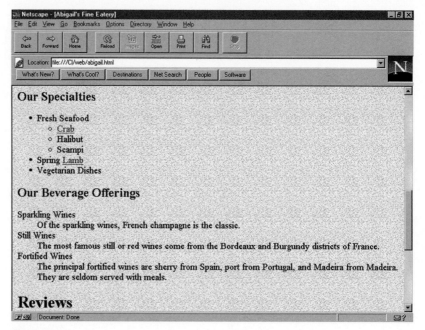

Figure 7.5

8 Now you'll make a link back to the *abigail.html* page from the *lamb.html* page. Open the *lamb.html* document in your editor and find the words Return to Menu. Surround this text with **<A HREF="abigail.html">** and **</A>** tags as follows:

```
<P>
<A HREF="abigail.html">Return to Menu</A>
<P>
```

Figure 7.6 shows the source code for this change.

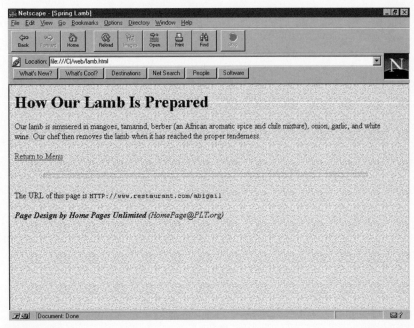

Figure 7.6

9 Test the link back to the main *abigail.html* document in your browser. The link should appear as a visited link (see Figure 7.7).

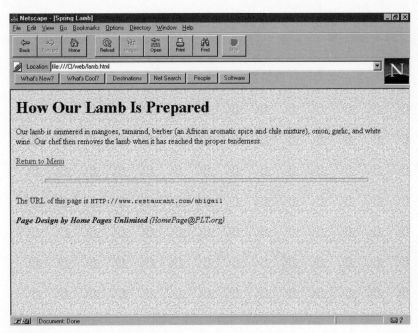

Figure 7.7

10 Close the *lamb.html* file. Keep the *abigail.html* file on-screen for use in the next exercise.

LINKING TO DOCUMENTS IN OTHER LOCATIONS

You might want to link your Web document to other Web documents. For example, if you have a Web page posted on the topic of Traditional African Music, you may want to create links to other Web pages dealing with the same or similar topics.

To link to Web documents located on different servers, you must include the complete URL or address. As you learned in the Overview, a complete URL has three basic parts–the protocol, the name of the server where the file is stored, and the path and filename, as in the following syntax:

`http://Web.site.com/path/filename`

So far you have probably used only the HTTP protocol, which tells your browser to use HTTP to access the file. World Wide Web servers use HTTP to send HTML documents over the Web. Some of the other popular protocols include Anonymous FTP, FTP, Gopher, e-mail, and newsgroups. Each of these protocols is described in Table 7.3.

Table 7.3

Protocol	Description	Example Address
Anonymous FTP	Links to an FTP server and allows you to login without a password	`<A HREF="ftp://ftp.com/path/filename">`
FTP	Links to an FTP server that lets you login and use your ID and password	`<A HREF="ftp://username:password@ftp.com/path/">`
Gopher	Links to a Gopher server	`<A HREF="gopher://gopher.com">`
E-mail	Prompts the user for a subject and body and automatically addresses the e-mail	`<A HREF="mailto:e-mail address">`
Newsgroups	Links to an entire newsgroup	`<A HREF="news:name of group">`
	Links to a specific article, using the ID of the article from its header	`<A HREF="news:article ID">`

To create a link to a document on a different server, the syntax is
`<A HREF="http://Web.site.com/path/filename"> text </A>`

To link to another document in a different location on the Web:

1 In the *abigail.html* document, find the heading `Location and Atmosphere` and type tags around the word `Location` like this:

`<A HREF="http://www.awl.com/he/is/html/ericksen/index.html">Location</A>`

Figure 7.8 shows the HTML source code.

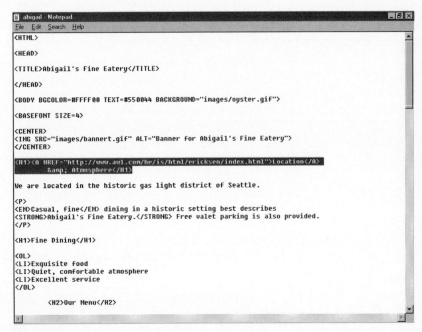

Figure 7.8

2 Save your work and check out the results in your browser. As Figure 7.9 shows, when you point to the Location link in the Abigail's page, the linked address is visible in the status bar. Clicking the link (if you're online) connects you to the linked document.

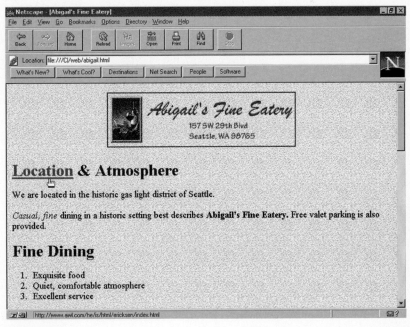

Figure 7.9

If necessary, you can exit the editor and browser and continue this project later.

LINKING TO EXTERNAL IMAGES

In Project 4, you learned how to use and link images within the same document. Sometimes you want to link to images contained in other files. For example, you can include a small version of an image on a home page and then create a link to a larger version of the image stored in a different file, so that visitors can view the larger image if they want to do so.

To link to an external image, include the name of the full-size image in the link and the name of the small version in the image definition. The format is

```
<A HREF="images/cap-2.gif">
<IMG SRC="images/dollar.gif">
</A>
```

The small image will appear, as shown in Figure 7.10.

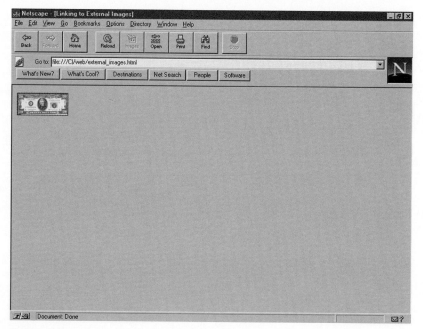

Figure 7.10

When the visitor clicks the small image, the full-size image is loaded, as shown in Figure 7.11.

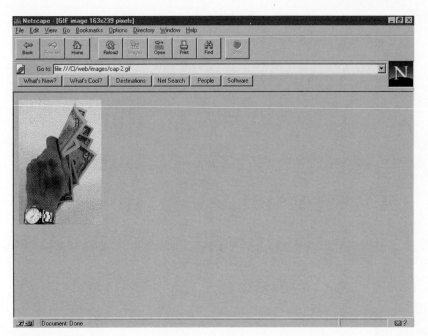

Figure 7.11

Web designers often include information about the size of the file and sometimes the format, so that visitors can decide whether they want to take the time to load the large image. You can include text along with the image, using a command like this:

```
<A HREF="images/cap-2.gif">
<IMG SRC="images/dollar.gif">The full size image is 8340
bytes
</A>
```

The added text is shown in Figure 7.12.

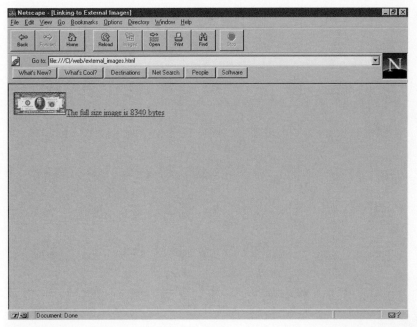

Figure 7.12

To link a small version of an image to the larger external version:

1 Open a new file in your editor.

2 Type the following HTML code lines (with the usual extra spacing added for readability as desired):

```
<HTML>
<HEAD>
<TITLE>Test</TITLE>
</HEAD>
<BODY>
<H1>This document is a test document</H1>
<A HREF="images/cup.gif">
<IMG SRC="images/cupicon.gif">The size of the file is 5000
bytes</A>
</BODY>
</HTML>
```

Figure 7.13 shows the code.

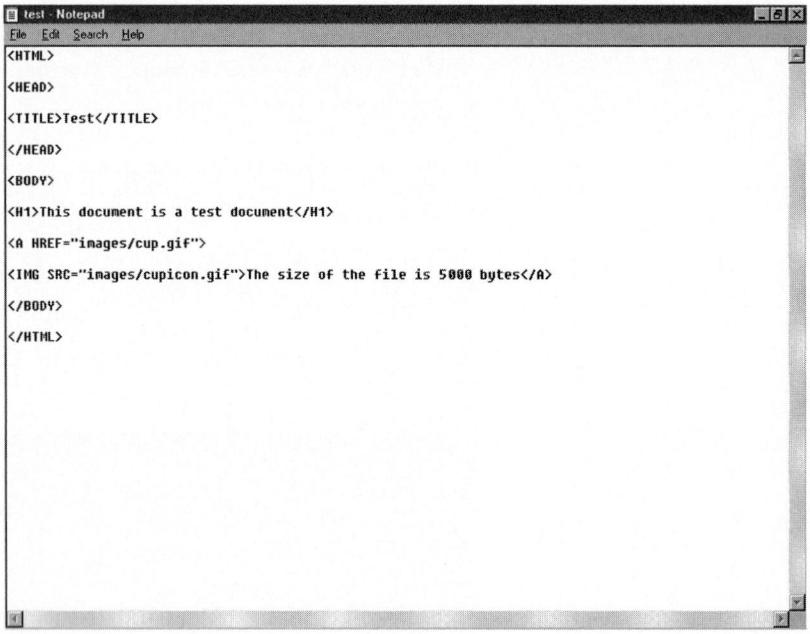

```
test - Notepad
File  Edit  Search  Help

<HTML>

<HEAD>

<TITLE>Test</TITLE>

</HEAD>

<BODY>

<H1>This document is a test document</H1>

<A HREF="images/cup.gif">

<IMG SRC="images/cupicon.gif">The size of the file is 5000 bytes</A>

</BODY>

</HTML>
```

Figure 7.13

3 Check out the results in your browser.

The document displays the small version of the image, as shown in Figure 7.14.

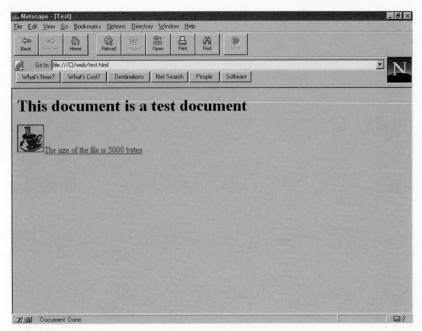

Figure 7.14

When the visitor clicks the small image, the full image appears, as shown in Figure 7.15.

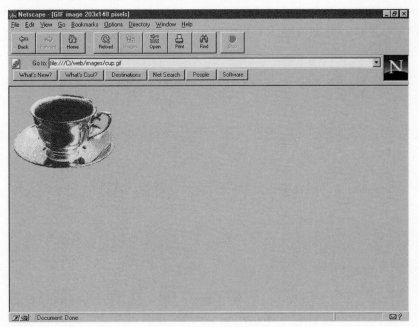

Figure 7.15

  If necessary, you can exit the editor and browser and continue this project later.

LINKING TO SOUND AND VIDEO

You can also link your Web document to sound files. For example, if you are creating a Web document about traditional African music, you might want to include examples of the music. You can record sound files or find commercial sound files.

Reminder If you record music or purchase files, you must get permission to use any copyrighted work.

Only one sound format is used by all platforms: the *AU* format developed by Sun Microsystems. This format is 8-bit technology, however, and is quite low quality. The standard sound format for Windows is *WAV* files, and the standard format for the Macintosh is *AIFF*. You can include these higher-quality sounds on your Web page, and people with the proper system configured for sound can hear the sounds. One technique many designers use when incorporating sound on their Web documents is to include several formats and allow the user to click the appropriate sound file for her system. Just as you can use graphics programs to convert graphics to other file formats, you can use sound programs to convert sound files to other formats.

To include sound on a Web document, you use a command like this:

```
<A HREF="sound.wav">Mbira music—Windows format</A>
```

You could also include an icon for the user to click to hear the sound. Here's an example:

```
<A HREF="sound.wav"><IMG SRC="images/casset.gif">Mbira
music—Windows format</A>
```

The icon appears on the screen for the user to click, as shown in Figure 7.16.

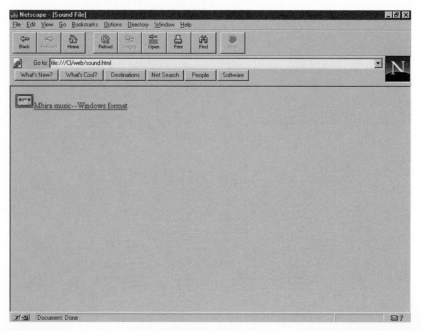

Figure 7.16

You can also include a link to a video file on your Web document. You can purchase commercial video or make your own.

Reminder The copyright laws that apply to video also apply to sound and graphics.

Only one video format can be used on all platforms: **MPEG format**. Files using the MPEG format use the extension .MPG. You can also use AVI files for Windows and QuickTime video format for the Macintosh. Just as with sound files, you should provide your visitor with information about the file size and format so that she can decide whether she wants to take the time to use the file. Video files tend to be very large and slow. Here's how you link to a video file:

<A HREF="video.mpg">MPEG format video–5MB</A>

The visitor would click the text to view the video.

To link to a sound file:

1 In the *abigail.html* file, find the text <HR SIZE=6 WIDTH=85% ALIGN=CENTER> and type the following line above it:

<A HREF="sound.wav"><IMG SRC="images/casset.gif">Surprise! · Sound file in Windows format</A>

See Figure 7.17 for the HTML source code.

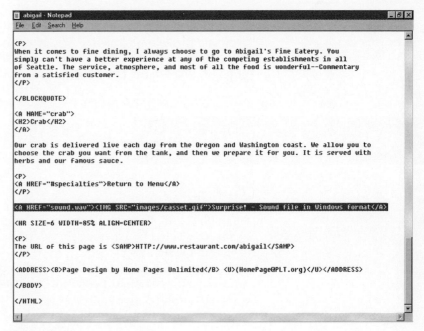

Figure 7.17

2 Save your work and view it in your browser. The results should be similar to Figure 7.18.

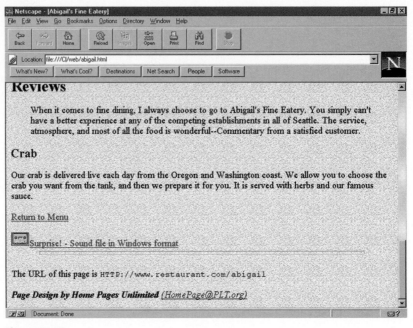

Figure 7.18

THE NEXT STEP

If you have the equipment to hear sounds or view video, spend some time browsing the web for sound and video libraries.

This concludes the project. You can either exit your editor and browser or go on to work the Study Questions, Review Exercises, and Assignments.

SUMMARY AND EXERCISES

Summary

- To link to an external file (another document, a graphic file, a sound file, or a video file) include the address of the file in quotation marks within the link tag.
- It's best to use relative addresses rather than absolute addresses for external files, so that if you move the files the links aren't broken.
- When using relative addresses, use the <BASE> tag in the head section to include the base address of the main document.
- To link to a document on a different server, include the protocol, the name of the server, and the path and filename within the anchor tags.
- To link to an external image, include the name of the full-size image in the link and the name of the small version in the <IMG SRC> tag.

Key Terms

absolute address

AIFF format

AU format

AVI file

base address

external element

MPEG format

relative address

WAV file

Study Questions

Multiple Choice

1. The base address is located in the
   a. body section.
   b. address section.
   c. head section.
   d. inside address section.
   e. closing section.

2. A complete URL is made up of
   a. the protocol.
   b. the name of the server where the file is stored.
   c. the path.
   d. the filename.
   e. all these answers.

3. When linking from a small image to a larger version of the image, it's a good idea to include
   a. text describing the large image.
   b. a menu.
   c. a sound file.
   d. text describing the size of the image file.
   e. both a and d.

4. The video format supported by all platforms is
   a. MPEG.
   b. WAV.
   c. VID.
   d. AVI.
   e. MOV.

5. Relative addresses
   a. provide directions to the file to link to from the current file.
   b. allow you to move files without destroying the links.
   c. separate directories with forward slashes (/).
   d. are the safest type of links.
   e. all these answers.

6. HTTP is a protocol that
   a. is used with Gopher files.
   b. is used with Anonymous FTP.
   c. is used with HTML files.
   d. is out of date.
   e. all these answers.

7. To create a link, the address in the link tag must be
   a. in quotation marks.
   b. in single quotation marks.
   c. in brackets.
   d. in capital letters.
   e. all these answers.

8. You can link your Web document to external
   a. graphics.
   b. sound.
   c. video.
   d. documents.
   e. all these answers.

9. The sound format used by all platforms is
   a. GIF.
   b. AU.
   c. WAV.
   d. AIFF.
   e. HTM.

10. Absolute file addresses
    a. are in relation to the current file.
    b. start with a forward slash.
    c. are the best to use for files stored in the same directory as the current file.
    d. are used only for sound files.
    e. all these answers.

Short Answer

Place the appropriate tag or attributes around the text.

1. Create a base address for a document you are creating:

   ```
   <HEAD>
   </HEAD>
   ```

2. Create a link to the file *picture.gif*, which is saved in the same directory as the base address you specified in question 1.

3. Create a link to the file *picture.gif*, which is saved in the *pics* directory under the current directory.

4. Create a link to the file *picture.gif*, which is saved in the directory immediately above the current directory.

5. Create a link from the small image *icon.gif* to the large image *picture.gif*.

6. Add the text `The full sized image is 60K` to display with the *icon.gif* image.

7. Create a link to a Web file saved on the *EFN.ORG* server in the *nonprofit* directory and call the file *index.htm*.

8. Create a link to a sound file called *birds.au*.

9. Add the text `Song birds of the Northwest—Windows format` to the link you created in question 8.

10. Create a link to a video file called *flight.mpg*.

For Discussion

1. Why would you include sound files in various formats in the same document?

2. Explain the difference between relative and absolute addresses.

3. Explain the term *external element*.

4. Discuss circumstances in which you would want to include sound files in your Web document.

5. Discuss circumstances in which you would want to include video files in your Web document.

Review Exercises

Linking the Alphabits Bookstore Web Page to Another Document

Create the following file and save it as *parents.html* in the same location as the Alphabits Web document:

```
<HTML>
<HEAD>
<TITLE>Children and Books</TITLE>
</HEAD>
<BODY BGCOLOR=FFFFAA TEXT=0000CC LINK=FF0000
VLINK=00AA00>
<H1>How to Read to Your Child</H1>

<P>
You should find a time every day to read to your young child. This
should be uninterrupted time. Make sure that both you and your
child are comfortable and that this is a pleasant experience.
</P>

<P>
Return to Main Menu
</P>
</BODY>
</HTML>
```

Figure 7.19 shows this source code. Notice that it specifies the same <BODY> attributes as in the *alphabit.html* page to be consistent in style with that document.

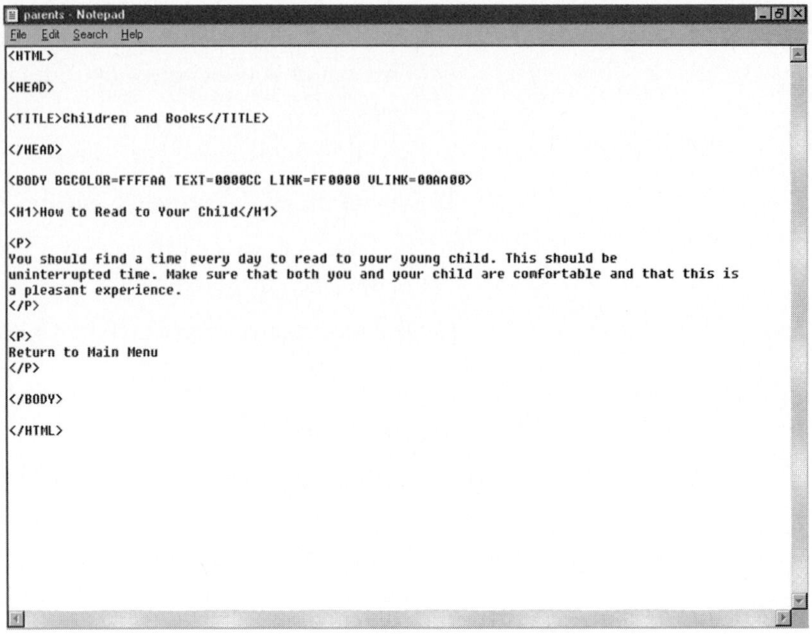

Figure 7.19

Close the *parents.html* file and open the Alphabits Bookstore Web document, *alphabit.html*. Above the `<ADDRESS>` tag, create a relative link to the *parents.html* file (see Figure 7.20). Test the link in your browser to make sure that it works.

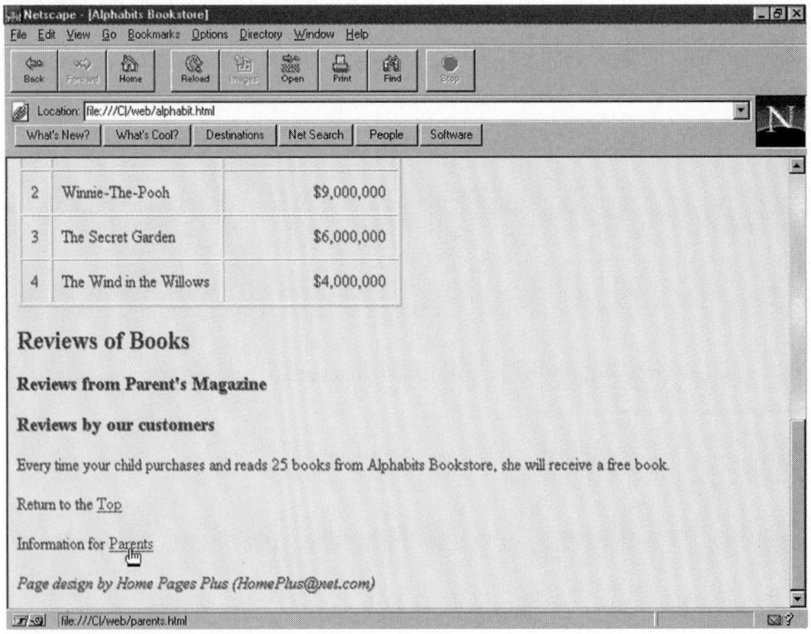

Figure 7.20

Reopen the *parents.html* file and create a link from the text `Return to Main Menu` to the *alphabit.html* document (see Figure 7.21).

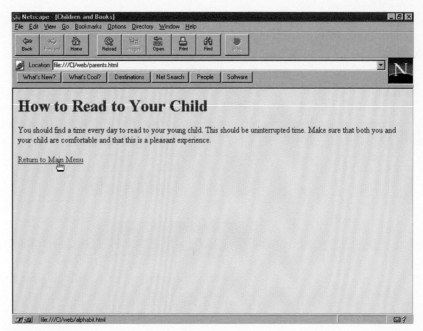

Figure 7.21

Linking the Animal Web Page to Other Pages

Create a link to other Web pages that have similar topics to those in your animal Web page. For example, if you are working on endangered species, you could link to a zoo that is preserving that species, or if you are working on a breed of dogs, you could link to a breeder that provides services.

Assignments

Linking Your Personal Web Page to Sound Files

Record a message and create a link from your personal page to the sound file. Include various formats for the sound file and include text that explains each link.

Linking the Organization or Nonprofit Web Page to Other Pages

Create a link from your organization to other organizations that provide similar services or to organizations that provide funding for your organization. For example, if your organization is part of United Way, you could create links to other United Way agencies in your area.

> **What Is PPP?** *PPP* stands for *point-to-point protocol*. When you set up a PPP connection with your Internet service provider, you're connected directly to the Internet, rather than connecting to a computer that will then give you access to the Internet through a shell account. The advantage to point-to-point protocol is that it allows you to see graphics, hear sounds, and play videos.

PROJECT 8: CREATING FORMS

In this project, you will learn how to create forms that allow the user to interact with your home page—rather than just read the information.

Objectives

After completing this project, you should be able to:

▶ Understand forms

▶ Create a form

▶ Define text fields

▶ Define radio buttons and check boxes

▶ Create list box options

▶ Get the user's input

CASE STUDY: BUILDING FORMS TO GATHER INFORMATION

In preceding projects, you created static pages with which the user can't interact except by clicking links. In this project, you create a form for the user to provide you with information. You create the form, enhance the form, and learn how to have the user e-mail the form's content.

Designing the Solution

Forms provide the capacity to get input from visitors by allowing them to enter information into blank areas and make selections from options. This type of interaction with visitors is a powerful feature.

Using HTML to create forms is no more difficult than creating any other part of a Web document. However, the processing of information that a visitor inputs into a form requires some programming. These *CGI (Common Gateway Interface) scripts* or programs provide the interaction between forms and other programs. CGI scripts gather the data input by the user and then provide the means for the data to be used by other programs. Scripting languages are becoming easier to use, and they will probably make dealing with forms much easier in the future.

Tip Because this isn't a programming text, you learn how to create forms and then simply receive the information from the user by e-mail. You should consult with a CGI programming book for further information on CGI.

CREATING A FORM

You can easily create an interactive form like the one shown in Figure 8.1 that will mail the user's input to a predetermined person. This is the syntax:

```
<HTML>
<HEAD>
<TITLE>form title</TITLE>
</HEAD>
<BODY>
<FORM ACTION="mailto:owner@site.com" METHOD="POST">
     body of form
     </FORM>
</BODY>
</HTML>
```

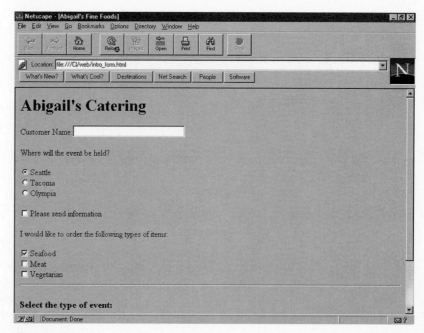

Figure 8.1a

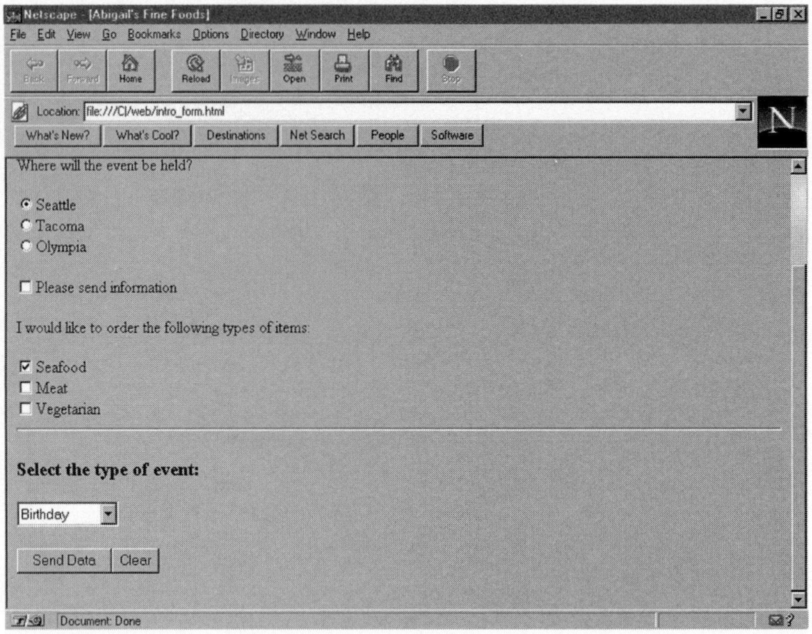

Figure 8.1b

The form is created between the opening and closing <BODY> tags, and the entire body of the form is contained between the opening and closing <FORM> tags. The ACTION attribute is mandatory because it specifies the URL where data from the form is to be sent. Although the action here is simply to mail to an e-mail address, you will often see an absolute path to a CGI program that will process the information. The METHOD attribute has only two possible values: GET and POST. When you use GET, the default value, the data is added to the end of the URL and sent to the server as a variable. POST sends a separate stream of data to the server.

When the visitor fills out this form, the information will be sent to the owner of the page at the e-mail address specified by the ACTION attribute. Notice that there are no spaces in the ACTION section of the tag.

To begin a form:

1 Open a new document.

2 If you don't have an e-mail address, find out the e-mail address of your instructor.

3 Type the following code lines, adding space as necessary to make the HTML code easily readable:

```
<HTML>
<HEAD>
<TITLE>Abigail's Fine Foods</TITLE>
</HEAD>
<BODY>
<FORM ACTION="mailto:email address of instructor"
METHOD="POST">
```

This is just some text.
</FORM>
</BODY>
</HTML>

Figure 8.2 shows how the HTML code should look.

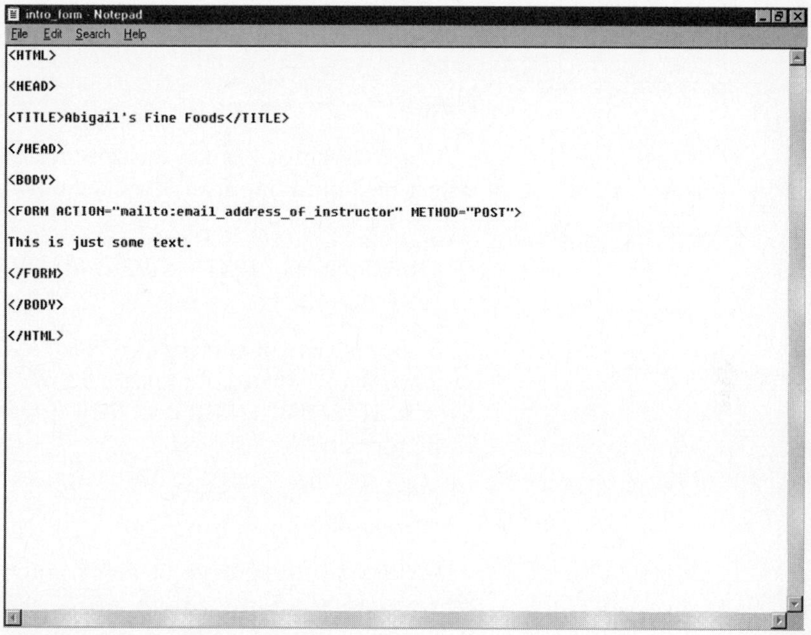

```
intro_form - Notepad                                                _ 8 X
File   Edit   Search   Help
<HTML>

<HEAD>

<TITLE>Abigail's Fine Foods</TITLE>

</HEAD>

<BODY>

<FORM ACTION="mailto:email_address_of_instructor" METHOD="POST">

This is just some text.

</FORM>

</BODY>

</HTML>
```

Figure 8.2

4 Save the document as *intro_form.html* if your operating system has long filenames or *intrform.htm* if it doesn't, and keep the document on-screen for use in the next set of steps.

DEFINING TEXT FIELDS

After setting up the opening and closing </FORM> tags, you're ready to define the ***user input fields*** (data elements) that will appear on the form. Form ***fields*** are the same as fields used in database software or in the address file for a mail merge. That is, they're the individual elements that make up the data for one person—for example, *Last Name* might be one field, and *City* another field.

You receive input from the user with the <INPUT> tag. You need to specify the type of input by using the TYPE attribute. The most common type of input is TEXT. This is the format for the <INPUT> tag:

    <INPUT TYPE="TEXT">

This command places a text input box on the form for the user to type a response to you. You can further define the text input with attributes. Table 8.1 lists the attributes.

Table 8.1

Attribute	Description
SIZE	Defines the size of the text input box on your form, in number of characters. The default setting is 20 characters.
MAXLENGTH	Defines the number of characters that will be accepted (because the user can actually type more characters than the size of the box).
NAME	Gives the text input box a data element name that identifies the information.

The following example sets the size of the input box as 30 characters, with a maximum input of 40 characters from the user. The name of the text box is username:

```
<INPUT TYPE="TEXT" SIZE="30" MAXLENGTH="40" NAME=
"username">
```

A special type of text input box is PASSWORD, used for security. As the user types a password, it appears on the screen as asterisks. You can also use the SIZE, MAXLENGTH, and NAME attributes with the PASSWORD tag. This is the format:

```
<INPUT TYPE="PASSWORD" SIZE="8" MAXLENGTH="8" NAME=
"password">
```

If you want the user to be able to input a large amount of text, create a *text area* on the form with the <TEXTAREA> tag. As with other text fields, you can use the NAME attribute to define the <TEXTAREA> data, and you can also define the size of the area. The default size of the text area is 40 characters wide by 4 rows long. To change the size from the default, use the COLS and ROWS attributes:

```
<TEXTAREA NAME="response" COLS="20" ROWS="10">
        default text that will automatically show up in the box
</TEXTAREA>
```

When you create a large text area, the area has scroll bars. Note that the <TEXTAREA> is a separate tag from the <INPUT> tag and requires a closing </TEXTAREA> tag.

To add a text box to a form:

1 In the *intro_form.html* document, replace the text This is just some text. with the following lines:

<H1>Abigail's Catering</H1>

<P>
Customer Name:<INPUT TYPE="TEXT" NAME="customer"
SIZE="30">
</P>

Figure 8.3 shows the HTML source code.

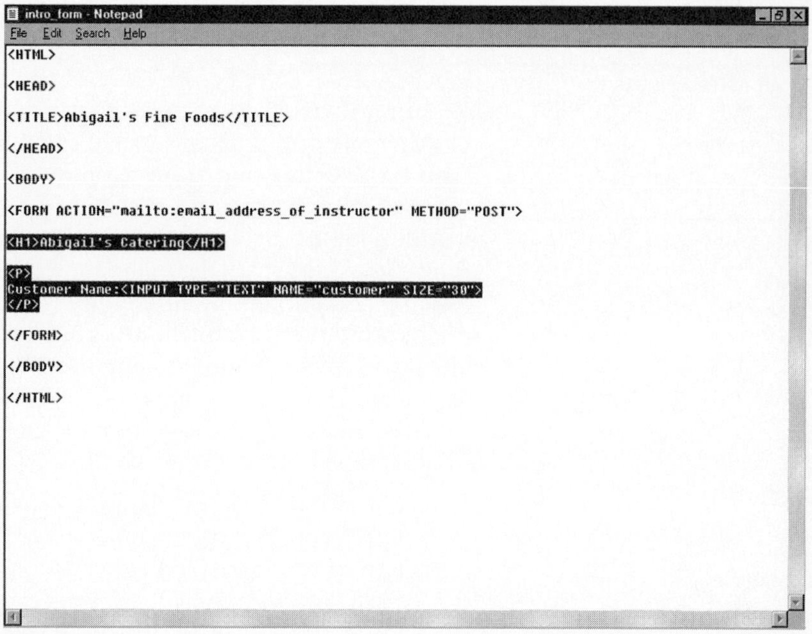

```
intro_form - Notepad
File  Edit  Search  Help
<HTML>

<HEAD>

<TITLE>Abigail's Fine Foods</TITLE>

</HEAD>

<BODY>

<FORM ACTION="mailto:email_address_of_instructor" METHOD="POST">

<H1>Abigail's Catering</H1>

<P>
Customer Name:<INPUT TYPE="TEXT" NAME="customer" SIZE="30">
</P>

</FORM>

</BODY>

</HTML>
```

Figure 8.3

2 Save your work and check out the results in your browser (see Figure 8.4). Notice that the text box appears on-screen. Try to enter data into it.

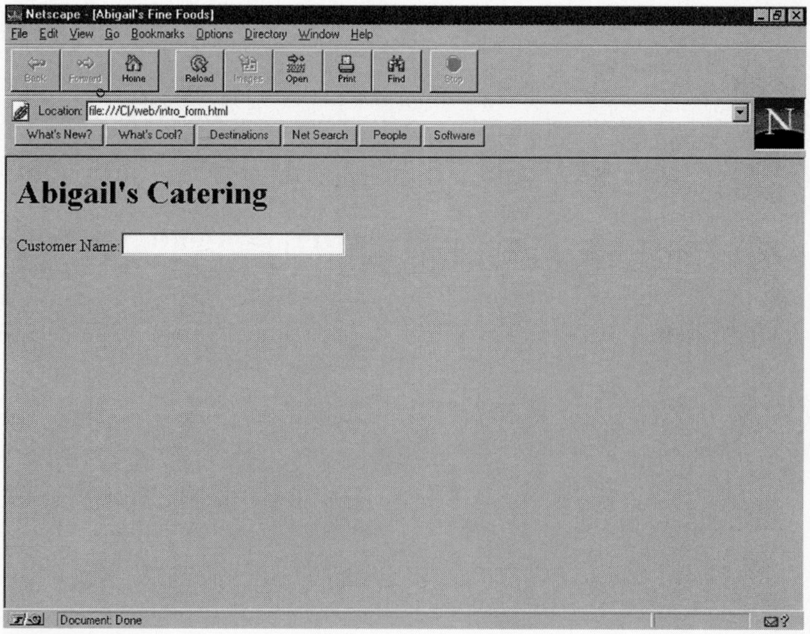

```
Netscape - [Abigail's Fine Foods]
File  Edit  View  Go  Bookmarks  Options  Directory  Window  Help
```

Abigail's Catering

Customer Name: [   ]

Figure 8.4

If necessary, you can exit the editor and browser and continue this project later.

DEFINING RADIO BUTTONS

You can make your form easier to use by providing *radio buttons* for selecting one option from a group of options. You also can provide *check boxes* for selecting one or more options in a group.

To create radio buttons, specify the <INPUT> type as RADIO. You must provide a NAME attribute for the group of radio buttons—for example, using the word *City* as the name for a group of buttons.

For each radio button in the group, you must supply the name of the group, using the NAME attribute. Then specify the individual buttons contained within the group by using the VALUE option. The text following the closing angle bracket (>) appears on-screen after the button.

Here's an example of a set of radio buttons. The name of the button group is *City*:

```
<INPUT TYPE="RADIO" NAME="city" VALUE="Seattle">Seattle
<INPUT TYPE="RADIO" NAME="city" VALUE="Tacoma">Tacoma
<INPUT TYPE="RADIO" NAME="city" VALUE="Olympia">Olympia
```

Reminder With all radio buttons, the user can choose only one of the radio button options in any set.

To add radio buttons to a form:

1 In the *intro_form.html* document, add the following code lines as shown in Figure 8.5:

```
<P>
Where will the event be held?
</P>

<INPUT TYPE="RADIO" NAME="city" VALUE="Seattle">Seattle
<INPUT TYPE="RADIO" NAME="city" VALUE="Tacoma">Tacoma
<INPUT TYPE="RADIO" NAME="city" VALUE="Olympia">Olympia
```

2 Save your work and view it in your browser (see Figure 8.6).

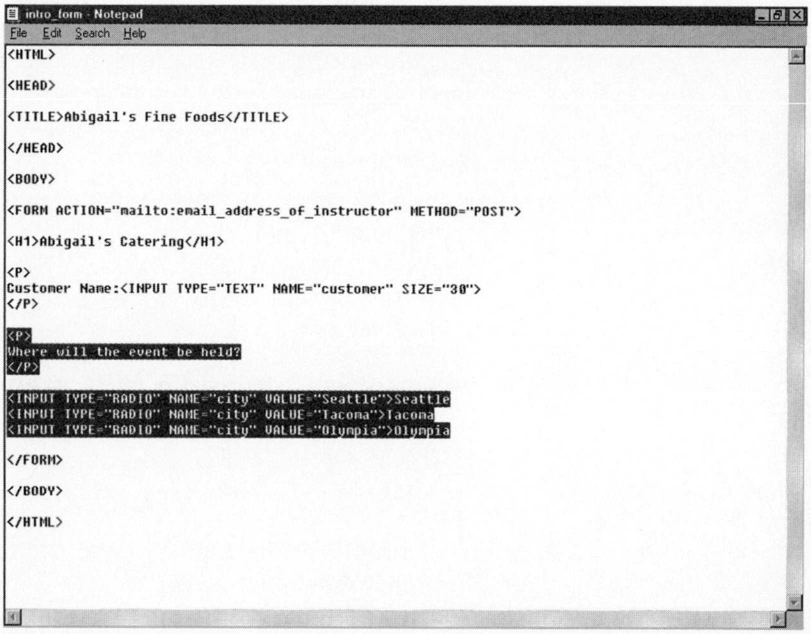

```
intro_form - Notepad

File  Edit  Search  Help

<HTML>

<HEAD>

<TITLE>Abigail's Fine Foods</TITLE>

</HEAD>

<BODY>

<FORM ACTION="mailto:email_address_of_instructor" METHOD="POST">

<H1>Abigail's Catering</H1>

<P>
Customer Name:<INPUT TYPE="TEXT" NAME="customer" SIZE="30">
</P>

<P>
Where will the event be held?
</P>

<INPUT TYPE="RADIO" NAME="city" VALUE="Seattle">Seattle
<INPUT TYPE="RADIO" NAME="city" VALUE="Tacoma">Tacoma
<INPUT TYPE="RADIO" NAME="city" VALUE="Olympia">Olympia

</FORM>

</BODY>

</HTML>
```

Figure 8.5

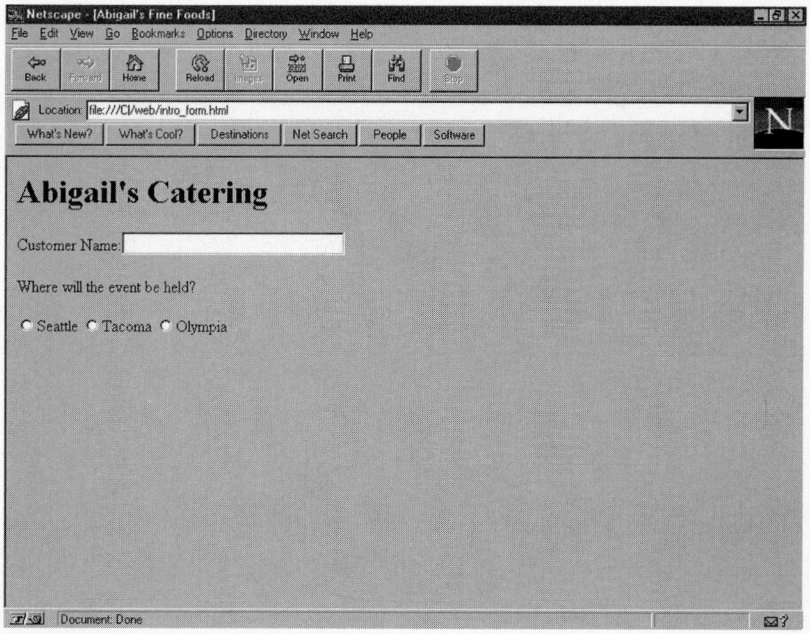

Netscape - [Abigail's Fine Foods]

File Edit View Go Bookmarks Options Directory Window Help

Back | Forward | Home | Reload | Images | Open | Print | Find | Stop

Location: file:///C|/web/intro_form.html

What's New? | What's Cool? | Destinations | Net Search | People | Software

Abigail's Catering

Customer Name: [   ]

Where will the event be held?

○ Seattle ○ Tacoma ○ Olympia

Document: Done

Figure 8.6

If necessary, you can exit the editor and browser and continue this project later.

If you want one of the radio button options to be selected automatically instead of making the user choose one, you use the CHECKED attribute with the option you want selected. For example, if your business is located in Seattle, most of your clients may be located there also, so having the Seattle option already selected saves the user time. But if the client is from Tacoma or Olympia, she will need to select the proper button, which will also deselect the default Seattle button. To have the first option selected, for example, you use this code:

```
<INPUT TYPE="RADIO" NAME="city" VALUE="Seattle"
CHECKED>Seattle
<INPUT TYPE="RADIO" NAME="city" VALUE="Tacoma">Tacoma
<INPUT TYPE="RADIO" NAME="city" VALUE="Olympia">Olympia
```

To preselect one radio button in a set:

1 In the *intro_form.html* document, add the word CHECKED at the end of the Seattle radio button tag so that it looks like this:

```
<INPUT TYPE="RADIO" NAME="city" VALUE="Seattle"
CHECKED>Seattle<BR>
```

2 At the end of each line, add the <BR> tag so that each option appears on a separate line. This will give the buttons a better appearance on the Web page.

Figure 8.7 shows the HTML source code.

3 Save your work and view it in your browser. The first radio button, labeled Seattle, is selected, as shown in Figure 8.8.

```
intro_form - Notepad
File  Edit  Search  Help

<HTML>

<HEAD>

<TITLE>Abigail's Fine Foods</TITLE>

</HEAD>

<BODY>

<FORM ACTION="mailto:email_address_of_instructor" METHOD="POST">

<H1>Abigail's Catering</H1>

<P>
Customer Name:<INPUT TYPE="TEXT" NAME="customer" SIZE="30">
</P>

<P>
Where will the event be held?
</P>

<INPUT TYPE="RADIO" NAME="city" VALUE="Seattle" CHECKED>Seattle<BR>
<INPUT TYPE="RADIO" NAME="city" VALUE="Tacoma">Tacoma<BR>
<INPUT TYPE="RADIO" NAME="city" VALUE="Olympia">Olympia<BR>

</FORM>

</BODY>

</HTML>
```

Figure 8.7

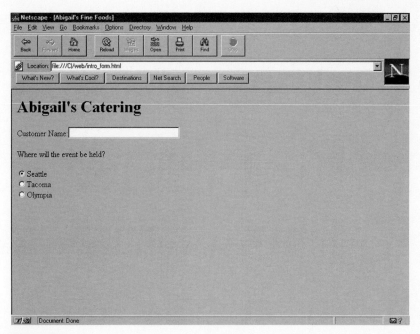

Figure 8.8

 If necessary, you can exit the editor and browser and continue this project later.

DEFINING CHECK BOXES

The only difference between radio buttons and check boxes is that the user can make multiple selections in a set of check boxes. The procedure for creating check boxes is similar to the one for creating radio boxes. To create check boxes, you use the CHECKBOX attribute. You can have a single check box for the user to select one option, or you can provide a group of check boxes. Check boxes are also grouped together using the same NAME attribute, and you define the value for the check box with the VALUE attribute. You can also include the CHECKED attribute if you want the box to appear selected. The following example displays one check box with the caption Please send information:

```
<INPUT TYPE="CHECKBOX" VALUE="information">Please send
information
```

 To add a check box to a form:

1 Add the following line below the radio buttons in the *intro_form.html* document:

```
<INPUT TYPE="CHECKBOX" VALUE="information">Please send
information
```

Figure 8.9 shows this addition.

```
intro_form - Notepad

File  Edit  Search  Help

<HTML>

<HEAD>

<TITLE>Abigail's Fine Foods</TITLE>

</HEAD>

<BODY>

<FORM ACTION="mailto:email_address_of_instructor" METHOD="POST">

<H1>Abigail's Catering</H1>

<P>
Customer Name:<INPUT TYPE="TEXT" NAME="customer" SIZE="30">
</P>

<P>
Where will the event be held?
</P>

<INPUT TYPE="RADIO" NAME="city" VALUE="Seattle" CHECKED>Seattle<BR>
<INPUT TYPE="RADIO" NAME="city" VALUE="Tacoma">Tacoma<BR>
<INPUT TYPE="RADIO" NAME="city" VALUE="Olympia">Olympia<BR>

<P>
<INPUT TYPE="CHECKBOX" VALUE="information">Please send information
</P>

</FORM>

</BODY>

</HTML>
```

Figure 8.9

2 Save your work and view it in the browser. This line of code places a check box with the text *Please send information* on the form, as shown in Figure 8.10.

```
Netscape - [Abigail's Fine Foods]

File  Edit  View  Go  Bookmarks  Options  Directory  Window  Help

Back  Forward  Home  Reload  Images  Open  Print  Find  Stop

Location: file:///C|/web/intro_form.html

What's New?  What's Cool?  Destinations  Net Search  People  Software
```

Abigail's Catering

Customer Name: [   ]

Where will the event be held?

◉ Seattle
○ Tacoma
○ Olympia

☐ Please send information

```
Document: Done
```

Figure 8.10

If necessary, you can exit the editor and browser and continue this project later.

To preselect a check box, add the CHECKED attribute, like this:

```
<INPUT TYPE="CHECKBOX" NAME="choices" VALUE="Seafood"
CHECKED>Seafood<BR>
```

In the following set of steps, you will add three check boxes to the form for the Abigail's Web page.

To add a set of check boxes to a form:

1 In the *intro_form.html* document, add the following code lines:

```
<P>
I would like to order the following types of items:
</P>

<INPUT TYPE="CHECKBOX" NAME="choices" VALUE="Seafood"
CHECKED>Seafood<BR>
<INPUT TYPE="CHECKBOX" NAME="choices"
VALUE="Meat">Meat<BR>
<INPUT TYPE="CHECKBOX" NAME="choices"
VALUE="Vegetarian">Vegetarian<BR>
```

See Figure 8.11 for the HTML source code. In this example, the first check box (Seafood) will be preselected.

2 Save your work and view it in your browser (see Figure 8.12).

```
<BODY>

<FORM ACTION="mailto:email_address_of_instructor" METHOD="POST">

<H1>Abigail's Catering</H1>

<P>
Customer Name:<INPUT TYPE="TEXT" NAME="customer" SIZE="30">
</P>

<P>
Where will the event be held?
</P>

<INPUT TYPE="RADIO" NAME="city" VALUE="Seattle" CHECKED>Seattle<BR>
<INPUT TYPE="RADIO" NAME="city" VALUE="Tacoma">Tacoma<BR>
<INPUT TYPE="RADIO" NAME="city" VALUE="Olympia">Olympia<BR>

<P>
<INPUT TYPE="CHECKBOX" VALUE="information">Please send information
</P>

<P>
I would like to order the following types of items:
</P>

<INPUT TYPE="CHECKBOX" NAME="choices" VALUE="Seafood" CHECKED>Seafood<BR>
<INPUT TYPE="CHECKBOX" NAME="choices" VALUE="Meat">Meat<BR>
<INPUT TYPE="CHECKBOX" NAME="choices" VALUE="Vegetarian">Vegetarian<BR>

</FORM>

</BODY>

</HTML>
```

Figure 8.11

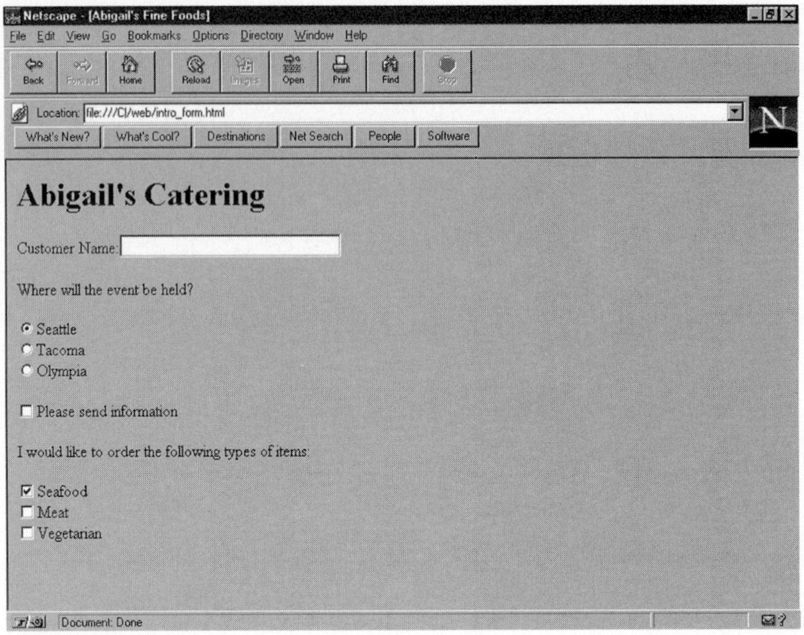

Figure 8.12

DEFINING LISTS OF OPTIONS

You can provide a user with several options by creating a list box and placing the options in the list for the user to select. You use the <SELECT> and </SELECT> tags to enclose the list options. When the user selects an option, the <SELECT> command sends the data in the form NAME=*value* to the server. You use the mandatory NAME attribute to identify the data. The *value* setting identifies the option selected by the user, and is not required. Each item on the list is then identified with the <OPTION> tag. In the following example, a list named County will be displayed, with the options Franklin, Lane, and Jefferson.

```
<SELECT NAME="County" >
<OPTION>Franklin
<OPTION>Lane
<OPTION>Jefferson
</SELECT>
```

The default setting is for one option at a time to be displayed in the list box. You can use the SIZE attribute to display more than one option. For example, if you want all three items to appear at one time, you add the SIZE attribute to the opening <SELECT> tag. For example, if you want all three county names to display by default, you would do it like this:

```
<SELECT NAME="County" SIZE="3">
```

If you want one of the items to be selected automatically for the user, include the SELECTED attribute with the <OPTION> tag. The following example automatically selects the second option, Lane county:

```
<SELECT NAME="County" >
<OPTION>Franklin
<OPTION SELECTED>Lane
```

```
<OPTION>Jefferson
</SELECT>
```

If you want the user to be able to select more than one option from the list, add the attribute MULTIPLE to the opening <SELECT> tag:

```
<SELECT NAME="County" MULTIPLE>
```

If the user wants to select more than one item in a list of this type, he must use the standard Windows keystrokes of holding down the [CTRL] key while clicking noncontiguous items or holding down the [SHIFT] key while clicking contiguous items.

To add a list box to the form:

1 In the *intro_form.html* document, add the following code lines before the </FORM> command:

```
<HR>

<H3>Select the type of event</H3>

<SELECT NAME="type">
<OPTION>Birthday
<OPTION>Wedding
<OPTION>Anniversary
<OPTION>Retirement
<OPTION>Graduation
<OPTION>General
</SELECT>
```

See Figure 8.13 for the HTML source code.

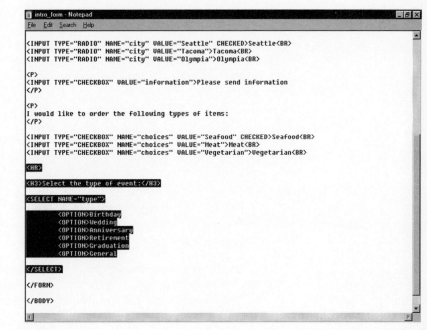

Figure 8.13

2 Save your work and check out the results in your browser. The form now includes a list box, as shown in Figure 8.14.

Keep the document on-screen for use in the next set of steps.

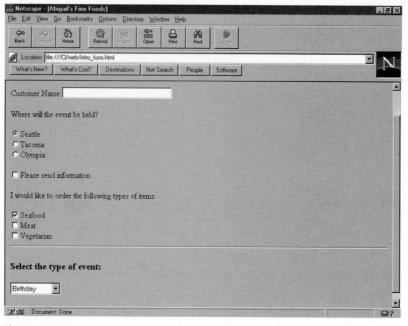

Figure 8.14

GETTING THE USER'S INPUT

The standard way for a user to send information on a form to the server is to use a Submit button. When the user clicks the Submit button, the form contents are sent to the URL defined in the ACTION attribute of the opening <FORM> tag. The Submit button's VALUE attribute allows you to define the text that appears on the button. If you don't include the VALUE attribute, the text *Submit Query* will appear on the button. This is the format:

```
<INPUT TYPE="SUBMIT" VALUE="Send Data">
```

When you include a Submit button on a form, you should also include a Reset button. The Reset button clears any fields in which the user has specified information, and resets all the form's default settings. You can also use the VALUE option to change the text on the Reset button. The default text is *Reset*. This command creates a Reset button with the name *Clear*:

```
<INPUT TYPE="RESET" VALUE="Clear">
```

An alternative method to the Submit button is to include an image on a form that the user can click to send the data to the server. When the user clicks the image, the X,Y coordinates of the mouse, measured in number of pixels from the upper-left corner of the image, are sent to the server. This serves as one way of completing a form, so you should place the image on the form after any other information you want to gather from the user, and explain to the user that when he clicks the image, the form information will be sent to the server.

You must include the name of the image with the SRC attribute, and the NAME attribute identifies the X,Y coordinates:

```
<INPUT TYPE="IMAGE" SRC="image.gif" NAME="location">
```

To add a Submit button and a Reset button to a form:

1 In the *intro_form.html* document, add the following code lines immediately above the closing </FORM> tag:

```
<P>
<INPUT TYPE="SUBMIT" VALUE="Send Data"><INPUT
TYPE="RESET" VALUE="Clear">
</P>
```

Your HTML code should look like that in Figure 8.15.

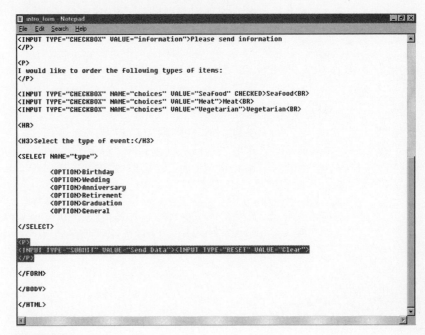

Figure 8.15

2 Save your work and check out the results in your browser. The buttons are added to the form, as shown in Figure 8.16.

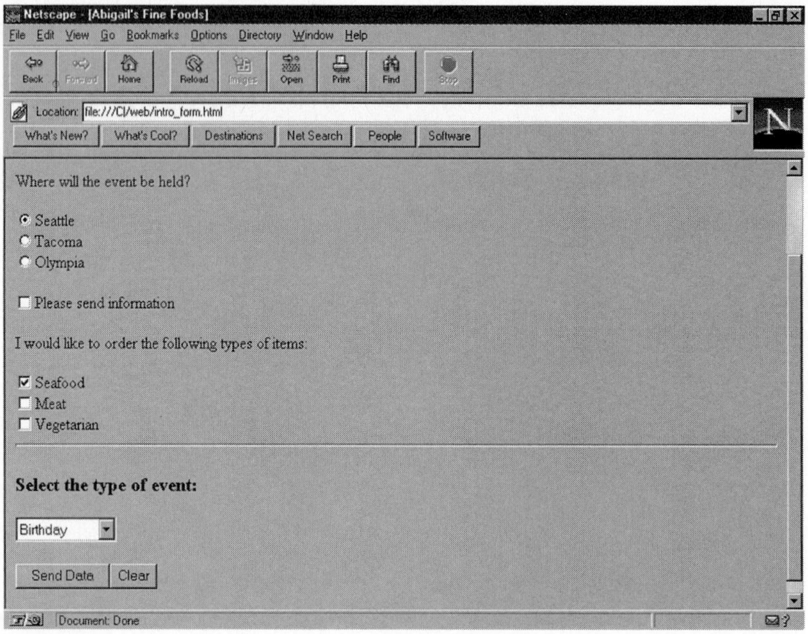

Figure 8.16

3 Type some sample data into the form to test it.

4 Submit the data.

5 Save and close the file.

6 Check out the data sent to your e-mail address or to your instructor's e-mail address.

> **Tip** To add to the consistency of your HTML pages, you can modify the <BODY> and <ADDRESS> tags in *intro_form.html* to match those of *abigail.html*.

THE NEXT STEP

Spend some time browsing Web documents to see how other people and businesses are using forms. Notice the type of data they request and the methods they use to collect the data.

SUMMARY AND EXERCISES

Summary

- The opening and closing form tags <FORM> and </FORM> enclose the entire form.
- The opening and closing <FORM> tags are both included in the body section of the Web document.
- The <INPUT> tag identifies the type of input: text, password, radio button, check box, image, Submit button, Reset button.
- A list box is enclosed between the opening <SELECT> tag and the closing </SELECT> tags.
- The <OPTION> tag defines each option in a list box and is used with the <SELECT> tag.
- The <TEXTAREA> tag creates an area on the form for the user to type a large amount of text.
- The Submit button sends the form to the address specified in the ACTION attribute of the opening <FORM> tag.
- The Reset button clears the form.

Key Terms

check box	form
CGI (Common Gateway Interface) script	radio button
	text area
field	user input field

Study Questions

Multiple Choice

1. The ACTION attribute in the <FORM> tag
   a. specifies the URL where data from the form is to be sent.
   b. specifies the fields on the form.
   c. specifies the type of input.
   d. specifies the type of buttons.
   e. specifies how the buttons will work.

2. The NAME option of the <SELECT> tag
   a. names the radio buttons.
   b. names the check boxes.
   c. names the list box.
   d. names the TEXTAREA.
   e. names the form.

3. Form fields
   a. are the same as fields in a database file.
   b. are the same as fields in an address file used as part of a mail merge.
   c. are the individual elements that make up the data for one person.
   d. are the location where the user inputs data on a form.
   e. all these answers.

4. The Reset button
   a. clears only button choices.
   b. submits the form.
   c. clears the entire form.
   d. clears only one field.
   e. submits the form and clears the form.

5. The CHECKED attribute in the <INPUT> tag
   a. preselects a radio button.
   b. preselects text.
   c. preselects a check box.
   d. preselects the Submit button.
   e. both a and c.

6. The <FORM> tags
   a. enclose the entire form.
   b. are used in the head section.
   c. have no attributes.
   d. are not paired.
   e. all of these answers.

7. INPUT TYPE can define which of the following?
   a. Text and password boxes
   b. Submit and Reset buttons
   c Check boxes and radio buttons
   d. Images
   e. All of these answers

8. Radio buttons
   a. can't have a default value selected.
   b. must contain the VALUE attribute.
   c. allow the user to select many options.
   d. are used rarely on forms.
   e. all of these answers.

9. A list box
   a. is contained within the <SELECT> tags.
   b. must have the NAME attribute.
   c. can display as many items as you want.
   d. uses the <OPTION> tag to define each choice.
   e. all of these answers.

10. The Submit button
    a. clears any fields that the user has typed.
    b. sends the form contents to the URL defined in the ACTION attribute of the opening <FORM> tag.
    c. must always appear with the text Submit Query on the button.
    d. must be an image.
    e. all of these answers.

Short Answer

1. Post this form to the e-mail address lindae@lanecc.edu:

   <FORM

   </FORM>

2. Create a text area:

```
<FORM>

</FORM>
```

3. Include an image on the form for the user to click to send the form contents:

```
<FORM>

</FORM>
```

4. Create a Submit button that says *SEND MAIL* on the button:

```
<FORM>

</FORM>
```

5. Create a list box with the following options:

```
<FORM>
<P>Make a selection from the following list:

       Have your address added to the mailing list
       Receive free information with no obligation
       Join our list of subscribers
       Become a sustaining member

</FORM>
```

6. Create a text box for the user to enter his or her address:

```
<FORM>

</FORM>
```

7. Create radio buttons for the following options:

```
<FORM>
       New member
       Renewing member
       Lapsed member
       Founding member
</FORM>
```

8. Create check boxes for the following options and allow the user to select more than one option:

```
<FORM>
       Single room
       Double room
       Nonsmoking room
       Suite
       Room with a Jacuzzi
       Kitchenette
       Room with access to the pool
</FORM>
```

For Discussion

1. When would you include a form on your Web document?

2. What's the difference between radio buttons and check boxes on a form?

3. Explain the `mailto` option.

4. What is CGI?

5. Discuss when you would use each of the user input types.

Review Exercises

Adding a Form to the Alphabits Bookstore Web Page

Create a form for the user to interact with the bookstore. The bookstore's e-mail address is `Alphabit@plt.org`. The form should include the following elements (see Figure 8.17):

- A text box for the child's name
- Radio buttons for the following options:
  - Age of your child:
  - 1–3, 4–6, 7–10, 11–13, Over 14
- Check boxes for the following options, which allow the user to select more than one option:
  - Select your favorite types of children's books:
    - Fantasy
    - Mystery
    - Poetry
    - Short stories
    - Illustrated books
    - Animal stories
- Include a Submit button and a Reset button

Use the same \<BODY> and \<ADDRESS> tags in this document as in the *alphabit.html* document. Save the file as *form.html*.

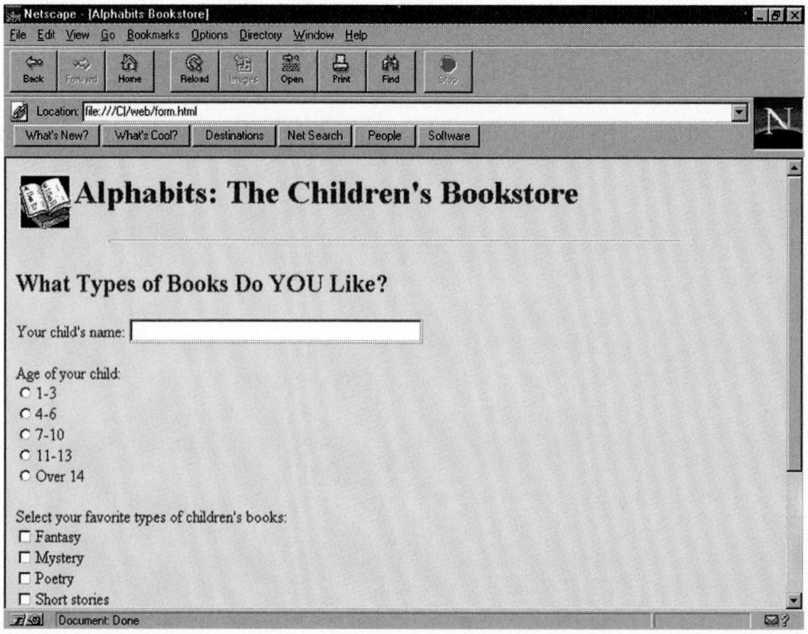

Figure 8.17a

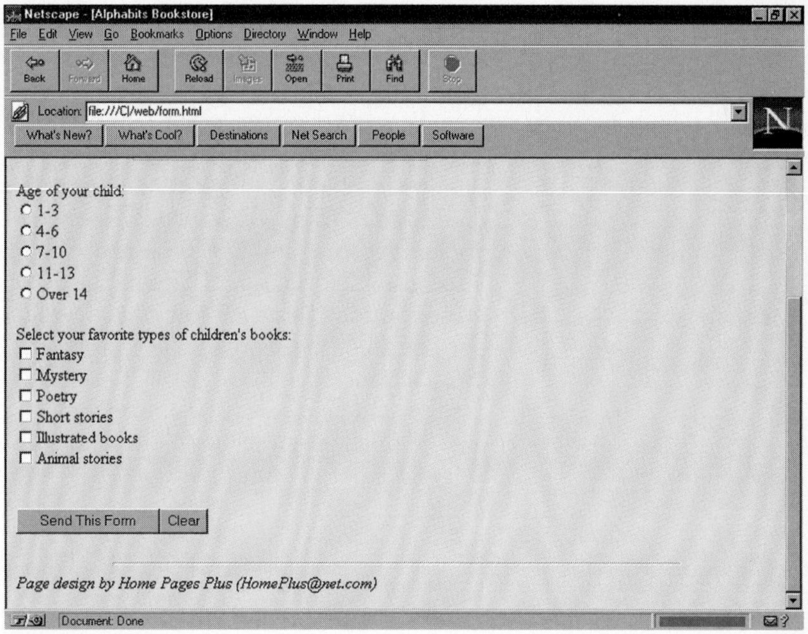

Figure 8.17b

Adding a Form to the Animal Web Page

Create a form so that the user can interact with you. If you're trying to sell animals, this will allow the user to let you know she's interested. If this is an animal information page, you can use the form to get a response to your page. Use an actual e-mail address if possible.

Assignments

Adding a Form to Your Personal Web Page

Now that you have a personal Web page to market your talents, you want people to be able to get in touch with you. Create a form so that the user can contact you. Use your e-mail address.

Adding a Form to the Organization or Nonprofit Web Page

Create a form for users to join the organization, receive more information, or perhaps pledge donations. Include the e-mail address for the organization.

What Is CGI? **CGI (Common Gateway Interface)** is a communications protocol that's an extension of the HTTP protocol. When a user fills out a form and submits it, the data travels from the user (client) to the server. The server recognizes the CGI protocol and directs the data from the form to the proper CGI application, where the data is processed. For example, the CGI application may be a database that processes and saves the data. Processed data can also travel back to the user from the CGI application.

These CGI applications are programs, also called **scripts**, written in **Perl (Practical Extraction and Reporting Language)**, C, or other languages.

Final Project

While learning how to use HTML tags and attributes, you have created home pages and worked with various HTML elements just to try them out. You may have included some elements just because you were learning how to use them.

Now take a good look at one of the home pages that you created. Redesign it, using all you know about HTML, so that the home page looks appealing and well designed. Start by diagramming on paper all the lists, graphics, links, and forms that need to work together. Look at other pages on the Web that you like—or that share the same topic as yours—for design elements that work. Using the Source Code feature in your browser, look at the code for these pages (now that you can read and understand it) to see how other people achieved their results. When you have a final design planned out, you are ready to create the page on the computer.

Appendix A:
Extended Symbols
Allowed in HTML

Symbol	Number	Character (if any)
†	&#134	
‡	&#135	
ˆ	&#136	
‰	&#137	
Š	&#138	
‹	&#139	
Œ	&#140	
□	&#141	
□	&#142	
□	&#143	
□	&#144	
`	&#145	
ʼ	&#146	
"	&#147	
"	&#148	
•	&#149	
–	&#150	
—	&#151	
~	&#152	
™	&#153	
š	&#154	
›	&#155	
œ	&#156	
□	&#157	
□	&#158	
Ÿ	&#159	

Symbol	Number	Character (if any)
¡	&#161	
¢	&#162	
£	&#163	
¤	&#164	
¥	&#165	
¦	&#166	
§	&#167	
¨	&#168	
©	&#169	©
ª	&#170	
«	&#171	
¬	&#172	
	&#173	
®	&#174	®
¯	&#175	
°	&#176	
±	&#177	
²	&#178	
³	&#179	
´	&#180	
µ	&#181	
¶	&#182	
·	&#183	
¸	&#184	
¹	&#185	
º	&#186	
»	&#187	

Symbol	Number	Character (if any)	Symbol	Number	Character (if any)
¼	&#188		Þ	&#222	Þ
½	&#189		ß	&#223	ß
¾	&#190		à	&#224	&aagrave;
¿	&#191		á	&#225	á
À	&#192	À	â	&#226	â
Á	&#193	Á	ã	&#227	ã
Â	&#194	Â	ä	&#228	ä
Ã	&#195	Ã	å	&#229	å
Ä	&#196	Ä	æ	&#230	æ
Å	&#197	Å	ç	&#231	ç
Æ	&#198	&Aelig;	è	&#232	è
Ç	&#199	Ç	é	&#233	é
È	&#200	È	ê	&#234	ê
É	&#201	É	ë	&#235	ë
Ê	&#202	Ê	ì	&#236	ì
Ë	&#203	Ë	í	&#237	í
Ì	&#204	Ì	î	&#238	î
Í	&#205	Í	ï	&#239	ï
Î	&#206	Î	ð	&#240	ð
Ï	&#207	Ï	ñ	&#241	ñ
Ð	&#208	Ð	ò	&#242	ò
Ñ	&#209	Ñ	ó	&#243	ó
Ò	&#210	Ò	ô	&#244	ô
Ó	&#211	Ó	õ	&#245	õ
Ô	&#212	Ô	ö	&#246	ö
Õ	&#213	Õ	÷	&#247	
Ö	&#214	Ö	ø	&#248	ø
x	&#215		ù	&#249	ù
Ø	&#216	Ø	ú	&#250	ú
Ù	&#217	Ù	û	&#251	û
Ú	&#218	´	ü	&#252	ü
Û	&#219	Û	ý	&#253	ý
Ü	&#220	Ü	þ	&#254	þ
Ý	&#221	Ý	ÿ	&#255	ÿ

Appendix B:
Partial List of Colors for Backgrounds and Text in Hexadecimal

Color	Number
antique white	#faebd7
aquamarine	#32bfc1
beige	#f5f5dc
black	#000000
blue	#0000ff
brown	#a52a2a
burlywood	#deb887
cadet blue	#5f929e
chocolate	#d2691e
cornflower blue	#222298
cyan	#00ffff
gold	#daaa00
goldenrod	#efdf84
green	#00ff00
hot pink	#ff69b4
indian red	#6b3939
ivory	#fffff0
khaki	#b3b37e
lavender	#e6e6fa
lime green	#00af14
magenta	#ff00ff
maroon	#8f0052
midnight blue	#2f2f64

Color	Number
misty rose	#ffe4e1
navy blue	#232375
orange	#ffa500
orchid	#ef84ef
pink	#ffb5c5
purple	#a020f0
red	#ff0000
royal blue	#4169e1
salmon	#e9967a
sea green	#529584
sienna	#ff8247
sky blue	#729fff
slate blue	#7e88ab
slate gray	#708090
spring green	#41ac41
steel blue	#5470aa
tan	#deb887
transparent	#000001
turquoise	#19ccdf
violet	#9c3ece
wheat	#f5deb3
white	#ffffff
yellow	#ffff00

Appendix C:
Alphabetized List of HTML Tags and Attributes Used in the Text

Opening Tag	Closing Tag	Attributes	Description
`<!-comment->`			Allows you to place, in the Web document, comments or documentation that won't display in a browser

`<A>`	`</A>`	`NAME=`
		`HREF=`
		`SRC=`
			Defines a link and anchor in the same document or to an external file

`<ADDRESS>`	`</ADDRESS>`		Places the name or e-mail address of the owner or designer of the Web page
`<B>`	`</B>`		Boldfaces text between tags
`<BASE>`		`HREF=`	Appears in the head section and defines the base address of the Web document
`<BASEFONT>`		`SIZE=value`	Changes the size of the font for the entire document to the number placed in the *value* variable
`<BLINK>`	`</BLINK>`		Makes text between tags blink
`<BLOCKQUOTE>`	`</BLOCKQUOTE>`		Places a long indented quotation in the document

`<BODY>`	`</BODY>`	`BGCOLOR=`
		`TEXT=`
		`LINK=`
		`VLINK=`
		`ALINK=`
			Identifies the second section of a Web document, encloses the body of the document; attributes allow you to change the background color and text colors

` `			Places text on a line by itself, without including any white space
`<CAPTION>`	`</CAPTION>`		Encloses the caption or title for a table
`<CENTER>`	`</CENTER>`		Centers text between tags
`<CODE>`	`</CODE>`		Used to format text such as computer codes
`<DD>`			Precedes the definition in a definition list
`<DL>`	`</DL>`		Creates a definition or glossary list
`<DT>`			Precedes the term in a definition list
`<EM>`	`</EM>`		Emphasizes text between the tags; browsers define the format of the emphasis

`<FONT>`	`</FONT>`	`SIZE=`*value*	Changes the size of the font for characters, words, or groups of words in a document to the number placed in the *value* variable
`<FORM>`	`</FORM>`	`ACTION=` `METHOD=`	Encloses an interactive form; you specify how you will receive the information and where to send it
`<H1>`	`</H1>`	`ALIGN=`	Heading 1—the most prominent of heading levels; you can change the alignment of all headings
`<H2>`	`</H2>`		Heading 2
`<H3>`	`</H3>`		Heading 3
`<H4>`	`</H4>`		Heading 4
`<H5>`	`</H5>`		Heading 5
`<H6>`	`</H6>`		Heading 6—the least prominent
`<HEAD>`	`</HEAD>`		Identifies the first section of a Web document

`<HR>`	`</HR>`	`SIZE=`
		`WIDTH=`
		`ALIGN=`
		`NOSHADE`
			Places a horizontal rule or line in the document. You can change the size, width, alignment, or shading of the line

`<HTML>`	`</HTML>`		Encloses an entire Web document
`<I>`	`</I>`		Italicizes text between tags

`<IMG>`		`SRC=`*name*
		`ALT=`
		`ALIGN=`
		`HSPACE=`
		`VSPACE=`
		`WIDTH=`
		`HEIGHT=`
			Places an image in the document that replaces the *name* variable; you can align the image, specify a particular size, and include more white space around an image

`<INPUT>`		`TYPE=`
		`SIZE=`
		`NAME=`
		`MAXLENGTH=`
		`VALUE=`
		`CHECKED`
			Specifies the type of input from the user of a form (text, password, radio button, check box, image, Submit button, Reset button); the size of the field; the name; the maximum length; the value; and, if the item is a button, whether it's selected

`<KBD>`	`</KBD>`		Used to format text to show an example of what the user should type
`<LI>`		`TYPE=`*value*	Starts each line of an ordered or unordered list; you can change the number or bullet for a specific line
`<OL>`	`</OL>`	`START=`*value* `TYPE=`*value*	Creates an ordered or numbered list; you can change the type of numbers or letters used and the starting value
`<OPTION>`			Identifies each menu item on a form within the `<SELECT>` tags
`<P>`	`</P>`	`ALIGN=`	Starts a new paragraph and includes white space; you can align a paragraph

<PRE>	</PRE>		Places preformatted text in the document
<SAMP>	</SAMP>		Used to format sample text for the user
<SELECT>	</SELECT>	NAME= MULTIPLE	Defines a pop-up menu on a form; you can name the menu and have more than one menu item displayed
<STRIKE>	</STRIKE>		Strikes out text between tags
<STRONG>	</STRONG>		Strongly emphasizes text between the tags; browsers determine the format of the emphasis
_			Subscripts text between tags
[	]		Superscripts text between tags
<TABLE>	</TABLE>	BORDER CELLSPACING= CELLPADDING= WIDTH= HEIGHT=	Encloses an entire table; you can change the border, the spacing between cells, padding from the text to the border of the cell, and the width and height of the table
<TD>	</TD>	 NOWRAP COLSPAN= ROWSPAN= ALIGN= VALIGN= WIDTH= HEIGHT=	Encloses a cell in a table that contains data; you can break a line, keep a line from breaking, span text over rows or columns, align text horizontally or vertically, and define the width and height of a cell
<TEXTAREA>		NAME= COLS= ROWS=	Defines a text area on a form. You can define the size of the area
<TH>	</TH>	 NOWRAP COLSPAN= ROWSPAN= ALIGN= VALIGN= WIDTH= HEIGHT=	Encloses a cell in a table that contains a header; you can break a line, keep a line from breaking, span text over rows or columns, align text horizontally or vertically, and define the width and height of a cell
<TITLE>	</TITLE>		Must appear in the head section; the title doesn't appear in the Web document, but rather in the browser's title bar
<TR>	</TR>	ALIGN= VALIGN=	Encloses each row of a table; you can align each row horizontally or vertically
<TT>	</TT>		Formats text in a typewriter font
<U>	</U>		Underlines text between tags
<UL>	</UL>	TYPE=*value*	Creates an unordered or bulleted list; you can change the bullets for the entire list

Index